HEALING HURTING CHURCHES

DR. DON HEBBARD

HEALING HURTING CHURCHES

The Economou Process

Healing Hurting Churches
Copyright © 2022 by Dr. Don Hebbard
All rights reserved.

Published in the United States of America by Credo House Publishers,
a division of Credo Communications LLC, Grand Rapids, Michigan
credohousepublishers.com

Unless otherwise noted, Scripture quotations are from the Holy Bible,
New International Version®, NIV® Copyright ©1973, 1978, 1984, 2011
by Biblica, Inc.®. Used by permission. All rights reserved worldwide.

ISBN: 978-1-62586-218-1

Cover and interior design by Frank Gutbrod
Editing by Donna Huisjen

Printed in the United States of America
First edition

“From the least to the greatest,
all are greedy for gain;
prophets and priests alike,
all practice deceit.
They dress the wound of my people
as though it were not serious.
‘Peace, peace,’ they say,
when there is no peace.
Are they ashamed of their detestable conduct?
No, they have no shame at all;
they do not even know how to blush.
So they will fall among the fallen;
they will be brought down when I punish them,”
says the Lord.

Jeremiah 6:13–15

This book is dedicated to Officer Jared Hebbard and Officer Hailey Hebbard Fisher, my son and daughter, who are my heroes serving as police officers on the thin blue line. They have supported me through all the church transitions I have led. They are the only two in the audience I strive to please.

This book is also dedicated to Marianne Economou Metropoulos. Marianne's stories of my birth father, Nicolas Economou, have been a gift to me words cannot describe. I was born Peter Nicholas Economou, and Marianne's love of my father has helped me connect with a man I never knew.

CONTENTS

INTRODUCTION

I was crossing the campus of Abilene Christian University with Dr. Paul Faulkner, Director of the new Marriage and Family Institute. I was his graduate assistant while finishing my master's degree in Communications. My life was planned. Complete my doctorate in Communications at OU, preach for a few years, then teach at a university. All that changed when he asked me, "Don, what are you going to do after graduation? I've taken the liberty of enrolling you in the new Marriage and Family Institute. I think you'd be a great marriage therapist." You didn't say no to Dr. Faulkner. That decision changed the course of my life.

A few years later I had opened one of the first Christian counseling centers in Dallas at a church when Dr. Tom Eaves contacted me. He knew I was pursuing my doctorate at TWU and wanted me to transfer into his new program in Adult and Continuing Education. "The tools we give you will change the way you work with organizations and the way you teach adults." Again, it was a life-changing decision.

Twenty years of local church work were spent opening counseling centers and family life ministries in Irving, Dallas, and Atlanta. Those were pioneer days when the local church was first admitting that Christian families really do have problems and the field of psychotherapy can be trusted. It was a rewarding and challenging experience to introduce a church to healing spiritually and emotionally.

At each stop, the congregation I served entered into a significant transition. The church was wounded and in need of a season of healing before it could move forward. The leadership would turn to me and ask if I could step into the gap and provide preaching and consultation to help them through.

There was no manual to rely upon. There were no models for healing a church. I drew upon the training I had received as a family therapist with Dr. Faulkner and my doctoral work in organizational consulting with Dr. Eaves. Both programs employed a new approach to human interactions, which was Systems Theory.

I was blessed to have a cadre of wise mentors who understood the dynamics of local church work. Dr. Dan Mitchell, Dr. James Cail, Dr. Charles Siburt, Dr. Royce Money, and Robert K. Oglesby were always available to take my calls and teach me how to be a "church doctor."

When I became a college professor and my Sundays were open, the phone started ringing. One church after another had a story to tell and a need to rebuild. It has been an honor to work with all of them.

It became clear that a book was needed on the subject of healing hurting churches. There are churches that go through an interim between one minister and another, and they are in need of an interim ministry. However, there are congregations that have been so wounded they cannot move forward without a season of healing. That is the work I have done for over thirty years and the subject of this book.

This book is written for the church leader struggling to understand what is happening in their church following a significant crisis. This book is written for the member in the pew who wants to understand why their church seems to be stuck in a destructive pattern. It is for the person who has left organized religion because they were hurt during a church transition. This book is also written for the individual who feels a calling to help hurting churches do better.

I have written *Healing Hurting Churches* in a problem-solution format. The first section will present six important ways churches can be wounded and the reasons congregations do not seek help.

The second section will offer a model for healing hurting churches that is biblically sound and grounded in solid theory and practice.

Along this journey I met my biological family. I was born Peter Nicholas Economou. I was introduced to my birth father, Nicholas Economou, through Marianne Economou Metropoulos's delightful stories. I learned that the Greek word *economou* in Luke 12:42 means "the faithful manager of the house of God." I realized that my birth name, Economou, was God's calling for my life. I was born to be a faithful manager of God's sometimes wounded house. God in his infinite wisdom decided that I was born to do this work.

Working with a wounded church is like doing therapy on a thousand people. The pain may be great, but the experience of healing can be remarkable. I never would have guessed on that day I walked across the campus with Dr. Faulkner that my life would be spent healing churches. His plans were much wiser than my own.

May God bless you as you seek healing for your church and as you strive to be an agent of His grace.

Dr. Don Hebbard

CHAPTER 1

THE WOUNDED CHURCH

I stood in the pulpit completely unaware of what I'd been saying for the past 25 minutes. My attention was not focused on the fifteen hundred people sitting before me, excited to be a part of a growing, rebirthing congregation. My focus was on the gentleman seated on the front row staring blank-faced up at me. His hands were quietly shaking as they held a single sheet of paper. On that page was an announcement that would change the course of history for that church and for my life as well.

Shortly before this I'd been given a private tour of the B-1 bomber used for low-level nuclear bombing missions. As I sat in the pilot's seat, the crew chief explained that they brought the plane in at treetop level and the bomb was released, attached to a small parachute that allowed it to float slowly to the ground before explosion. That morning I felt as though I were watching a bomb slowly floating over the church auditorium, waiting to explode in a few moments.

The page contained an announcement of the resignation of the minister of that church. His marriage was ending, and he was stepping away from ministry. It expressed the sorrow the leaders felt for him and his family, along with the confidence they had that God would see the church through this difficult time. It ended with a tear-filled prayer as stunned church members tried to bow their heads while shaking them in disbelief.

The shock waves of this announcement were enormous. A church that for years had been stagnant in growth had found a minister that had rekindled their passion for ministry. They had the momentum to grow and fill an auditorium they had built to house a much larger congregation. Now those dreams seemed dashed. A ministry family had been torn apart and was now silently hurting. A church leadership was in shock and struggling to find its bearings as members besieged them with questions they were not prepared to answer.

This was not a simple change in preacher. This was not a typical ministerial transition or interim period. This church was in shock and incapable of moving forward. Over a period of years, they had endured a number of disappointments, and all of this now culminated with this resignation announcement. They would need some intentional pastoral care to heal their wounds before they could move forward into the next era of ministry.

HEALING TRANSITIONS VS. INTERIM MINISTRY

Church life is filled with ministers coming and going like head football coaches at the local high school. This is a natural part of church life. Most of these changes in staff occur without shaking the foundations of the church. An interim ministry is appropriate for those congregations and will prepare them for the next chapter in their congregational life.

However, my experience has been that some congregations experience events or a series of events that lead them to require a "healing transition" to deal with spiritual and emotional wounds. If that season of healing can be given, the church will be ready to move forward. If the need is ignored, the church will limp along handicapped in its ability to function as a healthy body.

There are a wide range of congregational events that call for a season of healing:

- Sexual Misconduct
- Retirement of a Long-Tenured Minister
- High Levels of Congregational Conflict
- Financial or Ethical Mismanagement
- Extramarital Affairs
- Poor Match of Minister to Congregation
- Authoritarian Leadership
- Legal Difficulties
- Unexpected Death
- Changing Community
- Natural Disaster
- Personality Disorders
- High Staff Turnover
- Mismatch of Vision to Congregation
- Leadership Incompetence

These issues or a combination of them signal clearly that the church is in need of an intentional period of healing. Most church leaders will ignore this work and move ahead with little thought to the health of the congregation.

DATING THE FUNERAL DIRECTOR

Most church leaders, when confronted with one of the issues listed above, will opt for the "roll up your sleeves and get busy" approach to congregational care. "Let's just pray about it, get busy and find a new preacher, and just put all of this behind us. The sooner we can forget this ugly chapter, the better." As Jeremiah warned, "They dress the wound of my people as though it were not serious. 'Peace, peace,' they say, when there is no peace."

My adoptive parents were married for 53 years. My father died first, leaving my mother devastated. When we were leaving Restland Cemetery in Dallas, riding in the limousine together, I asked her, "Mom how are you doing?" What she did *not* say was, "Oh, just fine, honey. That cute funeral director was so nice. He and I are going to go out on a date tonight. I think it's time I moved on, don't you?" In our lives, marriages, and families we realize that there is a "time for every season under heaven." We realize that the difficult transitions in our lives require us to stop, catch our breath, and evaluate how we want to move forward with life. It was obvious my mother did not need to be searching for a new mate coming straight out of a major loss. Why, then, do we think a church can come out of a major loss, search for a new minister, and install him like an interchangeable sixty-month car battery?

It is shocking to me that church leaders ignore the very core principles of human need when it comes to church life. We treat the church as though it were bullet-proof emotionally and then wonder why it stumbles, worn out under the pressure of years of leadership mismanagement. The tried-and-true old prescription of just pray harder, do more, and put it behind you is espoused by leaders who lack the wisdom and skills to attend to hurting people, walk through conflict, or deal with issues in their own lives that may be hurting the congregation. Members sit wounded in the pews or silently leave out the back door—some leaving church life forever.

The red warning lights on the dashboard of the church may be lighting up, signaling that we need to stop and check the engine soon when the following exists:

- High levels of leadership or ministerial turnover.
- Church leaders seem to be managing one crisis after another.
- It seems as though we keep cycling through the same problems.
- Church members and leaders are in separate camps.
- There has been a major crisis event.
- There have been a series of events over an extended period of time leaving the church exhausted.

- Church is controlled by one group or individual whose pathology is endangering the institution.
- Core members or leaders are resigning and leaving the church.
- Key church "wise men and women" are saying we need outside help.

AFTER THE ANNOUNCEMENT

Following the announcement that Sunday morning, to my surprise, the leadership did not move full-speed ahead. They invited me into a conversation about healing the church. I had completed a master's degree in Marriage and Family Therapy at Abilene Christian University's new Marriage and Family Therapy program and had been counseling families in the church. I had just completed my doctorate in Organizational Consulting. They knew I was familiar with personal and organizational healing and said, "We don't know what it is you do, but we're going to give you the next year to help us get back on our feet. Tell us what we need to do." So began a thirty-year journey of my getting phone calls from troubled church leaders, saying, "We've had some serious problems here at our church. Can you help?"

I have been honored to work with all kinds of congregations—large, small, urban, and rural. Churches that were just starting out in rented facilities and churches whose auditoriums were built the year the Alamo fell. They have come from a wide range of faith groups but have all had one thing in common: they were all in the hospital emergency room and needed a season of healing. Some embraced the process of transition and did their work. They were able to move on to a new era of ministry. Others, like the clients I see in my practice, came for a few sessions and then decided they knew everything and didn't need help.

I get phone calls from former clients, saying, "Dr. Don, I saw you a couple of times several years ago and then never came back.

I wasn't ready to do the work then. I am now. Can we get together and talk?" Counseling works only when the client is ready to do the hard work of change. Churches are the same. If we ignore the wounds, if we ignore the pain, it doesn't go away. Like Israel's sin in the Old Testament, the pain just gets rolled forward. Eventually the issues and the pain must be dealt with, or they will bring the church to its knees. I tell my clients, "Deal with your pain, or your pain will deal with you."

OUR APPROACH

This book is written for the church leader or church member who finds they are navigating a difficult transition in congregational life. Your old resources and responses do not seem to be working any longer, and you are searching for a new approach. You may be a minister who finds yourself tossed into the deep end of a difficult church transition, and you are searching for tools to make sense of the changing dynamics. My approach will move from problem to solution.

In "Part One: The Wounds of My People," we will explore six typical patterns of congregational wounding. Wounds often occur around poor conflict styles, narcissistic behaviors, leadership incompetence, unpredictable borderline behavior, sexual misconduct, and congregational exhaustion. We will explore the typical responses these churches use to deal with these problems and why they fail.

In "Part Two, The Economou Model," we will explore the biblical basis for congregational healing and useful theories that help us make sense of church dynamics. We will explore the process and tools used in healing the church, along with the importance of endings and spending time in the wilderness, which is a place of unique opportunity. Treatment will revolve around an understanding that the church is a spiritual-emotional system, not an organizational flow chart.

TURNING LOOSE OF THE STICK

In all of this, I encourage you to rely upon God as the Great Physician. One of the greatest signs of spiritual leadership is to sometimes admit that we are powerless to change things we do not understand. Like the people at Pentecost, we proclaim, "Men and brethren, what do we do?" Putting God at the center of church life means that the rest of us have to step out of the spotlight.

I sat in the cockpit of that B-1 bomber with the crew chief as he described the process of a nuclear bombing run. He explained, "The unique thing about the B-1 is that you fly it with a stick, just like a fighter jet. On a bombing run, the pilot is flying at treetop level under the enemy radar. See that red button on the stick? That's the autopilot. They bring it down to a few hundred feet off the deck and hit the button, . . . then sit back and let the plane do its mission. The key decision for every pilot is "Can I hit the button when the stakes are so high and turn loose of the stick?"

For the church leader facing a crisis, the question is the same: Will I face this crisis by hanging onto the stick and flying the airplane as we always have? Or will I have the faith to hit the button and turn loose of the stick, to really believe that we walk by faith and not by sight?

PART ONE

THE WOUNDS OF MY PEOPLE

CHAPTER 2

THE TOUGH-BARGAINER WOUND

ORIENTAL TEA

Charlie was livid. That was not unusual, because Charlie was always angry about something. At the Central Church, members had learned to steer clear of him when he was in one of his moods. He frequently left bodies in his wake in the church foyer, not realizing how verbally abusive he was in speaking to members and even guests. He was hard to avoid because his aggressive leadership style had allowed him to take control of many key areas of church life.

Charlie was a successful, educated, and competent business leader. He had built his own company and enjoyed the financial fruits of a hard-driving work ethic. He was known around the office and in the community as being an authoritarian leader who was going to get his way. Charlie liked to win, and when opposition appeared, he had one gear—linebacker. But he wondered who he would leave his company to, as none of his adult children had much to do with him any longer.

The Central Church had experienced a leadership gap, with few men willing or able to serve. Charlie seized the opportunity to rescue this struggling church and could not understand why people were not more grateful for his sacrifices. They just didn't understand what it meant to be an effective leader. After all, look at everything he'd built.

It frustrated Charlie that he "had to do everything himself." When he came back to town after a business trip, he'd often feel a need to reconvene the church board to urge them to take a new vote on a measure he was opposed to. He had been instrumental in hiring the new preacher, but a rift soon occurred because the new minister did not appreciate Charlie's advice on preaching.

One Sunday, Charlie was fuming over the current crisis. The building program, which he had personally initiated and of which he was now chairman, was stalled due to neighborhood interference. Central was moving from its old home to a new location, but the new neighbors were not welcoming the change in zoning. The key leader was a spirited Asian woman named Ms. Cho with deep connections on the city planning and zoning committee. She had rallied a petition in opposition to the building of the church; held a press conference; and successfully painted the Central Church, and Charlie in particular, as "ecclesiastical bullies." The building was halted by the city, and Charlie was, predictably, furious.

After weeks of fighting in the media and threats of lawsuits, I was called in to mediate a conversation between the two sides. Charlie and I were invited to oriental tea at Ms. Cho's home. Charlie scoffed at the idea but then relented, and we found ourselves one bright spring morning sitting in her living room sharing oriental tea.

Charlie was prepared and launched into a long speech about the rights of the church and the damage her neighborhood group was doing to his congregation. He cited the financial costs that her delays had caused. He extolled the virtues of having a church adjacent to her neighborhood. He lectured her for thirty minutes while she sat patiently sipping her tea and listening to every word he spoke.

When he ran out of gas, she began speaking very softly and deliberately about her concerns. "Your site plan requires a retention pond to handle all of the run-off water. That retention pond is to be built directly behind this neighborhood. In fact, it will sit directly behind my back fence. Is that correct?" Charlie concurred that this was the plan.

At this point Ms. Cho called to a woman in another room to join us. In a few moments a nurse's aide appeared, wheeling a young boy in a wheelchair into the living room. The young boy was unable to walk and, we would learn later, unable to speak.

"This is my son Michael. Michael, when he was four, fell into a neighborhood pool and almost drowned. The accident left him paralyzed and has changed his life forever. The pool he fell into is just like the retention pond your church will build outside our neighborhood. When it fills with rainwater, there will be no fence around it to keep our children from wandering in there and risking an accident like Michael's. I couldn't prevent his first accident, but I can prevent another one from happening. I'm not opposed to your church building. I am opposed to risking our children's safety, and I'm disappointed that no one opened a conversation with us as your new neighbors."

For once in his life, Charlie was speechless. The conviction and compassion of this mother left me in awe of her strength and her ability to negotiate in the face of such an overpowering personality. The plans were changed. The retention pond was moved, and a security fence was built around it. But not before many people in the church and the community had paid a high price for Charlie's stubborn conflict-resolution style.

THE TOUGH BARGAINER

Conflict is a part of the life of every congregation. The early church was barely beyond Pentecost when the Grecian widows were complaining about their lack of service in the daily distribution of food. The apostles had their first major conflict to deal with. The church has been in the conflict-resolution business since that time.

I teach a graduate course in Conflict Resolution and Management at Amberton University in Dallas. One of the first principles we learn is that conflict is a natural part of every human system—family, business, university, or church. Conflict isn't good or bad; it just is. Our approach to conflict is a key to the health of any congregation.

We study a variety of different models used to explain how people approach conflict. Most of them explain conflict along two dimensions. The first is my commitment to getting what I want. It can be low or high, depending on the subject. The second is my commitment to the relationship, and that dimension can be low or high as well.

Mouton and Blake proposed a classic model of conflict resolution based upon these two dimensions—commitment to personal gain and commitment to the relationship. Combining the two, they proposed four conflict-resolution styles shown on the chart below.

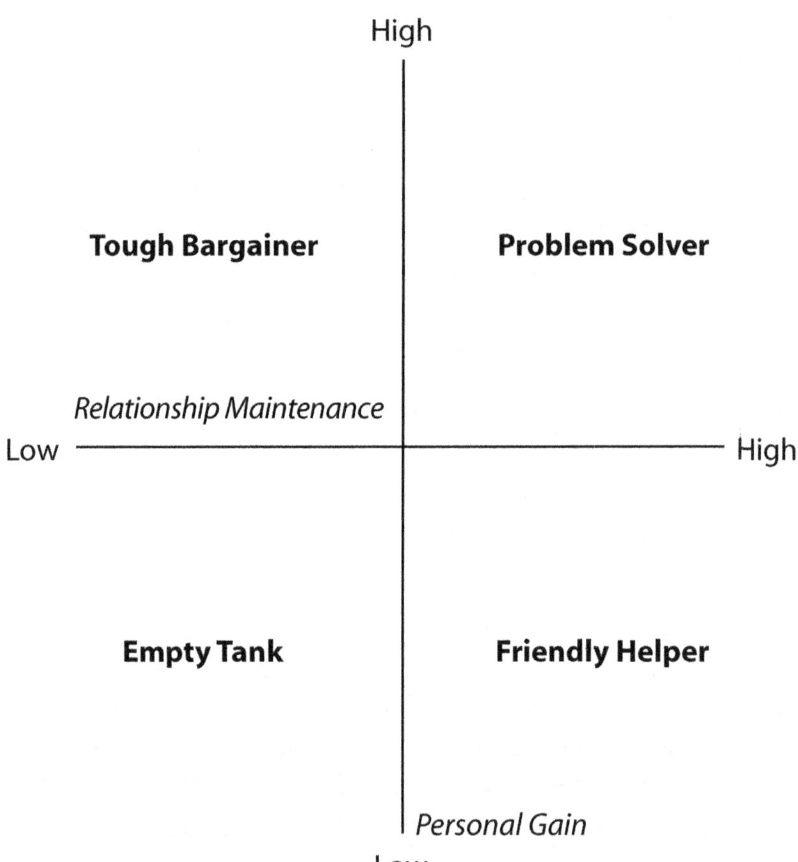

The Tough Bargainer is a church leader who is highly committed to personal gain and has a low commitment to relationship maintenance. They approach conflict resolution from a win-lose orientation, combined with a tough, no-nonsense, aggressive approach. Typically, relationships develop with this individual who is "going to have their say and get their way." Dealing long-term with a Tough Bargainer is exhausting for the rest of the church, because the individual has no social radar informing them how they are affecting others.

CHARACTERISTICS OF TOUGH BARGAINERS

- Tough, no-nonsense approach to decision making and conflict resolution.
- Say and do things that are offensive to others and damaging to relationships.
- No "social radar" informing them about the effects of their actions on others.
- Believe they "know better" than everyone else what needs to be done.
- Aggressive ambition will grab power to exert more control over a church.
- Monopolize discussions in meetings to control the power dynamics.
- Bully and badger others to get their way.
- Sulk and are highly offended when they do not get their way.
- Lack the "empathy chip," so they cannot feel the effects they are having on the church.
- Shocked when other leaders hold them accountable for their misuse of power.

TOUGH BARGAINER AND OTHER CONFLICT STYLES

Charlie's Tough-Bargainer style of conflict was complemented by another leader in the church who was a Friendly Helper. Carl's approach to conflict was one that valued relationships and tried to keep everyone happy, even if that meant sacrificing his own dreams. Carl, in the Mouton Blake Model, was high on relationship maintenance and low on personal gain. He was the perfect match for Carl's Tough-Bargainer conflict style. He was Charlie's wingman, coming along behind him, cleaning up bodies lying in his wake in the foyer.

The Tough Bargainer and Friendly Helper combination is typical in churches. The Tough Bargainer over-functions by demanding personal gain. The Friendly Helper over-functions by valuing relationships and avoiding conflict at all costs. They have a love-hate relationship, as Carl is forever hopeful that one day Charlie will wake up and see the damage he is doing. Charlie shows Carl disrespect because he considers his people orientation to be a sign of weakness. As we will see in Part Two, churches form systemic relationships that keep the dysfunctional patterns working. This is why churches do not change.

The healthiest approach to conflict resolution is the Problem-Solver style. This orientation values relationships highly but is going to be up front about what they would like to achieve. They "speak the truth in love." Problem Solvers are highly skilled at finding workable solutions to difficult problems, listening to everyone involved, and then communicating a solution in a clear and respectful manner. Problem Solvers can be very threatening to Tough Bargainers because they do not understand how they are able to get things done in a way that builds support and loyalty. In the opening case, Ms. Cho took a Problem-Solver stance toward Charlie. She listened politely as he vented all his hostility, and she did not react in an angry way. When she spoke, she presented her case with clarity and compassion.

I was consulting with a congregation that had a large leadership team. They had several Tough Bargainers in the group who were known in the congregation for being ill-tempered and stubborn. After one particularly egregious series of poor decisions, the congregation was up in arms. Members were demanding an audience with the leadership and were literally waiting in line one night to go in and "have their say."

An older, wise Problem Solver was a member of the church and had dealt with this leadership for many years. He watched the progression of bad decisions and the exit of members out the back door. He waited his turn in the outer office because he was the last one in line. The Tough-Bargainer leadership group knew they were in for a difficult conversation with this Problem Solver, so as he waited in the outer office, they quietly exited the building out the back door. They couldn't engage in a rational conversation, so they avoided the meeting entirely. A Tough Bargainer is a bully, and a bully is a coward.

WOUNDS TO THE CHURCH

The Tough Bargainer wounds the church in two ways. First, there is damage to the problem-solving and decision-making processes of the church. People complain that the church is controlled by one person or a small group of people. As we will see, that small group can be formally appointed leaders or informal leaders who work behind the scenes to control the church. The second form of wounding is to the fabric of relationships within the church. Church members carry the scars of years of painful conversations with the Tough Bargainer and need a way to process that pain. Ministry declines as more congregational energy is spent dealing with the Tough Bargainer. Paul urged the Ephesian church to "Be completely humble and gentle; be patient, bearing with one another in love" (Ephesians 4:2).

The wounding to the church may include the following characteristics:

- Low participation in meetings and decision making.
- Low participation in ministry.
- Stories are told informally about how people have been mistreated; lots of congregational gossip.
- Talented members (Problem Solvers) are on the sidelines or quietly leaving.
- One or more members repeatedly "takes on" the Tough Bargainer, resulting in rounds of open conflict.
- Congregation becomes "conflict habituated." They are negatively bonded by ongoing unresolved conflict.
- Membership is discouraged and in decline.
- Tough to recruit new leaders onto the leadership team.
- Relationships are strained and lack authenticity.

When I counsel parents, I tell them that if they use an authoritarian parenting style with their children, it will result in one of four outcomes. The same thing is true of a church subjected to Tough-Bargainer leadership. First, members may rise up in active rebellion. They will attempt to change the power structure and conflict processes but fail to do so. Second, some members will resort to "compliance with complaining." They will go along with city hall but fill their time talking about how badly the leadership functions. Third, members may opt for compliance with passive-aggressive retaliation. They will fight back by not following through on the jobs they are given. During Central Church's building program, the architect hired to design the building was so offended by Charlie's personality that he intentionally delayed the plans for several months, sending a passive-aggressive message that he would not be treated like a hired hand. The fourth response to Tough-Bargainer wounding is members exiting out the back door. My experience has shown that by this point it is questionable whether the congregation has the resources left to deal with the effects of the situation.

DEALING WITH TOUGH BARGAINERS

In Part Two we will explore a process for healing a church from Tough-Bargainer wounding. Here are some suggestions for dealing with Tough Bargainers in churches:

- Do not allow them in leadership.
- If in leadership, they should be removed as quickly as possible.
- Do not attempt to "reform" or "coach" the Tough Bargainer while they are in power. It will not work.
- Do not accept the Tough Bargainer's evaluation of you or a situation. It is skewed to fit their agenda.
- Limit your time with the Tough Bargainer and their access to you. Notice the effects they have on you physically, emotionally and spiritually.
- Find and cultivate emotional and spiritual reinforcement from others.
- Do not permit Tough Bargainers to offer pastoral care and counsel.
- Do not give Tough Bargainers a platform to speak.
- Pick your battles; they love a good fight.
- Be firm and unyielding on your own "non-negotiables."
- Be clear and firm on your personal and professional boundaries. Tough Bargainers will bend ethics to get their way.

CONGREGATIONAL HEALING

When I am working with a congregation healing from Tough-Bargainer wounding, I approach it as I would a very large, extended family that has been bullied by one member for many years. They need time and a safe space to recover from years of emotional and spiritual abuse. Some of the typical "Congregational Therapeutic Goals" we set include the following:

- Disempower the Tough Bargainer and his or her informal power structures in the church and find them help.
- Initiate active processes to repair relationship damage in the church.
- Provide time to identify healthy leaders, reconstruct the leadership team, and build new functional processes for decision making and conflict resolution.
- Help members process old offenses, tell their story, and find avenues of forgiveness to allow them to move forward.
- Empower members in a new decision-making process.
- Build trust between leadership and membership.

The postscript on Charlie's era of leadership was failure and disappointment. He and his team were eventually removed from leadership of the congregation. He and Carl never developed an authentic relationship. The architect quit in protest and had to be replaced, further delaying the building. Pledges to the building campaign fell off, and only a portion of the church building could be completed. Core long-term members left and went to other congregations, telling tales of mismanagement. The damage to the church's relationship with the neighboring community left permanent scars. The new minister resigned. The church, handicapped by a Tough Bargainer, stumbled into the next era of its history without momentum. Central Church was in need of a season of healing.

CHAPTER 3

THE NARCISSISTIC WOUND

Lights, camera, action. It's Sunday at Sundance Church. The praise band launched into a driving beat, the lights on stage lit up, the big screens filled with images of people raising their hands, and praise dancers moved across the stage. Twelve cameras began shooting the action from every angle, feeding the service live across the Sundance Sunday Celebration Network. Large Security Deacons roamed the crowd with Sundance Tithing Baskets and watched intently for disruptions. "Be sure to give now so God will give to you later," shouted the Associate Pastor. "And let's all welcome and bless Pastor Sandy as he comes to give us a word from the Lord!"

The congregation erupted in applause as a well-dressed, trim, and well-tanned man of forty moved briskly to the center of the stage and began waving his Bible affectionately at the crowd. "You all are so special," he proclaimed. "It's Sunday at Sundance, and we are here to claim all God's blessings." The auditorium was bursting with thousands of people crowding in to find a seat. From the foyer the gathering could barely be distinguished from a concert by the Red Hot Chili Peppers. It was Sunday at Sundance, and the show was on.

Pastor Sandy and his wife, Pastor Cheryl, had built Sundance from the ground up. Originating as an old, dying downtown church appropriately located on Sundown Ave, the elders hired Pastor Sandy and gave him "the keys to the kingdom." With his charismatic personality and ability to convince anyone of his vision, the struggling church began to attract scores of new congregants. Pastor Sandy called for the building of a "campus worthy of our calling," built his flock into a megachurch, and renamed it Sundance Church.

Sundance Church and Pastor Sandy had all the trappings of local church "success": a large campus, a huge staff of ministers and support personnel, thousands of local church members, a cable TV network, thousands of members online, and a budget that brought in millions each year in contributions. The image of Sundance was paramount.

Pastor Sandy was idolized and revered by his members. He could do no wrong, they believed. Look at how much he had sacrificed to build their church. His relationship with the congregation was a love fest—primarily in one direction. All Sandy had to do was mention how much he wanted to play golf at a particular course. *Poof*—that trip would be arranged by grateful members. He loved dining at a local restaurant, . . . and the invitation would appear. He had always dreamed of buying a luxury sports car. One arrived with a bow on it for Christmas. On his tenth anniversary at the church, the Pastor Sandy Prayer Garden was constructed in his honor, complete with a life-sized statue of the minister kneeling in prayer. Sandy basked in the love of his people.

Sundance provided every resource a believer could want. There was the Sundance Commemorative Bible that had all of Pastor Sandy's and Cheryl's favorite passages pre-highlighted for the reader. There was the Sundance Singles ministry, where Pastor Sandy and Pastor Cheryl provided dating rules for couples and conducted premarital counseling, even though neither had training in counseling, and Cheryl had become pregnant with Sandy's baby, necessitating a hurried marriage. And there was Sundance Fellowship, where lucky members were selected to meet for a picture with Pastor Sandy following the morning service and have their Sundance Commemorative Bible signed in *Koine* Greek by Sandy—the only Greek he had mastered was how to spell his name.

Pastor Sandy was not impressed with theological training or seminary education. He had dropped out of college after majoring in marketing and had entered sales. He could talk anyone into anything. After several less than successful jobs, he felt God's calling to enter ministry. Not long afterward, Sundown came calling. Sandy launched the Sundance Seminary, offering preacher training to gifted—and mostly very attractive—candidates for ministry. Sandy loved to wear vests, and each Sundance seminarian was supplied with a vest embossed with the church logo. The Seminary bestowed an honorary doctorate on Sandy, and his congregation loved to call him Dr. Sandy, though he'd never taken a single graduate course—or even completed his undergraduate studies.

Pastor Cheryl was a force to be dealt with. Intensely protective of her husband and their lucrative position, her hands were on the major decisions behind the scenes. If her husband were threatened, it was Cheryl who would come calling with her spiritual sword of revenge. The key ranks on staff were occupied by members of Sandy's family. His son was a CPA and managed the church's finances—careful to keep all financial matters strictly in the inner circle of leadership. His daughter was an attorney and ran the Sundance Strategic Vision Team, and his uncle was the Executive Pastor, who oversaw the staff. When asked about nepotism, Sandy dismissed it with a wave of his hand. "I just like working with people I know."

But all was not well in Camelot. Sundance members were categorized informally into a two-tier system. There were the general members who came, worshiped, gave sacrificially, and were expected to be loyal soldiers of the Lord. That meant sit down, shut up, and don't make waves. Another circle of "exceptional" members was granted access to the pastor and his family. Exceptional members typically had deep financial pockets, power in the community, notoriety, or a special talent that allowed them to reinforce the Sundance image. Sandy and Cheryl lived in a massive home justified for church fellowships, but few members in the first category every saw the inside of the house. It made a substantial tax deduction for the couple.

The ministerial staff was a roller coaster of disequilibrium. There were the staff members who "drank the Kool-Aid." They believed in Sandy and Cheryl and were unquestionably loyal to them. Then there was the revolving door of ministers. These talented and committed people would often join the Sundance team, only to discover that their ideas were not welcome or they were too talented and threatened the insecurities of the senior minister. One associate minister was told before filling in to preach for Pastor Sandy, "Preach—just don't do too good."

Sundance was under investigation by the IRS for possible mismanagement of funds and their status as a nonprofit. Several employees and former ministers had launched a website accusing the church of spiritual abuse. These charges were dismissed as Satan's attacks against the faithful, and Sundance steamed ahead, leasing the pastor a private jet for quick trips to conduct ministerial visits to satellite congregations.

But it was the ongoing rumor of sexual misconduct that was whispered in the hallways by members and ministers alike that kept the inner circle of leadership up at night. Sandy clearly had an eye for leggy blonds. His secretary, a loyal defender for twenty years, nonchalantly spoke of these women as "Sandy's church groupies." They would sit up front, hang onto every word Sandy spoke, and then request "pastoral counseling time" in the minister's private study. It was against this group that Cheryl was constantly on guard. Sandy's secretary, herself a leggy blonde, would just smile and say nothing. It was not uncommon for the senior minister to find jobs for these women in the church or among prominent members and spend a significant amount of time "discipling" them personally.

There was no time for negativity at Sundance Church. The place was rockin', and the church was growing, . . . so God must be pleased—right? They were celebrating the opening of another satellite church that morning. High-pressure Sundance Launch Teams had placed thousands of brochures on the windshields of every car in every church parking lot surrounding their new church plant. After all, we're Sundance; everyone wants to be a part of our fellowship.

FIRST AXIOM OF LEADERSHIP

There is an axiom of leadership: a system cannot be healthier than its leadership. If the leadership is functioning well, the family, church, or other organization will function better. If the leadership is sick, the congregation will mirror their pathology.

In the case of a Narcissistic Church, the leader has a core wound, and that wound is affecting every area of his life. Since he is leading a church, he is unconsciously projecting his own wounds and needs onto the congregation. The narcissistic leader is "running on empty." There is a hole in his soul, and he is trying to fill it by feeding his self-image. The church is organized around filling the pastor's internal wound with massive doses of attention, reinforcement, special favors, and the trappings of success. His self-image has become the altar to worship before.

Roger Kruger, in *The Proper Care of Snakes*, states, "Individuals with narcissistic personality disorder are preoccupied with self-image. Narcissists want or need little from others other than that which feeds their self-aggrandizement. They are full of big ideas, which they are gifted at describing in glowing terms but that, upon closer examination, often are lacking in specific details. They exude self-confidence and have an aura of nonchalance about them—until their confidence is shaken, when they are likely to respond with rage" (Kruger, 109).

PERSONALITY DISORDERS

The individual suffering from a personality disorder will have a number of common characteristics, including:

- The condition is pervasive—it affects all areas of their life.
- The condition is not amenable to change—it is not easily addressed, and the person does not seek help.

- The condition results in the individual being incapable of self-reflection—they assume it is everyone else who has a problem and they are fine.
- The condition causes them to be easily hurt or threatened and lack any coping skills to deal with others or problem-solve to correct the situation.

SIX CHARACTERISTICS OF THE NARCISSISTIC MINISTER

Pastor Sandy was functioning as a narcissistic leader for Sundance Church, with a combination of six very powerful personality traits that combined to create a congregational climate that appeared to an outsider to be very exciting but was deeply flawed spiritually and psychologically.

Charismatic Salesmanship with a Teflon Coating

Narcissistic ministers are charismatic speakers and inspirational leaders. They can convince a church that they are capable of doing great things and making significant sacrifices. When the plans fail or when the goal is not achieved, however, the minister will not be to blame. It is always someone else's fault. But not to worry: they are already off on their next "vision" for God's people.

Special Status

Narcissistic ministers believe they are in a special category. They are different from everyone else because they have been gifted with a special "calling from God." They should be awarded special privileges, and they are exempt from the rules that common folk must abide by. They baptize their arrogance with selected Scriptures that reinforce a haughty, self-righteous attitude. There really is a two-tiered system in their minds. With a casual wave of their hands, they exempt themselves from the IRS, ethical codes of conduct, counseling confidentiality, or sexual boundaries and marital vows of fidelity. "You just don't understand who I am and what I've been called to do with my life!"

Lacking the Empathy Chip

In Part Two we will explore the vital role empathy plays in the healing process of a church. However, there are ministers who lack what I call "the empathy chip." Empathy involves two steps. First, one must be able to recognize pain in another person. Second, one must be able to respond in a meaningful way to that condition. We want our ministers to be high in empathy skills. Narcissistic ministers are incapable of recognizing pain in others and therefore are unable to say or do things that would be helpful. In fact, they leave church members astonished at the things they say that are completely inappropriate. They are incapable of empathy.

No Conflict-Resolution Skills

Healthy leaders understand that conflict is a normal part of life in any church, and they develop skills. Narcissistic leaders, since they have a weak self-image, experience conflict as a threat to their self-worth. They may respond in rage with unexpected attacks over a small incident. They may respond with revenge, using a trusted colleague to exact vengeance on the poor victim. They may preach publicly against the people they feel are offending them—even addressing family members from the pulpit. Or they may crumble under the strain and publicly emote sobs of hurt and pain that are embarrassing to listeners.

Exploitation of Others

The narcissistic minister will attract others around him that are willing to do his bidding. They "drink the Kool-Aid" of his ongoing needs for attention and approval. As the church grows and is "successful," so will his needs. Members who can provide special favors, gifts of money or trips, are awarded attention and friendship by the pastor and his inner circle. As long as the gifts keep flowing, the access continues. However, the church has a long history of former members having been "used and cast aside" once their usefulness was over. Lacking empathy, the pastor sees them as former sheep who were never committed in the first place.

Incapable of Self-Reflection

When I begin working with a leader, one of the first assessments I make is their capacity for self-reflection. Can they step back and take a look at the role they play in the ongoing problems of the church? What do I do that contributes to the problem? Sometimes the answer is "I just didn't see it." That is still a contribution. The narcissistic minister in *incapable* of self-reflection. They are convinced that everyone else is to blame for whatever goes wrong. It is highly unlikely that they will be open to a consultant, or anyone from outside the church giving them input. They are highly resistant to therapy and rarely present themselves to my practice. When they do, it is to convince me of how normal they are and how badly everyone else in their world misunderstands them.

BUSINESSMEN MASQUERADING AS MINISTERS

The Narcissistic Church has many similar characteristics to a large, corrupt organization. The issues center on the big three—money, sex, and power. The church culture may be using "religious jargon" and "religious ceremony," but it is a thin veil for the corruption and abuse running just under the surface. Because self-image is the critical component to be defended, a great deal of energy goes into crafting and protecting the public persona.

Dr. Carroll Osburn, in his *Lectures on Titus*, describes Jewish rabbis who traveled the diaspora, teaching outlying communities of Jewish people how to follow the Mishna and traditions. These supposed religious teachers were really driven by the profit motive. Dr. Osburn calls them "businessmen masquerading as ministers."

Titus 1:10–11 reads, "For there are many rebellious people, full of meaningless talk and deception, especially those of the circumcision group. They must be silenced, because they are disrupting whole households by teaching things they ought not to teach—and that *for the sake of dishonest gain*" (emphasis added).

Healing for the Narcissistic Church will require an assessment of the power, money trail, and patterns of sexual misconduct that we will explore in the next chapter. All three are difficult to accomplish; therefore, recovery for this church will be more complex and require more time than would other forms of congregational healing.

SECOND AXIOM OF LEADERSHIP

The first Axiom of Leadership is that a system can be no heathier than its top leadership. The Second Axiom of Leadership is that a leader in a dysfunctional role will produce other roles around them that are also dysfunctional. At Sundance Church, Sandy had surrounded himself with a group of co-conspirators functioning in maladaptive ways to facilitate his leadership. His wife, Cheryl, was both a defender and a detective, keeping an eye on his sexual indiscretions. His secretary was a gatekeeper, allowing only the upper-tier members to have access to him and guarding his secrets. The Executive Minister executed his bidding among the staff and cultivated the large contributors. The staff kept their heads down, performing their duties and saluting the Sundance flag.

Systems Theory, which we will explore in chapter 10, suggests that vulnerable individuals move into important roles in a dysfunctional system. These roles serve to counter-balance the role of the Narcissistic minister and keep the system in its dysfunctional balance or homeostasis.

THE ENABLER ROLE

This is an individual who is a chief facilitator of the narcissistic leader. Like an individual who is constantly picking up the check at the end of a meal at a restaurant with friends who are capable of paying, this person is paying a price for the misbehavior of another. Cheryl, Sandy's wife, is in an enabling role, as are his secretary and the executive minister. They "pay the bills" for the outlandish behavior of the narcissist.

THE DEFENDER

The defender is the individual who picks up the flag and defends the narcissist from attacks. Again, Cheryl flips into this role when Sandy is attacked because she alone is allowed to hold him accountable. Members can be powerful defenders of a Narcissistic Church and become highly offended if an outsider questions the methods, beliefs, or motives of the church.

THE PERFORMER

While Sandy plays the primary role of performer in this system, he is attracted to other talented performers. The church must use highly skilled staff and ministers to maintain its performance standards. However, this is a double-edged sword. The talented individual soon finds that they are threating the fragile ego of the narcissist and will be quickly shown the door. As the new associate minister discovered, "Don't do too good."

THE SCAPEGOAT

Narcissistic Churches are constantly identifying and persecuting individuals they perceive to be a threat to the congregation. An individual may ask the wrong question in a meeting. A staff member may become too popular with the youth group. A worship minister may be getting too much praise. The individual is targeted, and a campaign to "drive them out of the camp" is initiated "for the good of the church and our mission here on earth." At Narcissistic Churches, it is common to call upon the judgment of God as justification for hate, slander, and lying.

DEALING WITH A NARCISSISTIC MINISTER

- Stay out of contractual agreements and negotiations with them.

- Wounded narcissists are dangerous.
- Be friendly but keep a distance.
- When problems occur, stick to the facts and show alternatives.
- Remember that the other person will always be to blame in a conflict situation.
- Offer highly rationalized reasons for their bad behavior.
- Live by double standards—ethically, spiritually, and morally.
- Paint others black, both publicly and privately, who are a threat to them.
- Conduct a hidden life of lies, secrets, manipulation, and gaslighting.
- Keep in mind that the narcissist is incapable of exhibiting remorse for their misconduct of empathy for damage they have caused.
- Remember that, when relieved of their ministry, they will seek a quick new start without addressing their core wound.

WOUNDS TO THE CHURCH

The Narcissistic Church is a highly wounded group of people who may not know the full extent of the damage they have incurred. If the members have been in the church for an extended period of time, the dysfunctional patterns may be their "normal." Other individuals have left and carry their scars with them. They include former ministers who have been scapegoated and had their ministry careers destroyed. Also included are talented people who have given generously, only to be tossed aside when their usefulness was over. Faithful members sacrifice for years and work tirelessly, only to discover that, when they were sick, in a family crisis, or out of a job, the church was not there for them. Ultimately, this is a system built around fulfilling the empty hole in the senior minister—a hole that cannot be filled by other people. The narcissist has to do his work, and that work must be done away from the ministry setting.

Wounds to the church may include:

- Disenchantment with the role of the local church and ministry in general.
- Emergence of church secrets and ongoing crisis management.
- Revolving door of ministers and staff.
- Financial mismanagement.
- Ethical violations.
- Sexual misconduct.
- Shallow preaching that does not provide a balanced feeding of the Word of God.
- Nepotism is common within the church organization.
- The church is a closed world unto itself with an "us vs. them" mentality.
- Growing "alumni base" in the community of former hurt and disenchanted members.

CONGREGATIONAL HEALING

My experience is that the prognosis for the Narcissistic Church is not always hopeful. The congregational system is going to resist help and a healing process. First, the church views itself as a "special group of God's elect people." They are unique, and someone from the outside simply will not be able to understand them. Second, they reflect the distrust the narcissistic leader has of input coming from any source other than their own group. An outside church consultant will not be trusted, and it will be assumed that any information provided "applies to those other churches, but we are not like them."

A healing transition may be difficult because the church has become accustomed to immediate change. They do not have the spiritual or emotional discipline for the long process of ending the current leadership and rebuilding a completely new, healthy church system. When a narcissist church goes into crisis, perhaps when a pastoral offense goes public, they will either conduct an elaborate public repentance of the pastor and restore him to his throne or go in search of the next savior and hire another narcissist. Church systems tend to replicate themselves.

Some of the most rewarding work I have done as a therapist and a consultant is with former members of a Narcissistic Church. They come in wounded, discouraged, and angry at the mistreatment they have received. They are questioning themselves, the church, and God. They are in need of tremendous spiritual and emotional support to understand the abuse they have been through. The best we can often is to get people off the Narcissistic-Church ship before it sinks.

A CALL FROM DENNIS

My phone rang one morning at the church, and it was Dennis, our Executive Minister, on the line. "Can you come down here to my office right now, or are you doing a session?" In a few moments I was sitting in Dennis's office with a young couple who were looking pretty shaken up.

"Don, these folks have just come from the hospital. They've lost their baby—a little boy. The ministers at their church were there and told them, 'It was because there was sin in your lives that the baby died.' At this point the grieving woman sobbed. They need some help doing a funeral, and they need someone to talk to. Do you think we can help these kids out? My calendar is now clear."

When they left, Dennis told me where they attended. It was a local church known for high control, high public profile, and a high turnover of members. It was a hotbed of narcissistic excesses in the name of religion.

We buried that little boy in the children's garden at Restland Cemetery in Dallas one beautiful spring morning. The young couple's hearts were broken, and so was mine. Dennis choked through the service and held back his tears. To my surprise, their former church sent two ministers to the graveside service. I was appalled at their lack of empathy. They stood there in dark suits glaring at us and saying nothing. My first impulse was to chain them both to the back of my pickup and drag them down Greenville Avenue. I took a very deep breath.

I don't know whether that young couple recovered their faith in God and belief in the role of the local church. I know that when they were grieving, the only way their Narcissistic Church responded was with attack, blame, and guilt. We wonder why churches are not growing. Perhaps it is because of the invisible damage done in the guise of religion by sick leaders who are emotionally, psychologically, and spiritually abusive. Paul knew exactly what he was talking about when he commanded Titus, "They must be silenced."

CHAPTER 4

THE SEXUALITY WOUND

I was walking out of the coffee shop when I met the minister's wife, Karen, walking in. I was in town conducting a marriage seminar at her church, and she invited me to join her for coffee. "Your lecture last night touched a nerve with me," she shared. "I am a woman in pain," she blurted out, "and I cannot go on like this any longer." She proceeded to download her "ministerial family secret": Carl, the love of her life, had been involved in one affair after another over the course of a 23-year marriage. Sometimes he would be carrying on multiple affairs at the same time with women in the church and community. She was angry, tired, and ashamed of having put up with it for so long.

"Carl is beloved by this church," she went on. "He's been adored by every church we've worked for because he connects so quickly with people. They feel like he's their best friend after talking with him for five minutes. And that's the problem. He can connect with women so quickly. He seems to possess an intuitive sense of what's going on inside a woman without them sharing much. They come away from talking to him feeling like he understands them better than any other man they've ever met. Believe me, I know. I felt that way too when we first met in college. Carl can really turn on the charm when he wants to. He can make a woman feel like she is so special to him.

"I've tried everything to deal with his messing around. When I was younger and newly married, I thought I was imagining things.

Carl would be offended, saying I was accusing him falsely of things 'a man with his calling would never do.' Then I found sexual emails to the children's minister, and that blew the lid off the first time. He cried, he begged, he repented, and he swore to me it would never happen again. Right! Not until we hired the next children's minister.

"I've tried everything I know. I've tried ignoring it, and my resentment just builds until I'm livid at his level of disrespect. Honestly, Don, I could open my own detective agency I have spent so much time following him, checking his emails, and confirming he's at church conferences. At this point in my life, I'm exhausted, and he's showing no signs of slowing down. Right now, I'm certain he's involved with a young divorced woman in our single again program. They meet regularly for 'discipling' meetings, and he's helped her find a job in one of our deacon's companies. He talks about her constantly, and he doesn't realize he's doing it. The man has no self-awareness.

"I know you're a marriage and family therapist and are going to tell me to try counseling. Been there, done that. Carl, when I could badger him into going, would show up for a session or two and charm the therapist or dominate the session by showing off with books he's read. The man is all show, and there is no depth to him. I think he's addicted to the chase after a lover.

"When I finally get enough and get angry or break down under the weight of all of it and cry, he just looks at me like I'm crazy. It's as if he's 'missing the empathy chip' in his emotional makeup. He cannot feel the normal emotions other humans feel. That's a terrible thing to say about your husband and sounds bizarre to say about a minister, but it is the truth. The man does not have the ability to empathize with another person's pain.

"The elders of our church have long suspected something is wrong. They've heard the rumors flying around the church about Carl and his 'current girlfriend.' But the church is growing, we are attracting lots of new members, and our giving is off the charts. I think they are scared to say anything because they are afraid of what they know deep inside to be the truth. They went so far as to assign one of the elders to be Carl's accountability partner. This elder has an office at the church to 'keep an eye' on Carl, but he's as sleazy around women as Carl is! The whole thing is a sad, terrible joke.

"Don, you talked last night about marriages where there isn't a lot of 'gas left in the tank.' That's exactly where I am. I'm weighing my options now. Do I cash it in on a 23-year marriage that has always had at least three of us in bed? My kids are almost grown. Do I wait a little longer and give them time to get out of the house? Or do I wait for the day when one of Carl's former lovers goes public with her story and the secrets all come pouring out?"

She finished her coffee and looked me in the eye with the cold look of a woman who has survived years of sexual betrayal. "I'm a woman in pain. I have paid my dues—to this marriage, to this church, and to Carl's beloved ministry. This is going to stop. I'm going to get the help my children and I need. When the truth comes out, it will blow this church apart."

THE SEXUAL-ADDICTION CHURCH

The Sexual-Addiction Affair has been identified by Dr. Emily Brown in her book *Patterns of Infidelity and Their Treatment* as one of five forms of affairs that occur in marriage. These forms of affairs can take root in churches and cause tremendous damage if not treated properly.

The sex addict is suffering from a core wound, often an early attachment wound, that has left a psychic hole in their soul. Rather than do the hard work of confronting the wound, the sex addict treats the wound with one sex partner after another. This is similar to an alcoholic's addiction, except that the drug of choice is sex, not Jack Daniels. This pattern normally emerges in adolescence and continues, if untreated, throughout the addict's life.

The sex addict is powerless to stop the behavior on their own without professional treatment. No amount of monitoring, prayer, Bible study, or men's accountability groups will put a dent in this compulsive disorder. Sex addicts rarely present for therapy, and when they do, they make it clear that it is everyone else who has a problem—they are doing just fine. In my forty years of conducting therapy, I have never had a high-profile sex addict call me for help on their own.

The local church presents a safe haven and a target-rich environment for the minister or church leader who suffers from sexual addiction. Close friendships are encouraged. Church members are in social situations where personal and emotional information about their lives is shared. Members in crisis are in need of pastoral care and vulnerable to the grooming behaviors of sex addicts. My experience has been that, the more successful the church appears to be in terms of "nickels and noses," the more likely the leaders are to co-conspire to keep the sex addict from getting help. In the case of Carl and Karen, the church leadership was co-conspiring to continue his addiction and allow him access to unsuspecting victims in the church.

Karen, as a faithful spouse, tried for a long time to ignore the behavior and fell into a co-dependent role of keeping up the family image. Most of the spouses I've worked with are highly intelligent, talented women who are trying to navigate a situation that is impossible for them to resolve on their own. Some, like Karen, reach what I call "the Popeye Moment" when they say, "I've had all I can stand." They are done with the marriage and go public with the family secret of many affairs. Others become co-addicted to the money, prestige, and power that ministry affords and create a parallel marriage for themselves, separate from their husband's ministry. In either case, the local church is robbed of authentic ministry and is literally built on sinking sand.

THE LONG-STANDING AFFAIR CHURCH

Beacon Street Church was an institution in town. They had called me to consult with them about starting a counseling center after a string of high-profile divorces among the members and ministerial staff had rocked the church to her foundations. When I did an assessment of the congregation's families, I discovered that fifty percent of the Sunday-morning crowd reported a need for individual, marital, or family counseling. Beacon Street was a church in pain.

Beacon Street had been blessed by a long-term ministry from its "founding pastor," Brother Bob, who had started the church thirty years earlier. He was now the Senior Minister over a staff of fifty and also served as the chairman of the executive board of deacons. To say that Brother Bob ran Beacon Street would be an understatement. The church mirrored his personality and values.

Brother Bob was a ball of energy and enthusiasm. He was always on the go, promoting a new ministry or raising money for a needy family in the community. He was preaching, teaching, evangelizing, and promoting seven days a week. Staff half his age had trouble keeping up with Bob and often complained about the long hours and endless demands.

Assisting Brother Bob with the day-to-day operations of the church was his loyal assistant, Becky. Becky had begun working for Bob shortly after the church was planted and then aligned herself closely with him following the loss of her husband to cancer while she was raising two young boys. Beacon Street, and Brother Bob in particular, were her mission in life, and she defended him with undying loyalty. As the church grew, Bob needed a financial manager to oversee the complex operations of church finances, and he moved Becky into that role.

As I began working with Beacon Street, I quickly learned that I would have to schedule my meetings with Brother Bob around his daily conferences with Becky that would sometimes go on for two hours behind closed doors in his office. It was clear that there was no accountability for Bob's actions, and that informal rule had spread to the rest of the ministerial staff. As long as there were no obvious problems, ministers operated in an independent silo.

The first tremor occurred one morning during a particularly difficult couple's therapy session. While working with Beacon Street starting their counseling center, I'd agreed to start meeting with some clients because the need for therapy was so great. During the session, the husband revealed that he had been engaged in an extramarital affair for the past year. While these sessions are always difficult, this one was even more so because the woman he was now involved with was a minister on staff at Beacon Street Church. The wife felt betrayed by her husband and by the church.

A short time later, I was working with another couple from the congregation. Once again, an affair was revealed; this time the wife was carrying on an affair with one of the core leaders on the leadership team of Beacon Street Church. Once again, the betrayal and the pain were compounded by the fact that a church leader was involved.

In a short period of time, I was treating a large number of couples who were all experiencing the crisis of an extramarital affair, and all of them involved various members of the Beacon Street Church leadership and ministry team. As a family systems therapist, I knew that this was no accident and that it was symptomatic of deeper congregational systemic patterns across the entire church.

In time, I discovered that Brother Bob had been involved in a long-standing extramarital affair with his assistant, Becky, and that this affair had become informally "institutionalized" as an unspoken part of the congregational culture. It was the corporate congregational secret everyone knew about but no one talked about.

When I grow St. Augustine grass in my lawn in Texas, the grass sends out runners across the yard. When I start to pull up one strand of grass, I find that it is connected all the way across my yard. That is what occurred as I started unraveling the complex sexual history of the Beacon Street Church. Brother Bob and his long-standing affair with Becky had left a legacy of sexual misconduct. The leadership of the church had created a congregational climate in which sexual boundaries and sexual ethics were ignored. Sex, on the part of church leaders, was seen as a part of the "benefits package" of being spiritually successful. This was a sickness that had infected the entire congregation.

Emily Brown, in *Patterns of Infidelity and Their Treatment,* describes the Conflict Avoidant Affair as a form of affair that occurs when a husband and wife are unable to discuss their conflict. The couple ends up moving emotionally farther apart, and the problems build up under the rug. Brother Bob was unable to deal with problems in his own marriage because he was a conflict avoider. He believed in staying positive. When his own marriage was suffering, he turned to Becky and a safe listening ear. Over time, the friendship grew into an emotional affair and finally a sexual one.

In time, Beacon Street Church became a Long-Standing Affair Church. Affairs do not stay secret. People recognize them for what they are. The leadership of the Beacon Street Church was not willing to deal with Brother Bob's and Becky's affair. By ignoring the affair, they actually created a congregational context that made extramarital affairs "acceptable behavior" so long as no one talked about them. The First Axiom of Leadership maintains that a system can only be as healthy as its leadership is. In this case, Brother Bob was granting permission to his leadership team to do as he did, not as he said. Some of them willingly followed his lead.

THE FLIRTATIOUS-MINISTER CHURCH

"You are doing such a great job! And you are such a lovely young lady! What is your name? My name's Mark." I was meeting Mark for the first time at a local restaurant, but I was having a difficult time starting a conversation with him because he was so interested in our waitress—a young college student at the local community college. Over the course of our meal, he was able to learn her name and how she was doing in school and to share a couple of cute stories with her. Mark was clearly flirting with her, and she was happy to respond. Perhaps this would mean a bigger tip! At the end of our lunch, Mark shared his business card with her and thanked her for her lovely service.

It appeared to be an innocent lunch; however, Mark was not a college student at the local college—he was the minister of the

College Church and was a married father of three children. "That waitress seemed to like you," I remarked to him as we walked out the front door. "Oh, I'm just friendly with everyone—especially the women. Women are more likely to attend church, you know." And off he went, oblivious to the fact that he had just been having lunch with a marriage shrink who was attuned to people's unhealthy sexual boundaries.

A few months later, I received a call from Mark. He was doing some pastoral counseling with a member and wanted to pick my brain. Could I meet him for coffee? We met at a crowded Starbucks near a rail line. Mark, always the enthusiastic conversationalist, launched into a lengthy description of the situation, as I listened. This time it was Mark's nonverbal communication that struck me as rather odd. The entire time we talked, he could not maintain eye contact with me. His eyes would wander around the room. I noticed that he would pick up on the women entering or leaving the Starbucks and attempt to catch their eye. On several occasions he did, and a quick nod was exchanged between him and the woman. Nothing was ever said, but it was obvious Mark's radar for the opposite sex was constantly on. Once again, the therapist in me simply filed the information away.

Over the next several years, I had a steady stream of female clients come through my counseling practice who were former members of College Church. They all said the same thing: the preacher there just makes me uncomfortable. I can't put my finger on it exactly; he's never come out and said anything overtly provocative or sexual, but he's always right there on the line. I think the guy's a sicko, so I left!

Mark was sending seductive messages to women in his congregation and his community and defending this practice as "just a minister being friendly." When he was confronted with his inappropriate behavior, he would brush it off as people being overly sensitive and not knowing how to "take a joke from a friendly guy." The women he offended, and their husbands he disrespected, did not think it was appropriate behavior.

SIGNS OF A FLIRTATIOUS MINISTER

- Using sexually suggestive humor to bring sex into a conversation.
- Inappropriate and unwanted touch.
- Use their position to blur the boundaries of healthy sexuality.
- Often on the edge with inappropriate comments about appearance, appeal, and sexuality.
- May tell stories in sermons or bring up sexuality in public settings that seem odd or strange.
- Give off a sleazy vibe or air.
- Use their ministerial position to gain access to people and then use that access to meet their own needs.
- Develop a reputation among women as a man to keep their distance from.
- Poor verbal filtering.
- Violate nonverbal boundaries.
- Offended and shocked when confronted. Blame others for misunderstanding them.
- Spouse is embarrassed by comments and behavior or seems oblivious to it.

LIVING IN DUAL REALITIES

All three of these case studies—those of the Sexual-Addiction Church, the Long-Standing Affair Church, and the Flirtatious-Minister Church, share a common theme. All three require the minister to live in a dual reality. Many times, this dual reality extends to the congregation, as they are affected by a sexual wound.

THE RELIGIOUS-IMAGE REALITY

On Sundays we stand up and proclaim the Word of God and hold up the standard of spiritual and ethical behavior. However, this commitment is two inches deep. It has no substance to it because it is a religious image that is being maintained. As long as we look good, sound good, and go through all the right religious traditions, everything will be okay. The sexual addict in particular is feeding his core wound of self-image with sexual acting out. The flirtatious minister is soothing a lagging self-esteem with attention from the opposite sex. Tremendous psychic energy must go into building and maintaining a fake religious image to hide behind.

THE SEXUAL REALITY

In some churches, sex, money, and power are the "big three addictions." We simply baptize their addiction in spiritual terminology and ignore the damage they do to the church. Sex, money, and power are seen as legitimate parts of the ministerial "benefits package." As long as the co-conspiring church leaders can maintain the dual reality, they will do so, hoping that the scandals do not become public. Some of the most vicious leaders I've dealt with have been those who are co-conspiring to hide sexual misconduct in the church. They are dangerous enemies when threatened because they know the stakes are so high if the truth becomes known. Sadly, the local church loses its soul and acts like any other corrupt organization.

Years ago, *D Magazine* ran a cover story on the decline and fall of a high-profile local Dallas minister who had a pattern of sexual addiction. When the affair went public, it was as though one had pulled up a runner of grass, and all the other sexual partners he'd had during his tenure began to step forward. In that article, the author described the change in the thinking of the minister as "rapture of the deep." It was as though the rules that apply to everyone else did not apply to him. And he thought no one would notice. Ministers like this are drowning. Sadly, many of them take the church down with them.

HOW TO CONDUCT A SEXUAL COVER-UP

I have worked with a large number of churches that are dealing with sexual wounds. An affair of a high-profile minister or church leader has gone public, and the church is now reeling with the aftermath of the betrayal. At this point, congregations confront a fork in the road. If they are to be a client church of mine, we will move forward with a plan of treatment that is transparent, responsible, and provides appropriate treatment for the minister, the minister's marriage, the leadership, and the church. The minister's time there in ministry is over. Period. It must end in order for healing to occur within the congregation.

Some churches feel as though they are exempt from the normal rules of human relationships. They are "specially gifted" by God and know how to deal with matters internally better than anyone from outside the congregation. After all, hasn't that been their mode of operation all along? Remember, sick leaders will continue to make poor decisions, even when the house is burning down around them. They choose a fork in the road that closes the church to outside consultation and helps ensure that the sexual wound will be a permanent scar on the history of that church.

The sexual cover-up is designed to move the church as quickly as possible through the crisis and restore the minister to his place of ministry, so members can all "get on with the work of the Lord." The cover-up is instigated by leaders who lack the ability to walk through high levels of conflict and instead apply "simplistic answers to complex problems," such as the minister's affair. The thinking is: "Maybe if we pray enough, ask God to restore this marriage and ministry, and come together in forgiveness, this will all just go away." This is simplistic thinking that ignores the hard work of dealing with the pain in the life of the minister that gave rise to the sexual behavior in the first place. If that pain is not dealt with, it will be repeated.

The plan to move quickly through the crises and cover up the wounds progresses in four phases:

Phase One: Denial in Pre-Crises Mode

Prior to an affair going public, the leadership and membership are in denial regarding the sexual behaviors going on within the church. They may be ignoring the behavior or functioning as enablers actively working to keep things covered up. Denial is a powerful force within the church, and this will be the fallback position the church system relies upon to avoid doing the hard work of healing the church.

Phase Two: Crisis Mode

In crisis mode, the affair has now gone public, and leaders are dealing with the aftermath of the affair or affairs. Leaders are struggling to "get the story" so they can begin to do damage control. One of the realities of doing affair counseling that I've experienced is that it takes months to piece together a full narrative of what happened over the course of an affair. Everyone involved is invested in *not* disclosing what happened. It is typical for leaders to be struggling with a new crisis each week, as they try to navigate while the story is constantly changing.

Members are asking questions that cannot be answered. Leaders are concerned about who will preach this Sunday and wondering how they are going to move forward. If churches are not careful, leaders who themselves are wounded and over-functioning will step into the gap and make matters worse. It is difficult to do surgery on oneself, but they are determined to try.

Phase Three: Quick Repentance

A church conducting a sexual cover-up will opt for a quick repentance on the part of the minister. He will make a public confession of wrongdoing, often accompanied by his wife, who is still in shock. The church leadership, supported by key enabling members, will call upon the church to practice forgiveness and "obey what the Bible teaches." A great show will be made of his contrite nature, and dispersions will be cast on the reputation of the woman who lured him to this uncharacteristic moral failure.

If marriage counseling is required by the church leadership, the minister in the Sexual-Addiction Church, or the Long-Standing Affair Church, will lobby for an intensive weekend session where they can go away and "quickly get this behind us." They return from the experience proclaiming that the marriage has been saved and the church may move forward, neglecting to do any follow-up counseling or implement any of the suggestions made by the therapist. An accountability group may be assembled, but the addictive minister will lobby for close allies and friends to be members of the group. It is not about doing the work; it is about restoring the image of the minister and the congregation.

Phase Four: Accelerated Restoration

To everyone's delight, the minister has made remarkable progress in therapy with his accountability group. After consultation with the church leadership, he is now ready to step back into the pulpit and lead the congregation to new and greater heights. He's a changed man. He may even deliver a series on marriage-based sermons on his recent struggles! All this has happened within a matter of a few weeks, and all is back on track again. The episode of the whole ugly affair becomes just an unfortunate blip on the screen in the history of the church—never to be mentioned again.

The sexual cover-up strategy fails in its attempt to restore the minister, to heal the marriage, and to assist the church in moving forward. It puts a band-aid on a cancer that often reappears within a short time. I have talked with hundreds of church members in such congregations who will describe in vivid detail the sexual misconduct of a minister or church leader that occurred twenty or thirty years earlier. They have never been allowed to process the damage that the affair did to them emotionally and spiritually. If the Church of God is worthy of its calling, then it is strong enough to walk through the pain of healing. To do less is an insult to God's people. "They dress the wound of my people as though it were not serious."

THE AFFAIR SYNDROME

Dr. James Cail, my friend and colleague at Oklahoma Christian University, is a pioneer in the field of marriage therapy. Early in his career he observed the patterns of people involved in extramarital affairs and proposed *The Affair Syndrome* as a way to explain the stages people move through as an affair develops. The Affair Syndrome is especially helpful when we try to understand how affairs occur in churches.

Stage One: Proximity

Dr. Cail notes that people typically have affairs with other people they are regularly in contact with. Proximity is the first determinate of who a person is involved with in an extramarital affair. Coaches have affairs with players, teachers have affairs with students, doctors have affairs with nurses, and ministers have affairs with members. The internet has changed the impact of proximity. If an individual wants to meet someone and have an affair, they can construct a fake identity and meet someone from another town; however, most church affairs are the result of poor boundaries and people meeting at church in proximity to one another.

Stage Two: Mutual Awareness of Attraction

We all carry a template of attraction. This template is a set of physical, emotional, and psychological characteristics we find attractive. We are romantically drawn to that person. For most people that radar of attraction never goes off. When we decide to date, the radar is on, and we attend to those men or women we find attractive. People swipe through profiles on their phone, eliminating 99 percent of the matches; however, when we see one and the radar turns on, we know it immediately.

When we marry, or are in a committed relationship, we turn that radar down. It never fully goes off, but we put a governor on its engine, and when it does go off, we don't attend to it. My minister friend

Mark would not control his attraction radar, so he was constantly sending out messages to women he found attractive. When two people are aware of their attraction, but hold it in check and maintain a respectful friendship, they are using healthy boundaries.

In cases of sexual addiction, the radar is constantly on. The church provides the addict a target-rich environment to explore. If both people experience mutual attraction, and one or both of them fails to shut down the radar, the syndrome may progress to stage three.

Stage Three: Seductive Message Is Sent

When I was in the sixth grade, I had my first crush on a girl in class. I sent Suzy the typical note: "I like you do you like me; yes or no-check one." As adults, we do the same thing, only in more complex ways. The two people have seen each other. Their radar has gone off, and they are aware of the mutual attraction. Now it is time to send a tentative message to the other person that says "I find you attractive."

One woman was standing in the church foyer visiting for the first time. The minister walked up to her and proclaimed her to be the loveliest woman he'd ever seen. The message was clear: I find you attractive; do you share my sentiment?

Normally, the seductive message is more subtle. The holding of a look a little longer than usual, the brushing of the arm or hand as one walks buy, or standing in the close presence of the other person, where one can be noticed, often are messages saying, "I'm here, and I notice you." Pastor Sandy at Sundance Church had his "preacher groupies" who sat up front and hung onto every word he spoke. They were sending and receiving seductive messages that reinforced the attraction. For some men and women, it is the excitement of the chase that becomes an addiction. It is the idea of something forbidden that becomes intoxicating.

If the message is sent, received, and reciprocated, then the relationship has started, and we are off to the races. The two people are telling themselves, "We are just becoming good friends," but the core attraction is driving them to spend more time together.

Stage Four: Increased Interaction

The two individuals will begin spending more time together. They will arrange to accidentally meet at the coffee bar at the same time every morning. They will be at the gym for the same workout class. At church, they will make a point of meeting and exchanging looks before class or worship service to check in with each other.

These casual encounters will become a regular pattern that the two people look forward to. One of the definitions of love is "an anticipation of being in the presence of one's beloved." They are looking forward to seeing the other person and being in their presence.

In time, they will exchange phone numbers, and the cell phone may become an important link to the other person as they text throughout the day. Ministers may invite the member to participate in one of his key ministries or take on a role at the church that allows them greater access to one another.

Stage Five: Downplaying the Marriage

Conversations between the two people become more personal and intimate. They are attracted to each other. They have reinforcement that the attraction is mutual, and they've both begun investing more time and energy in the relationship. Eventually, they begin sharing information about their disappointment with their marriage. The minister complains that he is tired of ministry, worn out from the pressure, and that his wife does not understand. The woman, recently divorced, discusses her failed marriage and her inability to find a "good guy on Match.com."

Ministers are particularly vulnerable to affairs when they place themselves in counseling relationships but are not trained to do so. They have not worked on their own internal issues and are unaware of the power of transference and counter-transference with counselees. Dr. Cail advises, "Do not be a therapist without a portfolio." At a training seminar for pastors I conducted for the Governor's Marriage Initiative in Oklahoma, in a class of two hundred ministers only ten percent had ever had one course in seminary on marriage, family, or counseling. Church leaders need to stay out of the counseling profession when they are not trained to do therapy.

Stage Six: Illusion of Invisibility

At this point in the relationship, an emotional affair is in full bloom. They are meeting each other on a regular basis. They have arranged their schedules so they can spend time with each other. They are making excuses and lying to their spouses at home about their activities. There are no boundaries now concerning the content of their conversations; they speak as lovers speak.

An interesting phenomenon occurs in Stage Six. Co-workers and friends begin to notice the chemistry that is occurring between the two. He looks at her from up on stage, and she begins to just glow from the inside out. They stare at each other from across the room. She laughs a little too long at his jokes and holds his forearm, keeping him close in the foyer. People see the attraction clearly for what it is—a budding romance turning into an affair.

The couple is oblivious to the messages they are sending out like a large billboard on the highway. They assume they have their new "best friend" relationship well hidden from pesky outsiders. Dr. Cail calls this "the illusion of invisibility." When an affair is blossoming into a full sexual relationship, the two people involved will assume that no one around them notices their behavior. Nothing could be further from the truth.

Sandy at Sundance Church assumed that no one was as smart as he was, a typical narcissistic assumption, and that he had his relationships well hidden. Karen, Carl's wife, had a fifty-yard-line seat for all of his sexual-addiction affairs and could map the progression of each one like a coach on the sidelines watching each play. Unfortunately, church leaders ignore the signs and continue in denial, hoping they are wrong and that all of this will just magically disappear. This is a fatal mistake.

Stage Seven: Taking a Position of "We Are Just Good Friends"

Eventually, the question is put to the one of the partners: "What's up with you and Katy? You're spending a lot of time together." Or the spouse complains about the time you are spending with this person or about inappropriate comments or gifts that are being exchanged. Their radar for the affair has gone off.

The couple moves to a defensive position now, realizing that the illusion of invisibility has been shattered. "We are just good friends" is the position that is taken, with an air of disbelief and offense. They cannot believe people would question their behavior or motives. "I've been spending time with her because she's a member of this church and has been through a terrible time in her life. You are crazy. You are so insecure. Once again, you have issues with trust!"

The "new couple" now has a pattern of spending time together. They have regular conversations in person, by phone, and through ongoing texts. They may have separate cell phones to hide the affair from spouses. Gifts are being exchanged as they each map their partner's likes and dislikes. This is dating behavior, only it is being conducted while one or both of them is married.

If the affair has not turned into a full-blown sexual relationship, which by this point it likely has, it soon will. They are fully engaged in an emotional affair, and the commitments they made to fidelity in their marriage are left far behind in the rearview mirror.

SIGNS OF AN EXTRAMARITAL AFFAIR

- Looking forward to seeing someone, anticipation of being in the presence of the other person.
- Mapping their likes and dislikes, habits and tastes.
- An urge to buy the other person gifts.
- Sudden desire to lose weight, go to the gym, or get in shape.
- Change in personal appearance or style of dress.
- Frequent mentioning of the other's name to friends.

- Disappearance of money.
- Unexplained disappearance of time.
- Contact on social media sites.
- Unusual texts, messaging, or calls that must be hidden or taken privately.

Affairs, whether they occur at church or in the office, do not occur Hollywood style. People do not meet in the hotel elevator, become aware of an immediate chemistry, and then throw themselves into each other's arms. Typically, there is a ramp-up of involvement that moves in stages, as described in *The Affair Syndrome*, and that progression can be tracked as the boundaries between the couple come down. Churches are vulnerable to this progression because they provide the social context for people meeting; the vulnerability of shared life experiences through emotional communications; and the absence of a professional, ethical code of conduct for ministers who make sexual behavior a violation of that code.

SORRY

Marsha was a young mother struggling with the typical pressures of raising six-year-old twin girls, keeping up with a job, a marriage to her college sweetheart, and caring for her widowed mom. She was typically upbeat, happy, and by all appearances well adjusted. She made an appointment because in the six months following Christmas her life had grown "progressively darker," as she described it.

She found herself moody and quick tempered with the twins and her husband. There were days she didn't have the energy to go to spin class—one of her favorite outlets. She was waking up at night after having nightmares, which she had never experienced before. Recently she had been watching a Disney classic movie, and when the little girl got lost in the film, she had unexpectedly broken into tears. She thought she was losing her mind!

I did an assessment and eliminated any immediate, obvious causes of these new developments, including changes in her physical health. She reported no unusual conflicts with her husband; she was happy at her job and absolutely adored her twin girls, Ruth and Rachel.

We began exploring her family of origin. Marsha had been raised in Ft. Worth in a faithful Christian family. Her dad worked for Lockheed, and her mom ran the office for a local dentist. Her older brother, Tim, was a standout athlete in town and made the papers occasionally. They were faithful members of the Rolling Hills Church and attended every time the doors were open. Dad and Pastor Frank were golfing buddies. She had graduated from high school with honors and attended TCU, where she met Mike; they married after their senior year. It was all rather bland—until the nightmares started, accompanied by crying jags over Walt Disney movies.

I asked her to reflect back to last Christmas, when the troubles had first surfaced. Had anything unusual occurred during the holidays? She reported that they'd visited family and friends, taken a quick trip to the hill country, and that the girls had collected their usual payout of Christmas gifts. This year they'd gone in big for Milton Bradley classic board games—Monopoly and Twister—and started having family game nights. The nightmares started soon after the first family game night.

We ended the session and scheduled another for two weeks later. She would be traveling, and I asked her to sit with the memories of last Christmas and, if she had any additional recollections, to bring them in to me. Two weeks later, Marsha arrived ready to share a piece of her past she had never shared with anyone else before. "I need to tell you a story about something that happened when I was a young girl," she began. "I've never shared the details with anyone, but I need to get this off my heart." With that, she began describing the details of her Sunday afternoon visits to Pastor Frank's home as a small girl:

"When I was a small girl, my mom and dad would sometimes let our preacher and his wife take me home after church to have lunch and spend the afternoon with them. They were trying to give my parents a break, they said. My mom and dad trusted Pastor Frank and his wife. I would go to church with my parents on Sunday mornings and go home with the preacher and his wife to spend the afternoon. It was during those afternoon visits things happened I've never talked to anyone about. It happened over several years. We would drive home to the preacher's house, and his wife would be in the kitchen cooking dinner. He had a study in the back of the house, and he'd take me back there alone and close the door. He'd then begin touching me and eventually work his hands under my panties and then begin touching himself. I was so young and terrified and confused. It happened many times, and I didn't know what to do—so I just kept it to myself.

"I don't know if his wife knew or not. She never said a word when we'd go back into his study. But, you know, Dr. Don, it's a funny thing. I remember he always had this weird tradition. We'd eat lunch together, just the three of us, and then Pastor Frank would want to play a Milton Bradley board game. And we always played the same board game after he'd molested me. You know what we played? We played Sorry. . . . He'd molest me in his study. and we always played to board game Sorry."

THE WOUNDS FROM SEXUAL PREDATORS

The case of Marsha and her pastor is tragically one I've heard repeated many times. An innocent child is sexually abused by a trusted friend or member of the family, who gains the trust of the family and is allowed unguarded private time with the child. Pastor Frank, a respected member of the church, is considered the last person anyone would ever suspect of committing these crimes. Yet Marsha's experiences fit the mold of so many victims of child sexual abuse I have talked with in counseling.

National statistics are both alarming and depressing as this silent epidemic ruins the lives of boys and girls in our churches, schools, and communities.

- One in four women has been sexually abused by age 18.
- One in six men has been sexually abused by age 18, although men report less often than women or girls do.
- There are 730,000 registered sex abusers in the United States.
- Fewer than 3% of abusers encounter our criminal justice system; therefore, upwards of 90–97% go undetected by the criminal justice system.
- The average age a sex offender will commit their first offense is 13–14, but the average age of first prosecution, if it occurs, is 30–40, leaving years of undetected activity flying under the radar.
- Male-to-male sex offenders average 150 victims before prosecution.
- Male-to-female sex offenders average 52 victims before prosecution.
- Criminal background checks are not the silver bullet. They identify less than 10% of the sex offenders.
- 90% of those who have been sexually abused were abused by someone they trusted.
- There is no "profile" for abusers; they come in any race, religion, age, sex, education, and neighborhood.
- We "guestimate" that 90% of abusers are male and 10% are female.
- The CDC confirms that 92–98% of outcries are legitimate, even if the victim later recants.
- Two-thirds of all victims do not tell their story, even in adulthood.

Churches are especially susceptible to sexual predators because they provide a population of children and teenagers who are involved in activities that include adult sponsors. Churches without proper policies and boundaries in place are at risk for facilitating sexual abuse among their children and youth. The case of Marsha and Pastor Frank illustrates several of the traps churches fall into:

AQUALUNG IS DEAD

Jethro Tull was wrong when he wrote about Aqualung "sitting on a bench . . . eying little girls with bad intent." You cannot recognize sexual predators. They come in all shapes, sizes, ages, and ethnicities. In fact, like Pastor Frank, they will do their best to appear as inviting and innocent as they possibly can to other adults. Sex offenders have been middle-school math teachers, CASA volunteers, children's ministers, and directors of missions programs.

GROOM THE GATEKEEPER

Molesters groom gatekeepers of children to gain their trust and eventual access to children. They groom a reputation as helpful, responsible, and trustworthy. They need alone time with the child. One of the best ways to do this is to offer help to the parents, often in the form of time or money. Once they are in the fence, the boundaries come down and the abuse can move forward. Pastor Frank groomed Marsha's parents into believing he and his wife were providing them with the gift of time away. The idea that he was a sex offender would have tragically never crossed their minds.

GAIN ACCESS TO ENVIRONMENT OR PROGRAMS

Sex offenders are drawn to a certain age and gender of child. They will seek out those programs offered to the kids of that age group and try to join those programs to gain access to children. They will target certain children and begin giving them special attention or gifts to gain their trust and the approval of the parent or parents.

TARGETING THE LONER

The child who is a loner or on the fringe of the youth group offers a prime target for the sex offender. They will build a relationship with that child and attempt to secure alone time with them to break down barriers. The sex offender will seek a career that gives them access to children or youth, or they may volunteer in those programs to give them access to the lonely child.

WHAT CAN CHURCHES DO?

In the face of these alarming statistics, churches can take important steps to protect their children:

- Cultivate a culture that battles institutional denial of the problem.
- Ramp up supervision in higher numbers across all children's and youth programs. No alone time with adults can be allowed.
- There can be no unseen places that children or youth can be, either with adults or with one another. The incidence of peer-to-peer sexual abuse has increased 300% in the past ten years.
- Communicate with supervising adults when shifts change to determine if there are any concerns.
- Provide appropriate monitoring of bathrooms, which some consider the number one place of concern for churches and schools.
- Dig deeper into résumés, references, and background checks for all full-time workers and volunteers.

I have witnessed repeatedly the devastation that sexual abuse brings on the victim; their marriage; their later adjustment in life; and, ultimately, their view of God. Many women have said to me, "The image of God the Father does not bring up a comforting image in my mind if you knew what my dad did to me."

But churches continue to bury their heads in the sand and proclaim, "It could never happen here." I was called in to consult with a church that had once had a sex offender on their staff. The damage he had caused was massive to the lives of many children. He had been convicted and sent to prison. When he returned from prison, he proclaimed himself "cured" and was reinstated onto the ministry staff of the church. The neighborhood was shocked and mounted a public campaign against the church, to no avail.

I spoke with a former counseling student of mine at Amberton University who now specializes in the treatment of sex offenders. "Was this a cure? Is this man now safe, since he is now in contact with children in their large preschool?" "Absolutely not," was her reply. "We would never put a convicted sex offender back into a situation where they would be tempted to do it again. It's like giving a recovering alcoholic a job as a bartender."

THE EFFECTS OF SEXUAL WOUNDS ON THE CHURCH

There are many effects that sexual wounds have on a congregation and its leadership, as the cases in this chapter have illustrated. However, I will categorize them under three broad headings: Crisis Management, Trust Issues, and Long-Term Rebuilding.

Crisis Management

When a sexual wound goes public, three groups in the church system are thrown immediately into crisis mode. First, the minister, his marriage, and his family are now in the midst of one of the toughest crises they will have to manage. I tell my client couples that, outside of the death of a child, there will be no greater pain one can go through than an extramarital affair.

Second, the leadership of the church is now thrown into crisis management. They are in shock dealing with the news themselves, all while trying to field a million questions from church members. They have few answers to give. They are trying to do what is best for the minister and his wife, while balancing the needs of the congregation and at the same time making interim plans. This is uncharted water for most of them.

To make matters more complicated is the issue of "staggered disclosure." When an affair goes public, the spouse who did not have the affair begins to put together a narrative of the events that occurred. Eventually that story begins to consolidate. Often, however, new pieces of the story come out that the person having the affair wanted to keep hidden. When this occurs, the new revelation throws therapy back to the very beginning, and we have to rebuild. Ministers and church leaders who have had affairs are highly vested in keeping as much of the story of their affair as hidden as possible. Church leaders trying to manage the crises find themselves dealing with "staggered disclosure" as weeks go by and new information appears. The congregation is taken on a roller coaster of emotional dysregulation.

Third, the congregation is in crisis-management mode. We will discuss the emotional nature of the church in Part Two, but a church can grieve, become angry, or suffer from congregational depression. The reaction of church members to the news of a sexual wound may include all three. People will react in their own emotional style and then demand that everyone in church feel exactly the way they feel and the church leaders do exactly what they would do. The congregation and its ministry have been stopped dead in their tracks by one announcement.

Trust Issues

A sexual wound is a betrayal of trust on the deepest level. Our sexuality represents the most intimate part of our identity. We trust that we are physically safe to be in the presence of our leaders. When trust is shattered, it cannot be rebuilt immediately. It will take time, patience, and a long season of rebuilding for the minister and his marriage, the congregation, the next minister, and the leadership.

Dr. Cail states, "Trust is the ashes from the logs of mutually shared experiences." Trust is a by-product of a relationship. It is based upon time and mutually shared experience. I do what I say I will do over an extended period of time. When you experience that as my partner or my church, then we will build trust. Trust is the ashes off the burned logs of the things I have done that match the things I say to you.

When a church or marriage experiences a sexual wound, all of the trust has been removed from the relationship. It is as though someone has gone in and used a wet/dry vac in the fireplace to remove all the ashes. There is nothing left. The spouse has no trust for the unfaithful partner. The church has no trust in the minister, or perhaps in the leadership that ignored the signs. No one trusts anyone else, and they won't for a very long time.

It is at this point that the offending spouse or unfaithful church leader takes a very unusual position. I have seen it hundreds of times in therapy. The unfaithful partner will demand immediate trust and want to hurry through the rebuilding process. "Let's just put this all behind us, forget it ever happened, and go on a romantic trip to the islands. When we get back, it'll all be behind us." The spouse is in the ICU emotionally, and the unfaithful partner is asking them to go to Six Flags.

I've seen ministers do the same thing with their church. Their affair has gone public. They are at risk of losing the one thing that holds their fragile self-image together, and that is their public ministry. So, they rally their loyal troops in the church; design a public repentance; do some quick "therapy"; set up a bogus accountability group; pressure their partner into agreeing to the insanity; and then are quickly back in the saddle, leading the church once again. It is ministry in reverse. The church exists to fulfill their needs; it isn't about their fulfilling the church's needs.

The church is left to stagger forward into the future with a massive wound on its collective soul that will never be spoken of and likely never be healed. An exodus of disenchanted members will slowly happen, and it will be blamed by those who are "higher and holier" for not being people who can forgive. We conveniently forget

John the Baptist's command, "Bear fruit worthy of repentance." In other words, don't tell me—show me.

Long-Term Rebuilding

If the ministers in this chapter and their spouses were to come to me for counseling, I would listen carefully to their story and then give them my little speech: "If we are going to put this marriage back together, it's going to mean several things. First, the affair stops today. There will be no contact, and your life will become completely transparent to your spouse. Second, I'm going to need to work with both of you weekly for the next year—maybe longer. Third, the marriage you had before the affair will look substantively different from the marriage you will have a year from now. There will be marriage book one, the affair, and marriage book two. When we are done, you'll prefer to never see me again because this will be a lot of work.

I make a similar speech to church leaders who call me to help with sexual wounds: "Your church must have a season of healing. It will take at least a year to move through that work, and that's if the church responds quickly. The minister and his marriage must have a plan of therapeutic intervention from licensed professionals. The leadership will need to undergo an assessment process to determine if they can continue, and we will have to explore whether patterns in the church led to the crises. The church that emerges from this wound will look substantially different from the church that went into it. This will be a difficult path, and there is significant work to be done."

Most church leaders opt to avoid the work. They hope that the wildfires will just burn themselves out. They reinstate the minister with a wish and a prayer that the abuse will not be repeated. Or they accept his resignation and immediately start the process of securing another preacher. When he is hired, he will inherit a congregation that is silently wounded, carrying unresolved emotional pain, and incapable of trusting him or the leadership that selected him.

EPILOGUE IN THE AIR

I was flying back from a speaking engagement when a professional-looking woman sat down in the seat next to me, extended her hand, called me by name, and introduced herself: "I'm Mary. You probably don't remember, me but I was a member of the Beacon Street Church when you worked with us. I was running a commercial real-estate business and in the singles program."

We chatted for a few minutes; then she looked me in the eye and said, "You do realize what a sexually inappropriate environment that church had, don't you?" She said this as though it were the most normal observation, like asking whether I attended the early or late service. I was somewhat stunned and replied, "Yes, I'm aware of that. Would you care to share your observations of the church as a professional single woman who attended there?"

At this point she began relating her experiences with the men of the Beacon Street Church. How many men had come on to her and solicited sex. How routine it was for both married and single men to hit on her at church. "Were you approached by members of the ministry staff?" She just smiled and said "Yes—so were most of the women in our singles group." She spoke with a detached disappointment about the time, money, and energy she had invested into the singles program and how disappointed she was with the church leadership.

A promotion had taken Mary away from Beacon Street Church to another city. She still carried the scars of disappointment in a church that had operated without sexual ethics and boundaries. When we landed, I wished her well but didn't have the heart to ask her whether she was still attending church. I already had my answer.

CHAPTER 5

THE BORDERLINE WOUND

Nancy had fired me as her therapist five times. It looked as though we were headed for number six. The reason was that I'd had the temerity to suggest that Nancy might have some responsibility in the failure of her four prior marriages. Her primal rage went from zero to eighty miles per hour in two seconds. "You have no idea what I've been through," she screamed as she stormed out of my office, slamming the door behind her. In a few weeks she was back, acting as though nothing had happened; she made no apology and declared me "the only therapist who ever understood me." Dealing with Nancy was a roller coaster of intense emotions.

Nancy was born into a prominent North Dallas family. She was educated at SMU, shopped at Neiman-Marcus, and lived in exclusive, upscale Highland Park. She married, the first time, a successful attorney who continued to provide her the lifestyle she adored. He was a fiery trial attorney, and when Nancy's own inner demons erupted, the arguments could be heard in Ft. Worth. The marriage ended abruptly and then was followed by another and another. At fifty-five, Nancy looked forty, could attract men, and showed no signs of slowing down.

Her inner demon was her Dr. Jekyll and Mr. Hyde personality. One minute Nancy would be calm, sophisticated, and even childlike in her vulnerability. The next she would erupt like Mt. St. Helens. She would fall in love quickly and become obsessed with her new "Mr.

Perfect." Then she would find a list of grievances that demonstrated he was not the man for her. She sabotaged relationships like a demolition expert. Mr. Perfect was taken on a roller-coaster ride of being alternately adored and hated by the woman he'd fallen in love with. He took the brunt of her anger and was left confused and rejected.

In therapy, Nancy was a paradox. One session she was the self-assured expert on her own issues, and the next she was crying and confused at the latest rejection. Another man had left her life. Nancy would coach me on how to do her therapy. After all, she'd been through so many therapists in the past. No one could tell Nancy anything. She was the confident authority on any subject. She offered elaborate rationalizations for the messes she created. The common thread to her stories was, "I didn't do anything, really. There just aren't any good guys out there." Nancy was unaware of her internal processes that were destroying her relationships. I would be fired the sixth time for mentioning them.

CONFIDENCE AND CONFUSION AT CALVARY TEMPLE

Calvary Temple had been great and glorious during its heyday. Now it couldn't keep a pastor. Once the "talk of the town," Calvary Temple had people flocking to its services and a gifted pastor who was on cable TV, writing books, and speaking nationally at conferences. Calvary Temple was proud of its heritage and basked in its "glory days." Longtime members could recite stories of overflowing parking lots, sermons that left members in tears, and missions programs that circled the globe. Now Calvary Temple went through ministers like New Yorkers going through the turnstile of a subway.

Calvary retained its overconfident congregational personality. The church's leaders were the experts on church growth. Listening to them tell stories of the past ten years, one might be persuaded that they had been victimized by a long series of inept ministers. Church leaders could analyze the faults of each of their former preachers and describe in detail the mistakes he had made. They were confident in their ability to "find the right guy the next time."

Calvary Temple, following the retirement of its legendary pastor, had "fallen in love quickly" with each of his replacements. They would quickly start a search for the next "living legend," compile a short list of high-profile candidates, and throw a large salary at the winner of this beauty pageant. When he arrived, he was expected to meet dozens of conflicting agendas in the leadership and solve all of the problems that had been shoved under the rug for years. When he was unable to do so, Calvary's love quickly turned to distain, and he was dismissed as a failure. Calvary could go from "I adore you" to "I hate you" in a thirty-minute meeting.

A board of deacons comprised the formal governing structure of the church. Many of them had held their positions since the glory days of the church. They were overly confident in their ability as leaders and were not open to outside consultation. At each minister's resignation, one deacon repeatedly offered his services as the new preacher, in addition to his role as deacon. Calvary Temple's leadership reminded outsiders of the statement Job made after he was visited by his three friends, Eliphaz, Zophar, and Bildad: "Doubtless you are the only people who matter, and wisdom will die with you!" (Job 12:2). The Temple was burning down around them, but they had all the answers.

The actual power source at Calvary was an influential, informal group of long-term members who made decisions behind the scenes. They held the church hostage through their financial contributions and considered Calvary "their church." Newcomers to the church, and especially outsiders, were viewed as a threat to this aristocracy. Members of this group would walk out during the minister's sermon and gather in the foyer if they were angry with him. The writing was on the wall if enough of them gathered to cast their lot for his departure.

It was the Dr. Jekyll and Mr. Hyde nature of Calvary Temple's personality that was so disturbing. The members and the leaders could appear victimized, confused, and hopeless. They could relate long narratives about all the misdeeds they had endured through the years at the hands of poorly equipped ministers. They were experts at pulling an outsider into the rescuer role. Once engaged, if the "new savior" said anything that implied they'd had a part in their own failures, he was met with a primal rage that destroyed the relationship.

The long cycle of love followed by divorce had been a drain on the congregation. Members sat in the pews wondering *What's going on here?* and *Why does everything blow up?* A congregational assessment would have shown that the church climate was in a nosedive, but no one on the deacon board was paying attention. There was a steady stream of former Calvary Temple members into other churches; however, the leadership was always confident they were going to find "just the right guy this time."

BORDERLINE PERSONALITY DISORDER

My client Nancy was suffering from borderline personality disorder. It is a significant personality impairment that has its roots in poor attachment patterns early in life. This leads to chaotic relationships in adulthood. Roger Kruger describes borderline personality disorder in this way:

> The relationship with an individual with borderline personality disorder is like a ride on a roller coaster. One never complains of boredom. Borderlines typically develop very intense relationships with others, but rapidly switch back and forth between expressing adoration and being generous to venting anger and acting punitively.
>
> The situation most likely to trigger the characteristics of a borderline personality is any in which the individual begins to experience either real or imagined abandonment.

> When not sustained by intense relationships, they have chronic feelings of deep emptiness and loneliness and will go to almost any length to avoid either real or imagined abandonment. This leads to impulsive behavior.
>
> Their demands are often unreasonable, and relationships with them will often be stormy. They will seldom apologize (Kruger, 97).

I have counseled high-functioning clients with borderline personality disorder working in medicine, law, ministry, and business. They cope well at times and then without warning have an explosion when their buttons are pushed. Their personal relationships take the brunt of their rage. It is like dealing with an adult who can go into a screaming infant mode at any moment.

THE BORDERLINE CHURCH

As an undergraduate ministry student, my first class was the Work of the Preacher. Dr. Warren described some churches as having three stages in their relationship with a minister: taste, chew, and spit. Eventually the situation deteriorates to simply chew and spit, he said. The old-time gospel preachers didn't know about attachment disorder, but they instinctively understood that some churches were not wired to build a long-term relationship with their minister.

The churches with whom I've consulted that possess borderline characteristics have often been in decline for an extended period of time. Martin F. Saarinen wrote in *Lifecycle of a Congregation* that churches experience cycles of growth and decline. As the decline deepens, churches enter the Bureaucracy Phase. Saarinen writes, "The major concern in the Bureaucratic congregation is maintaining one's own turf and prerogatives. Boundaries are marked by fences and any encroachment is met with hostility and defensiveness. Blaming individuals for the ills of the congregation is common. Any sense of shared ministry has been lost, and little attention is given to the work of the church" (Saarinen, 14).

As with Nancy, the paradox of a borderline church is their blindness to the central role they play in creating their own drama. Calvary Temple was its own worst enemy. It was caught in a loop of dysfunctional patterns that had been institutionalized over many years. The leaders were unwilling to look at the damage they had done to the lives of members and ministers. They functioned as a closed system, unwilling to accept help from the outside. They stubbornly maintained that they knew better than anyone else what they needed to do. They were addicted to the myth of their own glory and, as Jeremiah prophesied, called for "'Peace, peace,' . . . when there is no peace."

CHARACTERISTICS OF BORDERLINE CHURCHES

Impressive and Blameless

Borderline churches like to impress outsiders. They have a glorious history in the community. They have a beautiful building. They can cite the glory days when the church was growing behind the powerful preaching of a minister with an impressive reputation. To an outsider, this may seem like a church that really "has its act together." Like Nancy, who can still attract men after multiple marriages, the borderline church is an expert at putting up a good front. For this church, image is of paramount importance.

When I talk to leaders in borderline churches, the song remains the same: "We have been through one terrible situation with a minister after another." They relate in detail the failings of their past ministers and are quick to blame them. They take no responsibility for the failure in the relationship with the former ministers and are offended when I suggest there might be a pattern going on in the church that is contributing to this.

Borderline churches develop what I call "the Narrative." The narrative is a corporate congregational story the church tells itself about its history and its heroes, villains, and persecutors. The narrative is the way the church makes sense of its experiences. For most churches, that narrative has some basis in reality. For the borderline church, the narrative has been crafted to paint others black and retain their own position as the helpless victim. The power of the narrative keeps many borderline churches from ever seeking help.

Intense Relationships

Borderline churches, like my client Nancy, fall in love quickly. They have intense emotions, both positive and negative, and that is why they can appear so charming and entertaining. The borderline church will fire a minister and quickly enter a search for the new "savior minister" to replace the last failure. The hidden expectation is that he will bring the church back to its glory days and be the new incarnation of their beloved former minister. The new minister's entrance into the church will be marked with high hopes and fine-sounding promises from leaders. It won't be long before the second verse of the song begins.

Churches with borderline characteristics suffer from core attachment wounds. They don't know how to attach to the key figures in their lives, such as a minister, because they have experienced wounds in the past. Theirs is a core fear of abandonment. For all their pomp and impressive image, their core fear is being alone and having to deal with their own internal demons. They cannot be alone without a minister and do the healing work of a transition. They feel driven to "find the next guy" and push the problems off on him.

Borderline churches rarely embrace a healing transition. They are in a hurry to find the next candidate and "turn this thing around." They fight every suggestion of a healing process because it addresses their core wound, and that is terrifying to them. They attempt to control and rush the interim transition to avoid the hard work of dealing with their inner wounds.

"I Love You/I Hate You" Roller Coaster

Former ministers who have served borderline congregations speak of the roller-coaster ride the church took them on, often within a short period of time. During the interview process, there was no hint of the depth of pathology the church was experiencing. The narrative had been carefully crafted and communicated through key leaders in the informal and formal power structures. A handsome offer was made, and the minister saw this move as a real opportunity to help a church "get back on its feet." The church was definitely saying, "I love you."

Once inside the church, the minister was struck by the large number of competing agendas. There were groups at war with one another, and those conflicts had been going on for years. There were staff ministers undercutting every move he made. There were leaders now changing their stories. Promises he'd been made just six weeks earlier were now being publicly denounced in front of the church by the leaders who had hired him. The dynamics were so bizarre he felt as though he were going crazy. The church was now saying, "I can't be trusted."

When the minister makes the fatal error of discussing the incongruences with the leadership, he is given a front-row ticket to the Dr. Jekyll and Mr. Hyde demonstration. The emergence of anger and rage comes out with surprising intensity. Leaders who seemed to be his allies are now belittling him—have become sarcastic or verbally abusive. Others keep quiet and later carry out a passive-aggressive campaign against him behind his back. Staff ministers loyal to the old regime sabotage his efforts. He was to blame for all of this! What could they have been thinking when they hired him? The church is now saying, "I hate you."

Self-Importance

I was amused one Sunday as a song leader, known for his arrogant personality, announced, "Please turn to the hymn in the front of your hymnal, 'How Great I Am.'" The borderline congregation is singing that hymn to anyone who will listen. They have a core wound of abandonment and protect themselves with self-importance as a defense mechanism.

Borderline church leaders are the experts on every topic. Their heightened sense of self-importance is amazing as they oversee a congregation that is in danger of dying on their watch. They lecture me on how to do the consulting process. They want to control the preaching. They bring in other outside "experts." They agree to a transition process but then, a few weeks later, want to change its implementation. They are the master preachers, teachers, consultants, and church experts, yet every week their congregation is shrinking.

Lack the Empathy Chip

Nancy could say things to her partner that were verbally abusive when she raged or engage in passive-aggressive behavior that undermined the relationship. She would never apologize for the pain she inflicted on her spouse. The next day she would be cheerful and happy, acting as though nothing had happened as her husband struggled to heal from the hurtful things she'd said. Nancy lacked the empathy chip.

Just like individuals, congregations can operate without the empathy chip. They say things during announcements or sermons that are damaging to members emotionally and spiritually. They conduct meetings that leave members scarred for years. When a consultant points out the need for the church to stop this pattern of abuse and seek forgiveness from the people they have harmed, they scoff at the idea. They dismiss the consultant as being another inept individual who can't be trusted.

The transition for a congregation that lacks the empathy chip and has a history of damaging ministers and members needs to be longer than most transitions. It will take time to interrupt processes and help all those involved see the need to start a plan of restitution for the damage done to former members and ministers. They will need to learn new processes of communication, decision making, and conflict resolution.

Closed System

Healthy boundaries are like a good backyard fence. They let the good in through the gates but keep the bad out. Borderline churches have closed boundaries. They have a high, tight fence around their perimeter and don't allow outsiders access to the church system. You can attend and be a member, but the key areas of decision making are open to very few. These churches guard their access and are suspicious of outside input.

I was conducting a preliminary meeting with the leadership of a church that would ultimately display borderline tendencies. When they learned that I would be preaching a series of lessons designed to promote healing in the congregation, they were highly offended. One woman hissed, "We do just fine with our own speakers. We need to get back to doing what we always have done." And that's exactly what they did. Borderline churches will explore a healing transition, but very few will follow through with the process. The system will not open to allow change to occur.

The Shadow Church

The therapeutic process with clients is often blown off track when the therapist doesn't have the complete story or key people are not engaged in the counseling sessions. The same is true of consulting with churches. There are times when this happens when I feel there is a "missing piece" to the story, that events are transpiring under the table, outside normal decision-making processes. I know I am working with a "Shadow Church" within the congregation.

The Shadow Church is comprised of powerful individuals within the congregation who may not hold an official role in the church but maintain great influence over its direction. They have achieved their power through a variety of means. They may have made large contributions to the church. They may have donated land or buildings. They may have family ties going back several generations in the congregation's history. They may employ key leaders in the church and hold them hostage, owing them favors.

The membership of the Shadow Church may be small, but they are typically more powerful than those in the formal leadership structure and hold sway over their decision making.

At the core of the Shadow Church's belief system is a sense of entitlement. Calvary Temple had a small group of influential members who believed they held ownership of the church similar to that of a stockholder owning vast shares in a corporation. They were entitled to have their say and to get their way because of their tenure, status, or financial abilities. From a power-theory standpoint, this is raw coercive power being wielded in a religious organization. The results are deadly and devastating to a church.

Reversing the effects of the Shadow Church is almost impossible to achieve. First, members of the Shadow Church must be identified and then removed from access to information or decision making. This is difficult to do because these systems are informal and almost impossible to trace. Second, the existing leadership must be purged and a new leadership team assembled that holds no allegiance to the informal power structure. Convincing new leaders to step in when the past has been so toxic is difficult to accomplish.

The Shadow Church process can exist in any congregation, but it is very common among borderline churches in which lying, manipulation, and cheating are common. Some of the signs of Shadow Church operations include:

- A small group of individuals hold key positions of leadership or influence key positions of leadership in the church.
- Key areas of church operations, such as finances, personnel, and search committees, are held by the same group of people or those who owe allegiance to that group.
- Decisions are made using agreed-upon congregational processes then can be mysteriously reversed.

- Key decisions are made but never implemented. Change is never implemented.
- A core member who has stepped down from leadership or retired still holds significant sway over the existing leaders.
- Communications are guarded and unclear, as opposed to open and authentic.
- The congregational climate lacks openness and authenticity. There is guardedness to the interaction patterns among staff and leaders.
- It feels as though there is a "missing piece" to the story. Things just don't add up from an outsider's view.
- Key talent exits without warning.
- Talent exits with financial agreements that ensure their silence.
- Rumors frequently float about decisions and leaders.
- Meetings are scripted ahead of time, with voting arranged before open discussion can be heard.
- People are offended when they are confronted with their abuse of power in the church.

Wounds to the Church

I live close to Love Field in Dallas and watch the Southwest Airlines 737s take off and land. Periodically, they roll those big jets into a hanger on the west side of the airport and run specialized gauges over the skin of the aircraft. The mechanics are testing them for "metal fatigue"—hairline fissures in the surface of the plane. Put something under enough pressure, and over time it will crack.

Churches like Calvary Temple are operating under pressure for an extended period of time. If we were to put a gauge to the climate of the congregation, we would discover that the church is suffering from "metal fatigue." There have been self-inflicted deep wounds for an extended period of time. The church is self-harming and unaware of it.

Attracting Borderline Leaders and Members

Janice suffered from borderline personality disorder. She was married to Jerry, who was on the deacon board of Calvary Temple. Janice's radical mood swings could go from being friendly and engaging to verbally attacking in public. Janice decided that one young couple did not belong in the congregation. The woman had been married before, and Janice decided that all divorce was sin. When the young couple would be walking down the hall, Janice would cross to the other side of the hall and avert her eyes to avoid contact with them. At dinners, Janice would make a show of sitting far away from the young couple. Her public shaming of individuals she judged unfit for membership in "her church" caused many to leave Calvary Temple. Jerry, a sweet conflict avoider, would take the brunt of her abuse at home.

One of the rules of Systems Theory is that a system will attract individuals who are like others in the system. A healthy system tends to attract other healthy members. Calvary Temple had characteristics of borderline personality, so it attracted members who had borderline characteristics. The young couple left Calvary Temple, and the leadership was held hostage by this very sick individual.

Anger, Rage, and Verbal Abuse

Outbursts of anger are common at borderline churches. Members and leaders who trigger emotionally will dysregulate and become verbally abusive in meetings, classes, or public gatherings. These individuals have no verbal filter on the things they say and will make statements that leave the listener shocked and hurt. This lack of control is justified as "speaking the truth in love," but there is no love motivating them. Such an outburst is a momentary catharsis for the speaker that damages relationships with no intention of apology.

Passive-Aggressive Behavior

I was consulting with a borderline church, and one staff minister would visit with me every Sunday morning before I spoke, pleasantly sharing his view of the transition. He would then spend the remainder of his week sending emails out to the leadership decrying the need for the transitional process. To my face he was an ally. Behind my back he was undermining the process. Churches are susceptible to passive-aggressive individuals because they adopt a denial style of conflict resolution. Passive-aggressive individuals wreak havoc in churches because holding them accountable is like nailing Jell-O to the wall.

Gaslighting and Painting Black

Borderline churches are famous for making commitments and promises and a short time later feigning a case of amnesia regarding the entire process. Gaslighting is the habit of promising to do something and then acting as though the conversation never occurred. The partner is left speechless, thinking he or she must be going crazy.

Painting black is the habit of individuals in a borderline church of telling false negative stories about individuals they feel are a threat to them. Calvary Temple could paint black every former minister who had worked for them. They could paint black former members who had left their fellowship and staff ministers who had quit or been fired. In some cases, leaders would stalk the minister after he had resigned and attempt to sabotage his reputation among other churches. Once you were on Calvary Temple's blacklist, you were forever painted black.

Too Many Restarts

Members in the pew become exhausted from the ongoing roller-coaster ride of ministers coming and going. They grow to doubt the optimistic explanations from leaders who time after time try to put a positive spin on yet another crash-and-burn situation. The congregation begins to collectively look around and wonder, *Does everybody believe this stuff?*

The roller-coaster ride of emotions and poor leadership leads to a revolving door of members leaving for other churches. Many of these members carry the scars of verbal and emotional abuse at the hands of this dysfunctional church. Sadly, many have left organized religion entirely, citing spiritual abuse as the cause of their lack of faith in the local church.

Inappropriate Public Speaking

Survivors coming out of borderline congregations report a wide range of inappropriate things said or done publicly to confront, blame, or shame the congregation. Members who do not fall in line with the direction of the church may be shamed in public or in sermons. Leaders who oppose the minister may make a public display of leaving when he steps up to preach. Individuals may be confronted publicly in the foyer by an angry leader. Statements are made that are derogatory and hurtful, and then a week later the individual who was verbally abusive acts as though nothing wrong had occurred.

Individuals like Nancy, who suffer from a personality disorder, will lack the empathy chip to understand that the words they say can do permanent damage to a relationship. A church can suffer from the same pathology. Emotional dysregulation is a second hallmark of this disorder. Some individuals have no brake on the things they say. Toxic statements come spewing out, and they have no empathy to see how destructive they are being to others. This is a recipe for relationship disaster.

CONGREGATIONAL HEALING

Dr. James P. McCollough, a leader in the treatment of chronic depression, states that "Inflexibility is a sign of pathology." Inflexibility is the problem when trying to assist a Borderline Church. They stubbornly retain their old patterns that are deeply ingrained within the church system. They refuse to get better because, like Nancy, they storm out of the counseling office when they cannot control the process. They are the experts, even though they've been unable to right the ship for many years. The inflexible, closed system is a hallmark of the Borderline Church.

The inflexibility fuels a second issue: the rise of pain in the system. When humans experience a high level of pain, our bodies shut down. We cannot bear it. No system—whether it is a marriage, family, business, or church—can endure ongoing cycles of pain and survive. The wear-and-tear of the emotional roller coaster takes its toll on ministers, leaders, and members. There is an emotional drain as hopes rise and fall with each sad chapter. There is the emotional drain of too many goodbyes in a short a period of time. And there is the long-term impact of cover-ups, manipulation, and lying on the part of members who are trying to believe their church has an ethical base but see mountains of evidence to the contrary. Eventually, the pain builds up in the congregation and cannot be ignored.

When pain reaches a critical mass in a church, there are two options. First, the church may opt to ignore the pain and continue on the downward spiral that has characterized its trajectory. Denial is the primary coping mechanism church leaders elect to follow. Membership will continue to decline, contributions will fall off unless propped up by a few key contributors, confidence in the leadership will be gone, and people will exist in well-defined warring camps within the congregation. Martin Saareinen notes that the next stage of congregational decline after Bureaucracy is Death. A church that follows a borderline path will eventually die from the weight of its own pathology.

The second option available to the Borderline Church is to open its boundaries and seek outside help. The pain becomes a signal that "Something must finally change." If Calvary Temple were open to seeking help, it would require a significant commitment to major change on the part of top leadership, ministry staff, and the congregation. This would include:

- A commitment to an extended healing transition, providing time necessary to do the work of healing and reconstruction of the church and its processes.

- An assumption that there are adequate resources to complete the transition in terms of time, money, and energy. If a church waits too long, these resources may be nonexistent.
- An assessment of the current leadership team and openness to reconstruction.
- A dismantling of the informal Shadow Church and removal of its influence.
- An intentional process of healing congregational wounds from the past and present.
- A restorative forgiveness process to make amends for damage inflicted by the church on former members and ministers.
- New communication, conflict resolution, and roles with open accountability and appropriate ethical boundaries.

This is a significant process that will require the recrafting of the church from the ground up. Most churches will avoid this work and opt to deny the issues and continue to whitewash the decline. It is accurate to say that the church that emerges from this transition will look significantly different from the church that went into the transition. There will be church book one, the transition, and church book two.

Often, the best work that can be done dealing with a Borderline Church is helping people leave. They will need support, as they carry anger, confusion, and sadness. People carry the scars of spiritual abuse for years, and it affects their marriage, participation in another congregation, and ability to pass on a meaningful faith to their children, who have seen their parents suffer at the hands of troubled churches.

WE OWN YOU

I received a call from a young minister who had served in a troubled church I'd consulted with and was now asking to visit with me about his departure. He had been talented, dedicated, and energetic when I had first met him. The voice on the phone now sounded sad, tired, and confused. He was looking for some clarity with regard to his experience ministering in a borderline church.

He described the unrealistic demands that had been placed on him in terms of leading small groups. He told stories of the manipulation and passive-aggressive methods used by other ministers who seemed to delight in starting conflicts. He reflected on the contrast between the church's image and the reality of the inner workings of leaders who abused their power.

He had tried to be a good soldier. He had saluted the flag and worked hard. He had overlooked violations of his own beliefs, as well as of his moral and ethical codes. Finally, he had reached a point at which he could no longer sit back quietly. He had made an appointment with the Executive Pastor. He had laid out his concerns in a respectful way and asked for some modest changes in his ministry that would allow him to do his work more effectively.

The Executive Pastor, who had been with the church for many years, listened quietly, waiting for the young man to finish. Then he said, "There will be no changes to your job. You will not talk to anyone else about the things you've seen or shared with me. Is that clear? What you don't understand is this: we own you." The meeting ended, and the young man left.

The heartbreaking reality for people like Nancy and congregations like Calvary Temple is that they never get the help they need. They continue a pattern of self-destruction that impacts everyone who comes into contact with them. The best we can hope for is to limit their zone of damage and help their victims pick up the pieces and move on with their lives.

CHAPTER 6

THE INCOMPETENCE WOUND

Fellowship Community Church's vision stated that "It's all about Jesus." It should have read "It's just church." FCC was a church plant that had never taken root. The church was like an unmade bed. It wasn't that things there were really that bad. It's just that they weren't very good. Visitors would come away thinking that things at the church were disorganized and sloppy.

The worship service was reminiscent of Judges 21:25: "In those days Israel had no king; everyone did as they saw fit." Sunday morning was like open-mike live at a stand-up club. There was no predicting what anyone might say. Uncle Joe, an elder for thirty years, could turn five minutes of announcements into another sermon. The worship leader felt that stories about his two children between hymns were entertaining. The chairman of the missions committee spoke so long one morning that the guest speaker had to cut his sermon to only ten minutes. The worship service wore members out as they struggled to stay awake.

One never knew what might happen next on a given Sunday morning. The media ministry was constantly training new sound techs during the Sunday morning assembly. It was not uncommon for worship leaders to speak into dead mikes that would then scream to life with feedback reminiscent of George Harrison's guitar solo on the Beatles' "I Feel Fine." One embarrassed media tech accidentally loaded the wrong PowerPoint slides, and the slides for the minister's sermon on the Beatitudes were replaced with those of a fishing trip on the Arkansas River. It wasn't a big deal. Everyone laughed because that's just how things were at FCC.

The FCC auditorium, a converted storefront in a shopping center, was retrofitted with lights. A "special deal" was secured through a friend who installed the church lighting at a discount. However, for three years following the installation, a short in the system caused the two main spotlights to spontaneously strobe in the middle of services, turning "Night with Ebon Pinion" into "Night on Disco Mountain." "We've got to get that fixed one of these days," one deacon would say each time it happened.

During a storm one Sunday morning, as the preacher was concluding his sermon, a loud clap of thunder was heard. This was followed by a booming sound, as all the lights went dead. Not another sound was heard. Then, one by one, members lifted their cell phones and lit the auditorium so the flustered minister could finish his message.

The preacher, Minister Kevin, was an enigma to the members. Occasionally he could knock a sermon out of the ballpark, but most of the time he struggled on the edge of mediocrity. Therapists have long known that when people receive positive reinforcement, like a good sermon, but only on an occasional basis, the periodic positive reinforcement can actually be very addictive. Members would show up just to see whether this Sunday morning was going to be a homerun or a pop fly to the infield. His batting average was on the decline. Rumor had it that the minister's wife, Karen, a graduate of seminary, wrote his best sermons. Post-it notes in her handwriting were found in his Bible on Sundays when he took the cover off the ball. One frustrated deacon was quoted as saying, "We need to fire the preacher and hire his wife."

The youth minister and the preacher were united in the direction of their ministries. Neither of them kept office hours and could rarely be accounted for during the week. The preacher preferred to study at home, away from the demands of the church office. He had gone into business with his father-in-law, launching a chain of convenience store/car washes called the Sack and Suds. Members complained that "the sack" was exactly what he deserved. The preacher defended his business interests as an "opportunity to get out among the community and meet people."

To his credit, the youth minister was pursuing his education at a local Christian college. He had been working on a graduate degree for the past eight years. His problem was a lack of focus. First it was counseling, then spiritual formation, and now he was considering preaching. It would only be a few more years, he assured the leadership, and the church had been good enough to underwrite half of his tuition costs.

The elders at Fellowship Community were a great group of guys. They enjoyed standing in the foyer every Sunday talking to members, welcoming guests, and drinking coffee as people came to church. Most of the "big decisions" were made in hastily called meetings on Sunday mornings to put out the latest fires. FC elders preferred to operate in a free-flowing style of leadership. They didn't have regular meetings because all the men who served traveled for work, and some had lake houses they frequented on weekends. When they did meet, no one kept minutes. When decisions were made, they were often reversed if the announcement was met with a deluge of angry texts and phone calls. The FC elders followed an unwritten path of nonconfrontation. They avoided all conflict because the church is "supposed to be a community of peace." They practiced the Old Testament habit of rolling the sins of the people forward from year to year.

Ministries at FC behaved like a group of warring tribes competing for scarce resources of money, volunteers, and church attention. Each ministry was siloed into its own interest group, and there was no overall vision that brought them together. The mission's ministry lobbied their favorite elder for support and funding. The youth ministry lobbied their key elder for the same things. Competing ministries had staked out their turf in the church building and ran competing ads for congregational attention.

The Bible classes were a collection of little personality kingdoms. Each adult class was led by a director who acted as though the events in which their class participated were the most important activities in the church. Some classes welcomed new members, but others felt closed, and guests got the ecclesiastical cold shoulder for venturing into their space. Minister Kevin made the mistake of suggesting that all the Bible classes join him in a combined study of the parables. The elders' phones quickly lit up, as class directors let them know they were involved in an "important series right now" and could not participate. So ended the coordinated study idea. The tribes went back to "doing what was right in each man's eyes."

Mary Margaret had been teaching third grade since Fellowship Church was planted. Mary Margaret was great with kids but could be stubborn when dealing with adults. She decided that a field trip to visit the local nursing home one Sunday during the Bible class hour would be a great experience for the children. She got the keys to the van and took them away from the building. A crisis ensued when shocked parents, unaware of their children's departure from the building, arrived at Mary Margaret's classroom to discover that the room was empty. Mary Margaret was running late. Three angry couples who were visiting that morning never returned to Fellowship, but no one had the nerve to talk to Mary about the incident. The leadership was afraid of losing her as a teacher.

Tony convinced Minister Kevin that the church should offer a divorce recovery group to the community, and he volunteered to lead the new group. Never mind that Tony had been recently divorced and had no training in psychotherapy or group therapy. What he lacked in experience and expertise, he made up for in enthusiasm. Tony had a history of failed businesses and failed relationships. He'd been married three times and was currently installing seamless gutters for a living. The group met on Tuesday evenings at the church and was launched with a respectable turnout from the community. Tony found a book on divorce recovery and added his own experiences to the meetings, which soon turned into

Tony's testimonial time. He was unintentionally working out his own unresolved issues in the group. Women soon began avoiding the divorce recovery group when Tony began texting them for dates after the meetings. After a ten-week run, the group dissolved, and the church was thankfully not sued by angry group members for failure to supervise and for sexual misconduct. Tony returned to his gutter work.

Larry, the elder in charge of church finances, was a friendly guy but kept FC finances very secretive. No one really knew where the money was going, but the church never had enough funds to meet the bills. One month, the special collection for building homes in Honduras had to be spent on insurance for the building. The church was never informed of this switch. Other elders would recommend an annual audit, but that never happened. Ministry leaders were accustomed to spending whatever they wanted and just dropping off the receipts at the church office. Larry had a son who was deeply in debt following a failed business venture. The church had "bailed the boy out" once, and rumor around the halls was that Larry continued to siphon money off to support his son. No one checked this out.

Laura, Fellowship Church's only secretary, ran the office and kept the ship afloat. She managed the ministers and the competing demands of the various ministry groups. Everyone was afraid of Laura because she could "really go off on you" if she were having a bad day. Laura was dealing with chronic pain issues and was secretly addicted to pain medications. Laura was close to Larry, the elder in charge of finance, and word on the street was that she would occasionally dip into the Caring and Sharing funds to support her prescription-drug habit. Once again, no one checked into this because, after all, if she needed the help, maybe that was okay.

Every September, the Fellowship Community would host its annual town hall meeting. All members were invited to a potluck dinner following the Sunday services where elders and ministers would present a "State of FC Report." The report was always the same. FC struggled with the same problems year after year. Members would complain about the lack of planning and funds. Ministry leaders would promote their own needs above the needs of other ministries. There were never any solutions offered. A congregational depression seemed to have descended on the church, and no one knew what to do about it.

THE INCOMPETENCE WOUND

Growing up, my mother was famous for her lemon meringue pies. Think three-inch meringue with sugar droplets falling off the curlicue ends. Her flaky crusts were so delicious that I would beg her to make extras just so I could eat them like popcorn. When we'd go to church socials, her pie was the first one gone. At every social, the second choice after my mom's pie was a store-bought Morton's frozen apple pie. Folks at the end of the line were stuck eating a slice of pie that wasn't really bad; it just wasn't that good.

The problem facing Fellowship Community Church was that its ministry wasn't that bad; it just wasn't very good. No one was taking the time to "make things from scratch." It takes a lot of work to prepare an original sermon that is fitted perfectly to the congregation and the occasion. It's easier to download some famous preacher's sermon from the internet and change up a few of the illustrations. It is difficult to confront people who are misbehaving at church and walk into the jaws of conflict. It is much easier to rock along and let people do whatever they want to in the name of religion.

When I consult with churches that operate like an unmade bed, I find that incompetence falls into one of five categories:

Vision Incompetence

The vision does not match the church, or it lacks the motivating passion to ignite the energy of the church. Too often a minister had read a book and decided that what another church had done should fit the FC congregation. Leaders had attended a church growth seminar and come away armed with copycat ideas of how to help their church grow. Rather than doing the hard work of determining who they were, in that unique place, with those particular members, the church tried to borrow the vision of another congregation.

Loren B. Mead was president of the Alban Institute, a congregational-consulting group. He was the keynote speaker at the conclusion of a five-day church growth conference in Atlanta and was charged with sending the pastors home with a fire to change the world. Instead, he offered these words of wisdom: "When you get home, you'll find that none of these things you've heard the past five days are going to work in your congregation. They just won't fit. You're going to have to find out what works in your church because it may be very different from what works somewhere else." Mead understood that vision must rise from an understanding of congregational context and the giftedness of the members of that church.

I was starting a transition with a church whose preaching minister was retiring after a thirty-year tenure with the church. I was sitting in the audience listening to his final sermon to his flock and was shocked by what he said to them. I expected reflections on their ministry together, as well as thoughts about the impact of "marrying and burying" two generations of people, flavored with a few laughs and tears. What the congregation received was a book report. He had read the latest book written by a minister at a growing church and wanted to bequeath that church's vision on his people as he left. I was saddened and amazed. After thirty years of ministry, this leader had no idea how to craft a vision for his own people.

Work Incompetence

Fellowship Community just didn't want church to be that much trouble. After all, "it's just church." The media ministry missed cues. The lighting system went without needed repairs. Kids who needed a youth minister went without a well-planned summer program. Members who needed a hospital visit were told that the leadership was out of town and could not be reached. FC was an unmade bed.

It takes twice as much effort to produce an excellent worship service or ministry when working with volunteers. Trying to hold to high standards of excellence while not discouraging people who donate their time is an art. Churches that are growing have worship assemblies that are guided by a central theme. The music flows into the theme, along with the prayers, communion comments, and sermon. Such coordination takes extra effort, but, like my mom's pie, it is the service people stand in line to attend because they are edified by its continuity of purpose.

Personnel Incompetence

Fellowship Church had deep issues related to personnel incompetence. The ministers functioned without job descriptions, performance reviews, or an accountability system. The elders treated their role as an honorary position and showed up at church when it was convenient for them around their travel schedules. Ministry leaders like Mary Margaret and Tony were allowed to function without proper supervision, and there was a lack of accountability because the leadership was conflict avoidant. The membership could not be expected to perform at a higher level than the leadership, and this contributed to the downward spiral of growth.

Ethical Incompetence

There is not a code of ethics for ministers and church leaders, as there is for the professions. Perhaps there should be. We hope that people will apply the high standards of faith to their practice of ministry and then hold our collective breath when things fall apart.

Paul wrote to Titus on the island of Crete and told him to appoint elders in the church. There was only one characteristic Paul demanded: "An elder must be blameless" (Titus 1:6). He repeated this again in verse 7; all other qualities of an elder revolve around that one ethical requirement. Paul knew that Crete's culture was a moral and ethical disaster. He wanted Titus to find men to lead who did not have a lot of skeletons in their closets. Paul understood the damage ethical wounds can do to a church when they go public and destroy its reputation.

Fellowship's divorce recovery group was putting the church in a vulnerable position by offering services in the realm of therapeutic care led by a nonprofessional who had no training or supervision. Churches run a fine line of ethical malpractice by offering support groups and recovery ministries that are run by unlicensed volunteers. These ministries often attract individuals with significant dysfunction who will not seek professional treatment. My experience has been that these types of ministries also attract volunteers like Tony, who have not worked through their own issues and are inflicting their dysfunctionality on the church. It is wise for a church to consult with a licensed Christian therapist who can review curriculum, ministries, and volunteers to ensure that the program is safe and effective.

Financial Incompetence

The financial affairs of Fellowship Church were a tightly held secret subject to multiple forms of abuse. Larry, the elder in charge of finance, was siphoning off funds to help support his son. Laura, the church secretary, was dipping into the benevolence funds to help support her prescription-drug habit. Members were accustomed to approving an annual budget and then spending whatever they wanted to spend and expecting the church to pay for it. The elders were co-conspiring with the congregation by ignoring the situation and refusing to demand an outside audit of the books.

The danger in all these situations was the easy rationalization that each person made to justify their misuse of church funds. Larry could justify his actions by saying that the church had helped his son before. Laura could justify her stealing by saying that she was as worthy of the help as any of the benevolence cases the monies were intended to assist. The elders could rationalize their belief that Larry had everything covered, so they didn't need to worry about anything. The power of self-delusion is seductive when church leaders are in financial need and there is no accountability system in place.

It is rare for me to work with a congregation in transition that does not suffer from one or another form of incompetence. It is very common to discover that financial incompetence is occurring among all types of wounded churches.

WOUNDS TO THE CHURCH

Incompetence wounds a church in subtle ways over a long period of time. The Chinese art of Ling chi calls this process "death by a thousand cuts." There is a cumulative effect on the church over time, and once this process gains a foothold in the DNA of a congregation, it is difficult to reverse.

DOMINANCE OF INFORMAL RULES

Every human system has formal rules and informal rules. When I went to college as a freshman, I was assigned a dorm room and two roommates I'd never met. The college had formal rules for where I would live and who I'd live with. Sometime that first afternoon we got hungry and found our way to the campus cafeteria to eat dinner. No one told us where to go or when dinner was served; we simply found our way by watching the other students around us. We were learning the culture's informal rules.

Fellowship Community Church was a church system dominated by unhealthy, informal rules. The youth minister could be a student instead of a minister. If the preacher delivered a decent sermon occasionally, he wouldn't lose his job. The elders were allowed to show up when convenient for them and did not get in the way of the warring factions in the church. Mary Margaret and the other Bible class leaders could do what they wanted in their classes.

Healthy church systems have clear, fair, and ethical formal rules that define how people will live and work together in the church.

They define the boundaries in terms of worship, ministry, finances, personnel, quality of work performance, and legal responsibility. In healthy systems, there is not one group that abides by the rules and another that is exempt from them. The playing field is equitable.

LACK OF AGREEMENT ON DIRECTION

"In those days Israel had no king; everyone did as they saw fit." Mary Margaret decided to take her class off campus. Bible class leaders decided they did not have to follow a set curriculum for their classes. Elders decided they didn't need to meet or attend services regularly if this interfered with their travel schedules. The media ministry interrupted worship services with untrained workers blasting feedback into listeners' ears. The message was clear: this is Fellowship Community, and we are going to do things the way we want to, regardless of what anyone else in the church says.

The results were quick and decisive. This church plant stalled out in its growth cycle shortly after the launch stage. There was no agreement on vision, mission, and implementation. In fact, they took great pride in being what one member called "a rather difficult group to deal with sometimes."

COMPETITION FOR SCARCE RESOURCES

Every church has three main resources: people, energy, and money. If those resources are directed toward a common goal, then the church will be moving to accomplish its mission. Fellowship Community lacked a clear, empowering vision to call people toward. Such a vision would have defined the use of its resources. Ideally, though not on a practical, working level, people would be dedicated toward ministries moving the church toward its goals. Energy and time would be devoted to the accomplishment of those goals. Financial resources would be strategically dedicated to key areas of growth. Instead, Fellowship was a loose confederation of warring tribes that represented competing interests and met together for a common worship service each week, while spending the remainder of the time eyeing each other warily.

CONGREGATIONAL DEPRESSION

As indicated earlier, attending Fellowship Community was similar to eating a slice of Morton's pie for dessert at the church potluck. It wasn't really bad; it just wasn't very good. The church had consolidated around a core group of members who had their ministry and their group of friends. Outsiders would visit the congregation and experience distancing from veteran members, who would say all the right things about wanting new members but keep a cool, aloof social distance that sent the opposite message.

Congregations, like individuals, can suffer from depression. They are, after all, a collection of people with emotional needs. As leaders failed to deal with the problems at FC, they continued to push the unresolved issues forward and bury them under the rug. But problems do not go away; they simply build up. The anger, frustration, and resentment were building at Fellowship Community, but their conflict style was one of avoidance. Depression is anger turned inward, and this church was suffering from a case of congregational depression. If not corrected, the depression could become institutionalized and eventually lead to the death of the church.

CONGREGATIONAL HEALING

Many churches like Fellowship Community are wounded but never seek help because the damage occurs gradually over time. The congregational culture adapts to its own peculiar idiosyncrasies and develops an odd "insider and outsider" view of the world. "If you're one of us, you get it; if not, we can't help you."

The first order of business in any consulting process is agreement on the part of all leadership, as well as the congregation, on the need to engage in a transitional process. This is critically important for churches battling wounds of incompetence because they often fail to understand why people are so upset about the way things are going. "That's just the way we've always done things here." Healing can begin only when the church sees a need for things to change and personally takes ownership of their participation in the problems.

Objectives for healing a church struggling from wounds of incompetence would include:

- Formulating formal rules to replace informal rules in the life of the church.
- Creating accountability structures for the enforcement of formal rules for the church.
- Building a new corporate congregational work ethic that extends to all key ministries.
- Building an agreed-upon vision statement and mission statement for the church.
- Directing all ministries toward the accomplishment of the vision and mission of the church.
- Building a formal decision-making process within the leadership team.
- Creating communications processes that are open and inclusive to replace the informal communication chain in the church.
- Building job descriptions, accountability structures, and a review process for each minister and staff member of the church.
- Building job descriptions, accountability structures, and selection processes for each member of the elder board, deacons, or leadership team.

- Creating a culture by which the church walks through its conflict rather than avoiding conflict or experiencing congregational depression.
- Creating a culture that is inclusive of outsiders and welcomes new members.

ANOTHER ONE BITES THE DUST

Chris's CPA firm transferred him to town, and his family transferred their membership to Fellowship Community. He had been an elder for a church plant at a town close by and was drawn to FC's start-up reputation. Chris was a skilled teacher and an energetic leader and was asked to fill in for the auditorium class teacher, who had become ill. Chris was quickly embraced by the long-term members in the auditorium class and was invited to serve as an elder. His wife and two teenage daughters were adjusting well to their new school and church home.

Chris entered the leadership of Fellowship Community and began asking some simple questions: "Why are the worship services so disorganized? Why can't we seem to get some repair work done on the lights that pulse on and off during the services? Where is the youth minister during the week? Why does the church secretary seem frustrated with me when I asked for some information?"

Chris was encountering the informal rules of the congregation, and he was about to get punished by them. Being a CPA, Chris began asking questions about church finances. "Why does only one person sign the checks? When was the last time we had an audit? Who is checking the books on the benevolence fund that the church secretary is dispersing?" He was speaking as a professional CPA, but he was threatening the informal financial rules of the church. Chris gently but firmly confronted Larry about the financial dealings of the church in one of their rare elders' meetings. The room went silent, and Larry was livid.

Life for Chris and his family changed dramatically at Fellowship Community. The auditorium class was removed from his schedule of teaching and returned to the former teacher. Elders' meetings were being called informally, and Chris heard about them only after the fact. His two girls were quietly ignored by the youth minister. The ladies who had reached out to Chris's wife no longer called and politely declined her invitations. FC was sending the clear message: you've tried to change things here, and it's not going to happen.

The final straw occurred one Sunday morning as the elders read a public statement affirming the finance ministry, Larry as liaison elder for church finances, and Laura for her work in the benevolence ministry. Chris was never consulted on the statement, but the writing was on the wall. He resigned as elder, and a short time later he and his family began looking for a new church home.

Three years later, Chris was attending a men's conference hosted by his new home church. The events at Fellowship were in his rearview mirror. At break, he began talking to one of the men from his small group discussion. They discovered that they were both FC alumni. The man confided to him, "I made the horrible mistake of agreeing to be a part of their leadership team. I started asking too many questions, and they showed me the door quickly." Fellowship Community had once again been safely restored to its incompetent balance.

CHAPTER 7

THE EXHAUSTION WOUND

Three red blinking camera lights stared at Mike as he stepped up to the pulpit to deliver his Sunday morning sermon. Once they had been an afterthought as he gazed in the eyes of his congregation. Now they were his only connection to the congregation he'd served for only 48 months. Covid had hit, and his congregation had vanished, some never to be seen again. The world was in the grip of a global pandemic, and it might signal the end of this historic old church.

Grace Chapel would soon celebrate its centennial birthday—if it could keep its doors open. The church had been the first congregation of any kind established along the river when the city was founded. An historical marker near the entrance of the building marked the storied history of this pioneering congregation. As the city grew, church leaders had acquired prime downtown land and built an impressive colonial building with the tallest steeple in the state. Movers and shakers in city government, business, sports, and academics called Grace Chapel their church home. Grace was blessed by ministers who served with distinction for long tenures, missions programs that spanned the globe, and exemplary children's ministries that attracted young families. The two-thousand-seat sanctuary was filled to capacity every Sunday. Neighboring churches sent their staffs to study Grace's model of church growth. They were a pillar in the downtown community.

A series of events occurred over a period of time, however, that changed the fortunes of the church. Today Mike could throw a baseball across the auditorium on Sunday morning and not hit anyone. The pandemic had emptied his church, but the genesis of Grace's downfall had occurred years earlier as a series of events had signaled trouble ahead.

The first shift occurred geographically, as the city grew and established affordable neighborhoods outside the downtown area and new congregations were established in the suburbs. Young families with restless toddlers were less inclined to drive twenty minutes downtown and park in a parking garage, when there was a good church option just down the street from them. Developers were buying up older buildings and creating new urban loft apartments, but rebirth of the downtown area was slow. Grace's first challenge was the result of urban development and growth. Grace's ministers and leaders tried a host of things to entice members back downtown, and the ongoing discussion of whether the church should relocate was often on member's minds. The consensus was that no one wanted to give up their mission to the inner city.

The second shift occurred as downtown businesses and shopping moved to the suburbs and the local medical center began buying up property for expansion. The medical center added a new medical school, a cancer research center, and a children's hospital. Downtown streets were peopled with white-uniformed doctors and nurses changing shifts 24 hours a day. The sounds of ambulances arriving at the emergency room could be heard clearly in the foyer. Other churches that had once stood with Grace had sold their buildings one-by-one to the large corporate hospital chain. As Mike stood facing the red blinking lights, Grace Chapel was now flanked by the main hospital on one side and the children's hospital on the other.

A third shift had occurred in the life of Grace Chapel 36 months earlier, as two of the pillars of the church had passed away within six weeks of one another. Brother Manchester had served as the senior minister for Grace Chapel for 41 years. He was the beloved leader of the congregation and a well-known figure in the downtown community. His energy was boundless, and he had a heart for hurting people. It was not uncommon to attend a professional game and hear Brother Manchester leading the opening invocation. He was the embodiment of the phrase, "He went about doing good." The congregation was devastated when the announcement was made that Grace's beloved senior minister was across the street in the cancer-treatment hospital he had visited many times. He succumbed two months later. The congregation took a body blow at the loss of their leader.

The second loss occurred unexpectedly just six weeks after Brother Manchester's death. Brother Marcos had been the leader of Grace's international missions program and, like the senior minister, had been a ball of energy. At 65 he showed no signs of slowing down. For years, a proud congregation called them "The M and M boys" and marveled at their ability to get things done. Brother Marcos had established mission churches across Central America and traveled the U.S., tirelessly raising funds for famine relief, medical care, and building local schools. So, it was beyond belief when the church secretary received a frantic phone call from Brother Marcos's daughter with the horrific news that her father had taken his life. No one in the family reported signs of depression, and everyone was struggling to make sense of this tragedy. The church staggered forward, having received another body blow.

Grace Chapel appointed a search committee to find its first new preacher in forty years. Mike was called to Grace less than six months after the church had lost "the two boys." He inherited a church that numbered two hundred in an auditorium that held five times that many, a congregation whose average age was fifty-two and whose weekly budget was in decline. Fortunately for Mike, those two hundred core members held a lot of grit and determination. The finance committee had wisely set aside a deep congregational endowment for "a rainy day." That day had come. Covid hit just three months after Mike's arrival. Grace's new beginning had just been compromised.

Mike was tasked with the monumental challenge of trying to meet a congregation that had now vanished in the midst of a global pandemic. He tried phone calls and got members' voice mails, or worse, "This mailbox is full." He and the staff had implemented Zoom calls to check on members, but, given the age of many in his flock, found that they were averse to technology. He worked to improve the church's website and social-media footprint but was discouraged to see that a large segment of his church was not using it.

Covid hit Grace Chapel hard. During an 18-month time frame, there had been 12 funerals of church members—many without the comfort of a funeral service. Grace members who had family in retirement centers struggled with separation from parents who were quarantined. Grace Chapel's retired adults gathered in an active 39ers ministry led by an energetic deacon and his wife, who led trips and kept an active social calendar. Both the deacon and his wife succumbed to Covid, and the once proud 39ers group was left without its lead couple.

Mike stood alone in that cavernous auditorium and stared at the three blinking red lights on the mounted cameras. He was thankful that technology gave him access to his church every week, even though he barely knew many of his parishioners. However, he wished that his congregation was back to be a part of the service. Mike was tired of laughing at his own jokes and trying to fake his level of motivation. He felt the weight of the crisis bearing down on him. Right now he was just trying to get his church through another day. They would worry about the future once the world opened back up.

TRANSITIONAL DENSITY

Growing up in West Hartford, Connecticut, I was accustomed to snowfalls that began around Thanksgiving and stretched into March.

We lived on a hill, so the task of clearing the driveway after an overnight snowfall was a normal part of my daily routine. Before my dad bought a shiny red snowblower from Sears, my go-to tool was a flat metal snow shovel. Even when there was just a dusting of snow, my dad would order me to "clear the driveway." I learned quickly that even a small dusting could quickly turn to a heavy weight on my shovel. The accumulated snow would be so heavy I could barely lift my shovel. I was amazed at how something that looked so light and easy to get through could be so heavy to lift.

I have worked with clients in therapy who have had similar experiences as they have faced multiple life crises. They may have experienced the loss of a job, a change in health, the loss of a loved one, and/or a move to a new city. The changes they have faced may have included a negative stressor such as an unexpected financial setback or a positive stressor like getting married or graduating from college. Many times, the crises were unexpected, like contracting the Covid virus. At other times, as with a scheduled surgery, they could see the train barreling down the track toward them.

In these cases, it was the buildup of crises over time that eventually caused a breakdown in the individual's capacity to cope well. It wasn't one large hit to the body that took them out of the fight. It was the continually pounding stressors over an extended period of time that led to exhaustion. As with moving a snow shovel down a driveway dusted with snow, eventually the buildup of emotional and spiritual weight became so overwhelming the individual concluded, "I've had enough. I can't do this anymore. I think I need some help."

GRACE CHAPEL AND TRANSITIONAL DENSITY

Grace Chapel was a fine church. It had a proud history. However, a series of events, both external and internal, had left a coating of snow on its driveway, and the church found itself incapable of shoveling itself out of trouble. Grace was wounded by Transitional Density.

FACTORS IN TRANSITIONAL DENSITY AT GRACE CHAPEL

- Changing neighborhood and sociological shift from the city to suburbs.
- Downtown shift from cultural/shopping center to medical district.
- Unexpected loss of key senior minister and unprocessed grief.
- Unexpected loss of key missions' director and unprocessed grief.
- Accelerated search for senior minister without processing congregational grief.
- Covid pandemic, resulting in loss of fellowship, loss of worship connection, aborted onboarding of new minister, and loss of members.
- Unexpected loss of key deacon couple in 39ers ministry.
- Unclear vision and mission moving forward.
- Members and leadership adjustment to technology changes to maintain church functions.
- Congregational depression resulting from unprocessed grief.

Any one of the events listed above would be enough to stop a church in its tracks and require a healing transition. Add them together, and you have the makings of a congregational stress sandwich. The question was not How could Grace Chapel do better? Given all it had endured within a short period of time, the question was How could this church still be standing after taking so many body blows? It was a testimony to the remarkable spirit of a group of people dedicated to their church and city.

RX FOR TRANSITIONAL DENSITY

If Grace Chapel were my client in therapy, I would recommend the following treatment protocol to recover from transitional density.

Own the Cumulative Effect of the Events You Have Endured

There is a scene in the movie *Band of Brothers* where a young American GI runs into an abandoned bakery shop as they are clearing out a French village. A German rocket follows him in, and the shop explodes around the soldier, sending thousands of fragments of glass from the display cases into his face and body. He staggers out into the street and refuses help from his comrades, who see his face now in ribbons, though the wounded man is unaware of the damage he's endured. He's bleeding out but thinks everything is just fine.

I've worked with churches like Grace Chapel, who have endured one crisis after another and bravely walked through the pain. They are unaware of the buildup of stressors they have been exposed to and the damage it has done to them spiritually and emotionally. Like the wounded soldier, they walk out into the street and proclaim, "Don't worry about me; I'm just fine." I find that some churches avoid the hard work of healing because they believe it is somehow unspiritual to admit that we are worn out and in need of a season of rest. I remind them that even Jesus needed to "get away from the crowds," but some churches believe they need to do better than Jesus.

Time to Recharge the Battery

Grace Chapel needed some down time to recharge its congregational battery. They needed a season of congregational rest to recuperate from the losses they had endured. Some churches have a very difficult time slowing down and giving people time to lick their wounds. They believe that, if you are not busy all the time, you are not being a good Christian.

When my car battery starts to lose its charge, I take it to my mechanic, and he tells me I have one of two options. My battery may have some charge left in it, but we need to get the jumper cables and give it a jump start. A quick shot of electricity will do the trick. Or he may tell me we need to pull the battery out and hook it up overnight and give it a deep charge because the battery is so depleted. A jump won't do it this time.

Congregations are systems composed of people who have a certain amount of energy to expend. When that energy is depleted by a series of events that are traumatic, as in the case of Grace Chapel, it is imperative that the church receive a deep charge to restore them to healing. Attempting to jump-start Grace Chapel would have been a disaster.

Time to Process Emotions

I devote a chapter to the concept of congregations processing emotions. This is a critical step in maintaining congregational health, and one that is often overlooked by leaders. Grace Chapel was a congregation bathed in grief. The grief was layered one loss on top of another. The congregation had been given little time to catch its breath before the next loss was recorded. I'm certain that members sitting at home during Covid listening to the livestream church services were wondering, *What's going to happen next?*

Unprocessed emotions do not simply go away. They remain buried in our subconscious, waiting for the right trigger to bring them back to the surface. It takes a great deal of emotional energy to tamp down powerful emotions such as grief, anger, disappointment, and resentment. When a church does not deal with its emotional baggage, it's setting the stage for that material to emerge later on. When it breaks loose after building up to this degree, it will be even more powerful and destructive.

I've worked with many church leaders who have used denial as their main problem-solving tool. They would say, "Yes, we've lost our minister, our missions' director, our deacon who worked with 39ers, and a lot of dear members due to Covid. We are so sorry about that. But, you know, they're in a better place with the Lord, so the best thing we can all do to honor them is to just move forward." This is leadership devoid of a spiritual and emotional IQ.

Crafting a New Vision

Good leadership is an art and requires a sense of timing. Mike, Grace Chapel's new minister, knew that this was not the time to launch a new vision. He understood that the church was in survival mode, and he altered his leadership style to the demands of the situation. The church had not completed the process of welcoming him into his new role before Covid shut everything down. Mike understood that, once the current crises were over, there would be time to regroup and find a path forward.

A MEETING AND A SPEECH

Dean sat at the back of the auditorium listening to his fellow church members complain about the events of the past few years. Some wanted to pack up and move Grace Chapel to a new location. Others bemoaned the effects of Covid and the many losses the church had endured. You could feel the anxiety in the room.

Dean was a Grace Chapel "lifer." He was a third-generation member of the congregation. His parents had been raised in the church and married there. His grandfather, an early pioneer in the county, had donated the land where the church was now standing. Dean was approaching his eightieth birthday but retained a sharp mind and a keen ability to say the right thing at the right time. When Dean spoke, Grace Chapel listened.

The town hall meeting was winding down when Dean stood at the back, his hands gripping the rounded wooden pew in front of him. "I've listened to what everyone has been saying today, and my heart goes out to all of you. We've been through some tough times here, just like the rest of the world. But tough times call for tough decisions, and I think Grace Chapel has a real opportunity here. We were founded with a mission to help those in need in our city. This downtown area is our mission field. Once everyone in town came downtown to shop, see movies, and attend church. That's all changed. We are surrounded by hospitals, a cancer center, and doctors and nurses who are on the front lines fighting this pandemic every day. They cross the street in front of our church three times a day, going on shift trying to save lives. Lives of our own members, . . . and many of them are no longer with us."

Dean stiffened, and his voice grew stronger, "I'm eighty years old. I'll tell you this. It does no good to sit back and do nothing. Maybe through this terrible pandemic the good Lord is presenting us with an opportunity. Grace Chapel is surrounded by hospitals filled with hurting people. We watch every day as exhausted nurses and doctors struggle to do one more shift and try to save lives. What can we do to help them? What can we do to help these physicians in the name of the Great Physician? We have money in the bank, a huge facility that sits empty six days a week, and a heritage of people who have always stepped up to the needs of our city. We can sit around and wish for the old days, or we can deal with the reality of today. Folks, I think our mission has landed on our front doorstep, and we need to go down swinging." The silence in the auditorium was deafening as the old man took his seat.

Grace Chapel starting throwing some punches, but she didn't go down. The church was reborn. Fast forward 12 months, and the church was an entirely different place. Construction crews were putting the final touches on an unused education wing that had been gutted and would soon provide overnight housing to family members of Covid victims and cancer patients. A special grief-recovery support group ministry met several times weekly, and a psychologist in the church donated his time to meet with grieving families. The nursery was expanded, and a childcare facility was opened, fully licensed, for nurses and struggling medical students.

Families at Grace began an Adopt-a-Floor ministry and adopted the nurses and doctors on a hospital floor to offer them support, prayer, encouraging visits, and homemade treats. Especially popular was Grace's Front Steps ministry. Three times a day, at shift change in the hospitals, large tables were spread outside the front of the church, and coffee and doughnuts were provided for nurses and doctors.

Mike, the new preacher at Grace, felt a calling to minister to those who had experienced the loss of a loved one. Each week he and the worship ministry provided a socially-distanced memorial service for anyone in the downtown area who had lost a loved one due to Covid, cancer, or any other circumstance.

Grace remembered its "M and M boys," Brother Manchester and Brother Marcos. The Children's Ministry began visiting the Children's Medical Center and delivering gift baskets with packages of M&M'S to the children in their honor.

Grace was an aging church that reinvented itself by revisiting the original DNA that had given birth to it a hundred years earlier. The re-visioning process landed on its front doorstep, just as Deacon Dean had predicted in his speech. With time and healing, Grace Chapel was reborn.

CHAPTER 8

WHY DON'T THEY GET HELP?

I'LL KEEP MY SWAMP

Debbie's life had been an uphill struggle from the start. Her dad abandoned the family when she was five, and she had only faint memories of him. Her mother worked constantly and had a steady stream of boyfriends through the house. Debbie was expected to do laundry, cook dinner, and care for her younger twin brothers. She had vivid memories of sitting in the backseat of her mother's car at night, trying to keep her little brothers from crying or wetting themselves while her mom was inside a club picking up her next Mr. Right.

School was a challenge, and college was out of the question. There just wasn't enough money. She worked for a few years and then enlisted in the Army. Her service ended after a fall left her with a back injury that would plague her for the remainder of her life. Pain meds became her secret addiction.

Relationships with men were as dangerous for Debbie as the minefields in Iraq had been when she served in the military. Men never stayed around very long, and the ones who did left physical and emotional scars. She doubted there would ever be a man in her life and worried she was turning out just like her mother.

Tanner was the bright light in her life after all the failed relationships she'd been through. He was 11 now and entering middle school. They had always been close, but lately he'd been pulling away. He struggled in school and had been diagnosed with a learning disorder, and it was a battle to keep him on his medication. She wondered whether, had she herself been tested for a disability, school might have been different for her.

She'd never found a job she liked. She had bounced around from one to another trying to find work that excited her, but nothing seemed to work. Her current job working in a dental office paid well, but the office manager "seems to have it in for me and we get into arguments a lot," she reported.

Her current crisis was the entrance of her mother back into her life. They had gone for years without talking when a phone call came unexpectedly. Her mom had cancer and needed someplace to go where someone would look after her. Once again, Debbie was on call to "save the day" for her family. Her mom had moved in six months earlier, and her health was rapidly declining. The current situation brought back a flood of old, unresolved memories, and Debbie didn't like the way she was feeling.

Debbie had called me for a counseling session, and I listened to her story with interest and a sense of sadness. This woman had paid some heavy dues and had faced life alone for many years. She had not seen many good days. The future looked as though it would deal her the same hand as her mother's if she did not make some changes.

When she finished talking, I laid out a counseling approach to address her concerns. I explained that therapy meant forming a helping relationship and setting some goals to make her life different. I talked about how often we would need to meet and about how long the therapeutic process would take. I described some of the beginning steps she would need to take to change her life for the better.

Debbie listened quietly, and when I had finished, she said something most of my clients never say: "Yeah, I'm not going to do any of that." With a calm voice, she looked me in the eye and said, "Look, I'm not going to waste your time because none of that is ever going to happen. I'm just not going to do it."

I was slightly shocked at her forthrightness and somewhat amused by her candor. I told her that most of my clients listen politely, and, if they are not interested in therapy, I never heard from them again. They rarely tell me this to my face. Would she mind telling me why she was so sure she would not do the work?

Debbie spoke quickly and firmly: "Dr. Don, you need to understand something. My life is a swamp. I live in a swamp, and there are alligators that attack me regularly. You are asking me to risk leaving the swamp I know for a swamp I don't know. At least in my swamp I know where all the alligators live." With that she stood up and returned to her swamp. I was left to consider the question why some people embrace help and others give in to fear.

Matthew's Gospel describes a conversation between Jesus and a rich young man. The young man inquired, "Teacher, what good thing must I do to inherit eternal life?" He then quoted his "spiritual résumé" to the Master. Jesus replied, "If you want to be perfect, go, sell your possessions and give to the poor, and you will have treasure in heaven. Then come, follow me."

The prescription Jesus offed addressed the heart of the man's problem. He did many good things, but his life had an ongoing pattern that needed interrupting. He loved his wealth. The rich young man left Jesus disappointed. "When the young man heard this, he went away sad, because he had great wealth." Like my client Debbie, the rich young man returned to his familiar swamp. He was unwilling to risk the process of change to experience eternal life.

WHY CHURCHES DO NOT SEEK HELP

Some congregations seek help for their wounds. Many do not. The ones that do not seek help struggle on, following the same paths they have established in the past. As I visit with church leaders and we discuss the healing process, they avoid engaging in it for one or another of the following reasons:

They Don't Know Help Is Available

Many church leaders lead their church in isolation. They do not have access to good information about congregational life. They are surprised to learn that the patterns they are experiencing at their church are similar to ones experienced by other congregations. They are also shocked that there are approaches to identifying the problems in the church and finding solutions to them. One church leader told me, "I thought we were the only folks dealing with these kinds of things." For many of my client churches, the pain has built up to a point at which they are ready for any kind of help if they can just find the right resources to trust.

Comfortable in Their Patterns

Denial is the default setting for most church leaders dealing with wounded congregations. "If we ignore it, maybe it will all get better on its own." To walk into conflict is to acknowledge that it's there, and that might make it worse. Somehow it seems "more Christian" to ignore the pain than to deal with it head on.

Like Debbie and her swamp or the rich young man and his wealth, they have become what the band Pink Floyd called "comfortably numb." They may get attacked periodically by their alligator members, but that's better than risking change.

Healing a congregation will likely involve conflict. Old patterns will have to be confronted. Leaders who are dysfunctional will have to be removed. Ministers who are hiding out in ministry will have to decide whether they want to earn a living in a responsible manner or leave. These are tough conversations, but essential to healing a church. It is much easier for church leaders to look at the process and say "No thanks."

Congregations have an internal time clock for how long they will endure pain. I never know when that time clock will go off and people will say "That's enough." That's what I call the Popeye Moment; it's when people say "I've had all I can stand." At that point they require change.

The question at the Popeye Moment is whether there are enough resources left in the church for it to heal. Some church leaders wait too long, and too many members slip out the back door before they take action. The pain builds, and their denial continues. When they do wake up, it's too late, and the body cannot recover from the wounds. The congregation will eventually die from leadership denial.

Move Quickly into a Search

Many churches avoid dealing with their wounds by moving quickly into a search for a new minister or launching a new initiative. They hope to deal with the pain by focusing everyone's attention on a ministerial search or a new beginning. It's a nice sentiment, but it's based on faulty thinking.

I travel a lot in my work. I have a rule: I ask that you land the plane before we take off. I prefer you land at Love Field in Dallas and let me off before you take off again. I would rather not be dropped off at ten thousand feet, hoping I'll land in Bachman Lake on the north side of the field. Churches that move from one minister to another without time to heal are like a group of passengers that get thrown off an aircraft without a parachute.

The hiring of a new minister will not automatically change the old processes in the church. If anything, it will intensify them as he enters and tries to make some changes. The old patterns will emerge, shut him down, and throw the church into a higher level of conflict than before he arrived. He will be the lightning rod for the conflict, and the leadership will be blamed for "not hiring the right guy."

It is essential that congregational healing begin during the interim period between ministers. Problems that are not addressed do not simply go away. They roll forward into the next era of history and solidify as a part of the corporate congregational culture. Taking time to heal and examine church process will allow the new minister to enter the church on a level playing field. Otherwise, he will be blamed for many things from the past he had nothing to do with.

We Have All Knowledge

Job told his friends, "Doubtless you are the only people who matter, and wisdom will die with you!" (Job 12:2). Job confronted a group of friends who thought they had all the answers. You couldn't tell them anything because they had a corner on all the wisdom within their little group.

Systems Theory presents the idea of an open system, that of a church that has healthy boundaries and is open to new information. For any group to survive, it must take in new information and adapt to changing circumstances. Some church systems are open and adaptable, while others are closed and rigid.

I worked for a short time with a congregation that had as its mantra "Everything we need is in the house!" The preacher would say "We are facing tough times, but everything we need is in the house." They were not interested in a transitional process. They told me that everything they needed was already provided by God and was in their spiritual house. I respectfully accepted their conclusion and was sad to hear that they closed their doors two years later. Evidently everything they needed had not been "in the house."

Fear of Exposure

Churches avoid a healing transition because they fear exposure of processes and congregational secrets. John 3:19 states, "This is the verdict: Light has come into the world, but people loved the darkness instead of light because their deeds were evil." It is common for me to consult with a congregation and deal with moral, ethical, financial, or sexual issues that have been hidden for many years. These issues do not just go away. They remain as a cancer on the soul of a church and will destroy it.

In counseling, I work with couples who carry family secrets. It may be an affair, addiction, or misuse of family funds. There is a large elephant in the room that no one is talking about. Therapy threatens to interrupt that delicate balance and expose the family secrets. It's common to get a few sessions in and have clients bail on the process because they are fearful of bringing to light the events that have been in darkness.

I was consulting with a church that in the beginning seemed open and engaging. They had a terrible history of poor decision making and scores of members leaving for neighboring churches. We were trying to stop the bleeding. My contact person in leadership was at first helpful and engaging. Soon, however, I noticed that he was trying to control the consulting process. He was giving directions on how the preaching should proceed. He was asking for the results of survey instruments and then burying them when they proved to be embarrassing to the existing leadership.

It became clear that my contact person had been assigned to me to control the process and ensure that the work did not unearth any of the congregational secrets. This church had an informal power structure that functioned as a shadow church, and his role was to protect their interests. The formal and informal power structures feared exposure. I ended the consult when they refused to engage in a transparent process.

Addicted to Conflict

You've attended family reunions where one couple spends the entire time arguing with each other. Family members wonder what keeps them together. There isn't any warmth, affection, or respect. It is the conflict itself that keeps this relationship going. They stay together, bonded over the pain of their interactions. This is called a conflict-habituated marriage—a marriage in the habit of conflict.

This negative bonding process can also occur in churches. There are congregations that are bound together by their arguments, fights, and struggles. They keep score of old offenses and add new ones to the list. They exist to keep the conflict going. Often a church that talks a lot about grace, peace, and reconciliation will be the church that is tied up in knots of unresolved conflict.

Ministers and church leaders get caught up in the ongoing drama in the church. Ministry is traded for putting out the latest fire among the members. Energy that could be devoted to positive growth is lost in meaningless debates and arguments.

Paul warned Titus about the negative effects of a divisive person in Titus 3:9–11: "But avoid foolish controversies and genealogies and arguments and quarrels about the law, because these are unprofitable and useless. Warn a divisive person once, and then warn them a second time. After that, have nothing to do with them. You may be sure that such people are warped and sinful; they are self-condemned."

Simplistic Answers to Complex Problems

Churches that have been wounded by years of pastoral neglect, an affair by a leader, or the power abuse of a Tough Bargainer are walking wounded. The church will require a spiritual and emotional diet of care to be restored to health. It will take time to restore trust in leadership. The church will need to regain its sense of purpose and confidence so that it can move forward with a new vision.

Often church leaders will opt to apply simplistic answers to complex problems: "We just need to get busy and put all of this behind us." Some leaders will opt for a roll-up-your-sleeves-and-deny-the-ship-is-sinking approach to problem solving. Others will argue that there's a lack of spirituality on the part of the church. They have become spiritually weak. These are the compassionless individuals who tell parents who have just lost a child not to grieve: the child is in the arms of Jesus.

Jeremiah wrote, "They dress the wound of my people as though it were not serious. 'Peace, peace,' they say, when there is no peace." One of the most respectful things I do as a therapist is to treat my clients' struggles with the seriousness they deserve. When people are hurting, they want to know that the helper understands the pain they have been through. They do not need to hear platitudes from pseudo-leaders who recommend working harder.

On the first Sunday I spend with a congregation, I affirm the story of their history. I relate the stories that I've heard them share and I assure them that I take their concerns seriously. I assure them that I will listen to them and that the situation can get better. It will take some work, and that work won't be easy, but there is hope. I can feel a collective sigh of relief from the congregation because someone is giving more than simplistic answers to complex problems. Long-term members will greet me at the door saying, "We've needed this for a long time."

Cutoff Churches

Growing up, my parents would visit my aunt and uncle in Florida, and we would have to make an appearance at their church. My aunt and uncle were members of a mean little church that specialized in condemnation. There weren't many members, but what they lacked in size they made up for in hatred. My aunt would clue the preacher that my parents would be in attendance, and he would prepare a "special sermon" once a year to preach the Hebbard family into hell. The delightful experience resulted in my parents planning all year long how to visit another congregation when vacationing.

My relatives' church was a "Cutoff Congregation." There are churches that exist to be against everyone around them. They are cut off from society, cut off from relationships, and eventually cut off from one another. A Cutoff Congregation constructs a belief system or set of religious "doctrines" that is against everyone else. The members of these churches get their sense of identity from putting other people down. Likely, members of these churches were cut off in their family of origin. They replicate their relationship patterns with their family of origin at church. It's all they know how to do. They develop a congregational culture that is based on "us against the world."

Cutoff Congregations are filled with highly wounded individuals who will not seek help for their own core brokenness. The congregations are closed systems and highly defended from the influence of outsiders. A Cutoff Congregation will generally not seek help.

Cosmetic Change

I often get calls from church leaders asking me to speak to their church about transitions. "We've been through some tough times and are in transition right now. We are having guest speakers come in and talk to our church about how we can do better, and we'd like to have you speak one Sunday." I decline the invitation.

While getting some good information is a worthy endeavor, having a parade of guest speakers through during a transition will not alter the internal dynamics of a congregation. It may provide some good entertainment for a few weeks, but the church will continue on its trajectory. The leadership may pick and choose a few ideas to implement, but it will not be a systemic approach to dealing with the wounds of the church.

I've also found that it takes one key person to create a trust-based relationship with a congregation during a transition. While the idea of a team approach sounds promising, it often breaks down in implementation, resulting in "too many cooks in the kitchen," all with competing agendas. The task of healing a congregation is an art and a science built upon the relationship between the church and the consultant/preacher. Scheduling a parade of guest speakers, however noteworthy, will not address the core issues of the church and result in long-term changes. It is a practice in cosmetic change.

WHY DON'T THEY GET HELP?

I was giving a series of lectures at Pepperdine University, and a church in the area invited me to speak on parenting during their Sunday services. The minister introduced me and then sat down on the front row next to the worship leader and several of the elders. I was addressing a fan-shaped auditorium filled with people when a young woman walked into the back, carrying a large shopping bag. She was dressed in jeans and a black Harley-Davidson t-shirt, and her long, dark hair looked like it hadn't been combed in some time. She walked down the center aisle as I continued speaking, but I was keeping a wary eye on the stranger. She began talking to the audience in a conversational voice that grew louder and louder. Soon everyone's attention was focused on the woman.

She began shouting accusations at the church. She was berating the congregation for hurting her. She was clearly dysregulated, and I was worried about what she might be carrying in the shopping bag. I was a guest that morning and didn't know the leaders of the church. I kept waiting for someone to do something. No one on the front row moved. Everyone sat frozen in their pew, looking first at the troubled woman yelling and then at me. The vibe I got was an implied "You're the psychotherapist, baby doll. Time to Cowboy up!"

I moved to her side of the stage and called out to her, "Tell me what's wrong." She turned and began talking directly to me. She started describing the breakup she had been through with her boyfriend who was a member of the church. She was alternating between tears and anger. I kept looking around for someone to help me, but the leaders sat frozen on the front pew with a deer-in-the-headlights look.

I quickly decided that I was in this alone and needed to get her as close to me as possible. If there were a gun in that shopping bag, I stood a better chance of getting it if she were up on stage. "Why don't you come up here with me and tell me what's bothering you. Then everyone else can hear you, too." She joined me on the pulpit and placed the shopping bag at her feet.

By this time, I could see mothers streaming silently out the back of the auditorium, headed to the children's wing to rescue their kids. I was thinking, "Surely someone has called 911." I was on my own with a dysregulated woman, an auditorium full of people now in panic, and a group of leaders frozen, leaving me to deal with the crisis. The worship leader looked as though he were having a heart attack at this point.

I decided that my best approach was to engage her in conversation. Maybe that would take her mind off the shopping bag and I could wedge between her and its location next to the podium.

"What's your name? Are you from around here? How did you and your boyfriend meet?" I was trying to connect with her in any way possible to buy some time. I was secretly praying someone there would have the good sense to call the police before the situation spun out of control.

The woman accepted my invitation. She began sharing her story. She talked about her ex-boyfriend and the pain she felt when he broke up with her. *I can't imagine why!* Luckily for me, the poor guy was not in attendance that morning, or the woman's head would probably have exploded. Instead, she began a long rant about their dating relationship and how awful men are. I agreed totally! I kept thinking, *Why don't they get help?*

At the end of one of her rants, the woman bent down and reached into her shopping bag. Every nerve ending I had was now in fight-or-flight mode. I moved as close to her as I could in case I would need to tackle her if she pulled a gun or bomb out of her Bed Bath & Beyond bag. I thought, *In front of a congregation of people I've never met before, I'm about to be pounding the crap out of a dysregulated woman who was spurned by her boyfriend. This better be a pretty hefty speaker's honorarium!* The worship minister looked as though he were now in full cardiac arrest.

Instead, the woman pulled out a large framed 8" by 10" picture of a man and handed it to me. "This is Gary. He's the jerk that broke my heart." I placed it on the podium. She cried as she reached into her bag once again. I braced for what was coming next. Instead, she retrieved a second portrait—this time of the two of them on vacation. "He's such a liar. I hate him," she continued. I placed the second picture next to the first. We continued this dating photo show-and-tell until the bag was completely empty of pictures. We had a full array of photos now covering the stage. The congregation was treated to a photographic narrative of their entire dating life. I kept thinking, *Surely someone has called the police by now. We've emptied out the bag, and if I talked to her any longer I'd charge her for a session.*

The podium was now covered with pictures of the "happy couple." The woman had told her story and was now sobbing uncontrollably. Her bag was empty, and so was her heart. The worship leader now regained his senses and began softly singing "We Love You with the Love of the Lord." The remnants of the congregation left in the auditorium joined in. The police arrived during the second chorus, and, thankfully, the woman was escorted out. I called for everyone to reassemble in the auditorium from the children's wing and parking lots, and we spent the remainder of the morning processing what had happened.

That incident became metaphoric for my time with churches. Congregations faced with a challenge tend to freeze up or run away from the problems. They look for someone else to deal with the problems or try denying they even exist. I would find myself "alone on the podium" with a bagful of problems looking at a front row of church leaders who were having a collective heart attack and didn't know what to do. I developed a process for helping hurting churches unpacks their bags and heal. I call it the Economou Process.

PART TWO

THE ECONOMOU PROCESS

The Lord answered, "Who then is the faithful and wise manager, whom the master puts in charge of his servants to give them their food allowance at the proper time? It will be good for that servant whom the master finds doing so when he returns. Truly I tell you, he will put him in charge of all his possessions."

Luke 12:42–44

CHAPTER 9

THE ECONOMOU MODEL

"The Lord answered, 'Who then is the faithful and wise manager, whom the master puts in charge of his servants to give them their food allowance at the proper time? It will be good for that servant whom the master finds doing so when he returns. Truly I tell you, he will put him in charge of all his possessions'" (Luke 12:42–44).

In ancient times, a wealthy landowner would appoint a head slave or steward to be in charge of his estate and affairs when he was gone. This individual was responsible for the care of the other slaves and the wellbeing of the property. He was called the *economou*, taken from the Greek meaning *oikos*, or "household," and *nomos*, meaning "rule" or "law." This was a faithful steward or business manager who ruled the estate. Joseph is portrayed in Genesis as functioning as an economou for Potiphar's household; his responsibilities extended over every area of the household except for Potiphar's marriage.

"'With me in charge,' he told [Potiphar's wife], 'my master does not concern himself with anything in the house; everything he owns he has entrusted to my care. No one is greater in this house than I am. My master has withheld nothing from me except you, because you are his wife'" (Genesis 39:8–9).

Jesus was using the term *economou* to refer to church leaders who would oversee the affairs of the kingdom of God. Church leaders are expected to be wise and faithful stewards of God's kingdom on earth. Jesus was aware that faulty judgment or corruption could lead to abuse by church leaders. Fred Craddock, in his *Commentary on Luke*, says, "The servant in charge (church leader) is responsible for the management of the household. Places of leadership offer unusual temptations to the abuse of others and the misuse of power and leadership positions in the church are not exempt" (Craddock, 165).

I developed an approach to congregational healing that is based on the "Economou" model given by Christ in Luke 12:42–44. The model calls for the consultant to be a faithful and wise servant who uses the tools of healing to restore the body of Christ. The model is integrated and unites four key elements into one unified approach. Those elements are theology, inductive preaching, process consultation, and Systems Theory.

THE ECONOMOU MODEL

Congregations are complex systems. Not fully explainable in organizational terms or as a volunteer group, they possess their own unique characteristics that demand a multidisciplinary approach. When a church is wounded, the injuries are even more complex to deal with because they are spiritual, interpersonal, and emotional in nature. The Economou Model addresses "the wounds of my people" with the significance and severity they deserve. If a church needs to be in the ER, it does not need to "go home and take two aspirin."

The Economou Model is a combination of four key elements that address congregational wounds and lead to healing. The four elements, taken together, provide powerful agents of healing and change that can transform the spirit and the processes of a church. As with the faithful and wise steward in Luke 12, the affairs of the household will be restored to their proper functioning.

The Four Elements of the Economou Model

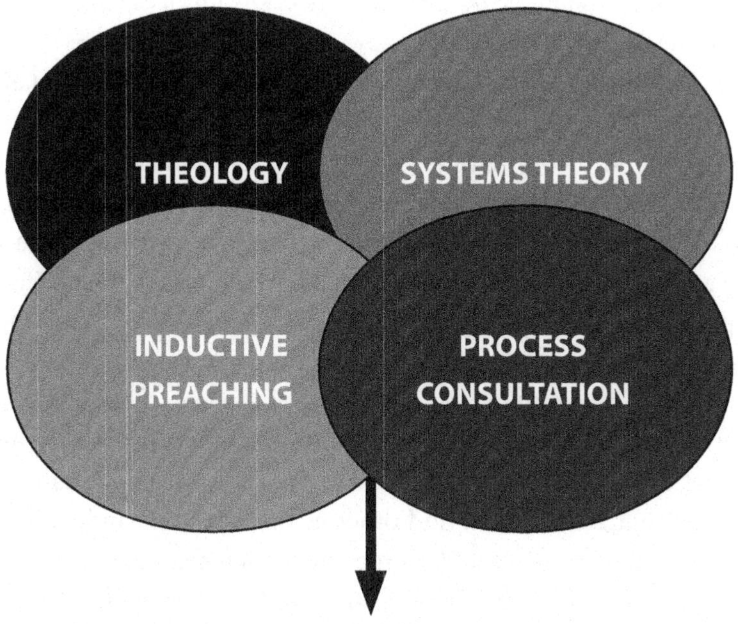

The Consulting Relationship

In the Economou Model, theology gives us the biblical basis for our approach, Systems Theory provides the overarching theory of change, inductive preaching provides a vehicle to deliver healing, and process consultation addresses important areas of congregational life. The consulting relationship is built around these four key elements. When they are utilized together, the church is restored, and trust in leadership can be rebuilt.

ONE THEORY, SIX MODELS

If you were to come to me for therapy, and, after listening to you for just a few minutes, I were to jump in and start making sweeping recommendations for change, you'd be very uncomfortable. Suppose that the next week I were to make more recommendations that seemed to contradict those from our first session? You'd begin to question my judgment. You'd think, *This guy doesn't know what he's doing; he's just shooting from the hip. He hasn't taken the time to get to know me.* You would be correct.

I tell my graduate students training to be marriage and family therapists, "You must ground everything you tell your clients in solid theory. Good theory tells us why we are doing what we are doing. It places every recommendation for change in a framework that makes sense. Too many consultants operate by shooting from the hip and lack a reliable and verifiable theory of change. Good theory explains a wide range of phenomena in an economy of terms and is understandable to the man on the street.

The first night of class, I tell my grad students, "Imagine I take one of you and dissect that person into all of their major systems. I lay out the circulatory, muscular, skeletal, and nervous systems here on the front table. I then add other elements of that individual—a personality inventory that tells me about their temperament, an IQ test that tells about their intelligence, and a résumé that describes their work habits. When I assemble all of those pieces, do I really have that person? Of course not! We must put all those elements together and add to them the spirit of life. We understand that human beings are an intricate blend of many complex elements that form our unique sense of self. Congregations are exactly the same. They are a complex blend of many elements that combine to form the unique 'sense of self' for each church. Like other human systems, they can be healthy or sick."

When I was in graduate school at Abilene Christian University in the Marriage and Family Institute, a powerful counseling theory was being adopted worldwide that helped make sense of complex dynamics in families. It is called Systems Theory. Systems Theory helps therapists understand the roles, rules, and relationships occurring in a marriage and family system. Later, as I was studying to be an organizational consultant at Texas Woman's University, my doctoral professor introduced me to Systems Theory once again. This time it was applied to larger groups of people—organizations, schools, and churches. Systems Theory works in those settings because they are simply larger groups of people, like big extended families. Those systems can be healthy or under stress. Systems Theory will be our overarching theory of change because it applies to a wide range of congregations, and it is highly effective in promoting long-term change in a brief period of time.

As I began working with congregations, I would encounter church leaders confronting the same challenges I had encountered in other congregational settings and asking similar questions:

- Can we reverse the decline our church has been in for many years?
- Can we resolve the conflicts we've experienced?
- How can we start growing again?
- How can we rebuild trust in the leadership of the church?
- How do we make sense of this transition we find ourselves in?
- What do we do when people overreact and go out of control?

I added a series of Models of Congregational Health that complement Systems Theory to help church leaders deal with these tough issues of church life. The models are drawn from some of the best experts in the field of transition management, conflict resolution, church lifecycle, church growth, trust, and trauma theory. Taken together, the Economou Model is built on a theoretical framework of Systems Theory combined with Six Models of Congregational Health:

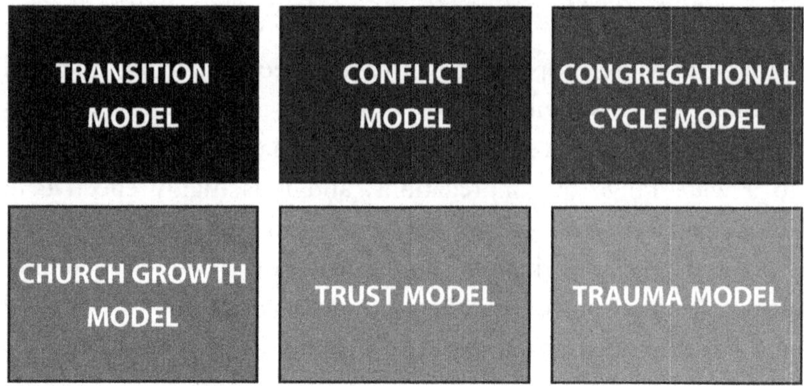

PLANE FLYING AT AN ANGLE

Imagine you go with me to Love Field in Dallas and board one of Southwest Airlines' 737s. We are taking a quick trip down to Houston, which takes about thirty minutes flying time. As we are taxiing to take off, the pilot announces, "Folks, we've got some rough air between here and Hobby Airport. Buckle yourselves in. I'm suspending cabin service. I'll try to find some smooth air, and we'll get you all there safely."

After takeoff, the air is turbulent, and the plane spends most of the flight with a noticeable lean to the right. We are flying straight, but we are flying at an angle. To compensate for this unusual angle of the 737, I lean back in the opposite direction to maintain my sense of balance. I don't notice I'm doing that; it's just my natural response to an unusual situation. I continue in that position for the duration of the flight.

As we land in Houston, the pilot comes back on the intercom and announces, "Thanks, folks, for your patience. I know this has been a rough flight. As we descend, we will hit smoother air. Thanks for flying Southwest." Sure enough, as we hit the outer marker, the plane encounters smooth air and levels out for the first time in thirty minutes. We are now flying level and straight.

An interesting thing occurs inside my head as I straighten up for the first time in half an hour. My body is now straight, but my mind is telling me I should be leaning to the side as I had been. I am upright, but it feels wrong! What had occurred during the flight was that my inner ear had recalculated my internal balance to accommodate this unusual lean in the aircraft. It reprogrammed by homeostatic balance to believe that leaning into the person sitting next to me was the normal way to fly! My mind had come to believe that flying at an angle was "the only way to fly."

I encounter the same phenomenon in churches. They have been "flying at an angle" for so long that their minds have recalibrated the situation to appear as though it were normal. The ongoing transitions, conflict, poor decision making, or confusing communications are the "norm" for the congregation. They've come to expect it. It's just the way things are.

Systems Theory presents church leaders and members with a way to understand how the plane is flying and what adjustments can be made to help it fly straight and level. It presents the church with a critical decision. They can choose to embrace the process of change. In other words, they can straighten up in their seat and wait for their inner ear to recalibrate to the new normal, or they can stubbornly choose to lean to one side and keep flying at an angle because "that's what we've always done." For churches that choose the former, it is an opportunity to choose a new flight path and stop flying at an angle.

SYSTEMS THEORY: A BASIC INTRODUCTION

Paul wrote the church in Corinth, "Just as a body, though one, has many parts, but all its many parts form one body, so it is with Christ" (1 Corinthians 12:12). I think of a church or a family as a set of wind chimes hanging on my porch. There are separate chimes, each with their own note, but they come together to make their own melody. As Dr. Richard Stuart observes, "For some the sound of their relationships is a sweeping symphony. For others it's the sound of rusty spikes hitting trash can lids."

We understand, as Paul did, that when you put all the elements of the body together, you get a uniquely functioning church. Dr. Stuart understood that when you bring together a group of individuals in a family, you get unique patterns of interaction. The first principle of Systems Theory is "The whole is greater than the sum of the parts." When you bring together a group of individuals, whether it's a family, school, or church, there will be a unique set of interactional patterns that are specific to that group of people.

The second principle of Systems Theory is "circular causality." Western education is based upon linear causality—one thing causes another. Two plus two equals four. Systems Theory takes an Eastern approach, which suggests circular causality. A impacts B, but B in turn impacts A. Two people in a relationship are both going to contribute to the dynamics of that relationship. In a marriage, a wife may want more connection and initiate conversations with her husband. The husband, wanting isolation, distances himself from his wife, causing her to pursue him more. They are in a dynamic loop.

In churches, a minister will preach a sermon that upsets some members. Members call their favorite church leader to complain about the preacher. The elder trying to placate the complainer will speak for the member to the preacher. The offended preacher will avoid the member or preach another sermon on the same topic just to prove he can do so. The preacher, elder, and member are caught in a dysfunctional dynamic loop. A healing transition attempts to identify these dysfunctional loops and offer new options for the church system to operate. The plane does not have to fly at an angle.

The third principle of Systems Theory is "structural and emotional relationships." In any group, there are structural relationships, which represent the formal roles that people occupy. I am a father, professor, therapist, and consultant, depending upon your relationship to me. However, within those structural relationships are deeper, more complex "emotional relationships." I confide in this person when I need advice. I share a funny story with another person when I'm in a good mood. I support another when they are going through a hard time. My life is filled with a complex blend of formal structural relationships and informal emotional relationships. I blend them, and most of the time I am not aware I'm doing it.

Churches are filled with complex structural and emotional relationships. I worked with a church that had a group of 13 elders and a formal decision-making process that they would vote and, regardless of the outcome, present a united front to the church. That was the formal structural relationship. The emotional relationship was that they would informally run every financial decision by the financial secretary, who had worked there for thirty years, to gain her approval. They were afraid of her disapproval and her informal power in the church. There were complex structural and emotional relationships that controlled the decision making of that church. Systems Theory offers us a way to make sense of them and change them if needed.

I will review some of the key concepts of Systems Theory as they apply to congregations.

Subsystems

Every congregation is composed of a number of important subsystems that represent the major areas of congregational life. Subsystems are where the work of the church is carried out. They can be working well or poorly, depending upon the health of the church. Some subsystems, like Worship or Ministerial Staff, may be core to the health of the church. Other subsystems may be less active or carry more dysfunction in them. When there is dysfunction or pain in one subsystem, it doesn't stay there. It tends to reverberate out into the rest of the church system. Examples of subsystems in congregations may include:

- Worship
- Ministerial Staff and Church Staff
- Leadership Team/Elders/Deacons
- Finance
- Youth
- Missions
- Media/Communications
- Outreach
- Disciplining
- Spiritual Formation
- Couples and Families
- Facilities
- Technology

A part of the assessment of a congregation's health is an examination of the various subsystems in the church and their relationship to each another. Churches that have been wounded will discover that those wounds are carried by the various subsystems, and their experience of those wounds may be vastly different from one subsystem to another. The consultant may enter each subsystem to assist but will not be triangulated into the conflict between one subsystem and another. The consultant works for the good of the whole.

ROLES

The role refers to the position we occupy within the church family system. Paul wrote, "If the foot should say, 'Because I am not a hand, I do not belong in the body,' it would not for that reason stop being part of the body" (1 Corinthians 12:15). Paul understood that there are various roles within the church and that each provides an important function. Church positions may include preacher, youth minister, deacon, and missions coordinator.

Within each position are a wide range of roles. I am a father, but within that position I'm my children's cheerleader, counselor, and confidant. I have a wide range of roles in that one position. My effectiveness in each role depends upon how comfortable I am in the role. A preacher may be comfortable as a "proclaimer of God's Word" but uncomfortable working the room at a potluck dinner. An elder may be great with Excel spreadsheets but awkward welcoming guests in the foyer. Those are issues of role comfort.

When I was a boy, I went to friends' birthday parties where we played Musical Chairs. The music would start, and we would walk around a line of chairs waiting to jump into one when the music stopped. The object of the game was that, once a chair was filled, people would move into another chair. Groups operate in much the same way. Once a role is filled, people tend to move into another role. In churches, I've found that individuals or entire subsystems (worship, youth, finance, etc.) may be sitting in a role when the music stops. Some of the common roles occupied in churches are:

The Hero

This is the person who holds the banner of the church high. We look to this person to make us proud and do the heavy lifting when things get tough. The hero is overly responsible and will take on everyone else's problems. In wounded churches, the hero will often be the person who calls me for help and is close to exhaustion, having tried to solve the church's problems for a long time.

The Scapegoat

As this Old Testament term suggests, this is the individual we blame for all our past problems and have "driven out of the camp." "They are the reason we are in all of this mess," church leaders and members will share, without regard to their own contribution to the situation. The scapegoat is the subject of many war stories I hear as I enter the church system.

The Rescuer

Similar to the Hero, this is the person or group we expect to swoop in and save the day. They function in an enabler or a co-dependent role. The rescuer pays the debts for the bad behavior of others in the system. In a Narcissistic or Sexually-Wounded Church, the many rescuers will operate behind the scenes to keep the false image of the church and its leadership intact. Rescuers like the Hero are often exhausted in a wounded church.

The Super Rational

This individual deals with pain in the congregational system by offering rational analysis. They do not know how to connect with others on an emotional level because they are disconnected from their own affect. They spurn emotion in religion and normally oppose a healing transitional process because it is a useless waste of time. "People need to just figure out what's going on and get on down the road."

My adoptive father was a Super Rational individual. He had been raised on a wheat farm, and when he was a young boy, he had two of his fingers cut off after they had been caught in the chair drive of a combine. When I was a boy, I asked him, "Dad, what did you do when that chain cut off your two fingers?" He stared at me blankly and said, "I don't know. I guess I picked up my fingers and walked to the house." I learned quickly to go to Mom when I was injured.

The Blameless One

As the name implies, the Blameless One is the person in the church who gets away with anything. They are never held accountable for their actions. They get a free pass to say and do whatever they want, regardless of whom they offend. Churches function according to a set of formal and informal rules, which we will discuss shortly. The Blameless One knows that those rules apply to everyone else but not to them.

I worked with a church that was strapped financially. They began the budget year in January, but ministries had to stop spending in May because they were out of funds. Except that one ministry continued spending each year because they were the Blameless Ones. A special contribution would be taken in November to make up for that group's annual overspending. Everyone would complain about their lack of fiscal responsibility. But everyone knew that next year the pattern would be repeated.

The Mascot/Comic

The Mascot/Comic hangs around and makes everyone feel good. We are not sure what he or she actually does. On staff, they may do just one thing each week and then walk around spending time in everyone else's office wasting their time or telling stories to keep the office entertained. Mascots may have deep family ties in the church. Those connections keep them employed. They under-function and may be incapable of obtaining employment outside the church.

Churches that are wounded and have experienced high staff turnover may have inadvertently promoted Mascots to positions of responsibility simply because they have been there a long time. Mascots will use the transition to further their own needs for power and money. They will detonate the healing process or be passive-aggressive in the change process because the result might mean that they have to give up their position of power and learn to be productive. Churches that ignore the healing transition process can find themselves spiraling downward if they are led by a mascot who is a "great guy" but totally inept.

The Arrogant One/King/Queen

This is the individual who acts as though the system were designed to meet their individual needs. They genuinely believe they are more important than others in the family, church, or organization. The rules apply to everyone else but not to them. They give themselves a pass to say anything they want, and when they offend others they will offer a halfhearted apology. They do things that are grossly offensive in social situations but are themselves offended by the slightest inconvenience.

Wounded churches can have individuals that function in this role, or it might be entire classes, ministries, or groups of people.

They lack the social radar that informs people they are being offensive. They operate without "the empathy chip." Wounded churches continue to be internally wounded by the Arrogant One who runs rampant in the congregation. In chapter 2 the Tough Bargainer was functioning in an Arrogant role in the church. The Arrogant One will not be open to change because they do not see the damage they are doing to others.

The Lost One

The Lost One or Ones are the individuals or groups in the church that have been ignored during all the trauma of recent years. These are the faithful members who sit quietly in the pews giving money each week, contributing their time, and trying to maintain hope. They feel invisible and powerless as the plane flies at an angle, and they remember a time when things did not operate this way.

The Lost Ones will eventually leave a wounded church and move to another congregation. They will grieve the loss of their church home. They may stop attending church entirely. Because they tend to be well behaved and faithful and do not make waves—it may be six months before church leaders discover they are gone. "What ever happened to the Johnsons?" someone finally asks. It is reported that they've been attending elsewhere for six months.

RULES

Churches are rule-governed systems. Some of those rules are doctrinal and theological. Many of the rules are interpersonal and relational. The interaction patterns of members of a church will follow predictable patterns. Sometimes those patterns are helpful, while at other times the patterns are unproductive. Systemic rules tell us what is permitted and what is expected in a church so those things do not have to be decided anew every day. The rules reveal what a church values.

There are two categories of church rules—formal and informal. The formal rules are the ones we can state openly and could post on a bulletin board in the foyer. Sunday worship starts at 10:00, we select new elders every two years, and "Talk to the finance committee for purchases over $500.00" are all examples of formal rules.

Informal rules are the rules we all know but no one talks about. No one is at the church building on Fridays, although that is a workday; Jerry, who is a deacon, never really does anything; and Brother Jones will lead 15-minute prayers every time he's called on. The informal rules are generally more powerful than the formal rules. When a church has been wounded, the informal rules often hold the pathology of the church and are in need of change.

The Biltmore Church was a merger of two congregations, Northside and Bailey Mills, but the two groups had never emotionally unified. On Sunday mornings, everyone knew that the former members of Northside sat on one side of the auditorium and former members of Bailey Mills sat on the other. The formal rule was "We are now Biltmore Church," but the informal rule was "We are still members of our former congregations." Healing for this church would involve unearthing the old informal rule and asking whether people wanted to keep living by it or to discard it in favor of a unified congregation.

The Biltmore Church never engaged in the process of examining their dysfunctional family rules, so they remained two separate congregations under one roof. This illustrates a systems tendency to resist change and remain stable in the condition one is in. This process is called homeostasis. A system will tend to stay in its current condition, resist change, and repeat the patterns of the past. The plane will continue to fly at an angle. When the pilot levels out the plane, passengers who are accustomed to leaning will complain until the pilot restores the old lean pattern. A well-functioning church is able over time to balance the two dimensions of stability and change.

Gary was the deacon in charge of building and grounds. He also liked to be the center of attention. Since his current role at the church did not put him in front of the congregation, he often found a way to get his needs met every Sunday by simply neglecting to set the thermostat in the auditorium correctly. As the worship service progressed and church members began to sweat in their pews, Gary would make a great show of coming from the back of the auditorium up to the front to adjust the thermostats located on each side of the podium. Members would grouse about the temperature, ministers would complain about Gary's showboating, and elders would listen to complaints, but no one was going to talk to Gary. The rule at the church regarding conflict was "If you don't have something nice to say, don't say it at all."

Some of the dysfunctional church rules I've encountered include:

- If you don't have something nice to say, don't say it at all.
- Good Christians don't have any conflict.
- Good Christians don't set boundaries.
- Anyone can say anything to anyone else, and they should just smile and take it.
- Be perfect; don't make mistakes.
- Don't ask for help.
- Strong Christians don't have emotional or spiritual struggles.
- Christian families don't have the same problems as other families.
- This member can do whatever they want.
- This member/minister is not accountable; they are the exception.
- The rules apply to everyone except . . .
- Stay away from __________ when they've had a bad day.

Paul states in 1 Corinthians 13:11, "When I was a child, I talked like a child, I thought like a child, I reasoned like a child. When I became a man, I put the ways of childhood behind me." For a wounded church, the healing process becomes an invitation to take out those old informal church rules that may not be serving us well any longer and discard them in favor of healthier, adult rules.

I have discovered that, when I'm consulting with a church and get a very strong reaction to a recommendation, I've trip-wired an informal congregational rule that needs to be changed. The church is denying this dynamic because to own it would be embarrassing to discuss.

A productive healing process with a consultant-preacher involves providing a church with new options. We work to identify those systemic rules that are working and reinforce them. We also work to identify those dysfunctional informal rules that are wounding the church and offer the opportunity to craft a new rule that is healthier.

BOUNDARIES

Every system has boundaries around it and within it. A boundary is an invisible line of demarcation that separates individuals, groups, or subsystems within the church, and the church from the community. Boundaries are defensive. They are not offensive. They protect what's in my yard like a backyard fence separating my backyard from my neighbor's yard next door.

Church boundaries can be open, closed, or permeable. When we moved to Dallas in 1968, a church was built two blocks from our house. It had a sign, and a few cars were around it every Sunday, but other than that there was no sign of life coming from that little group. It finally closed in 2010 and was torn down for a development. I always wondered who those people were. Their boundaries were closed.

Closed boundaries keep the good out and the bad in. Churches with closed boundaries have a bunker mentality: "It's us against the world, and I'm not sure you can trust all of us!" Churches with closed boundaries rarely accept help from the outside because those outsiders are not to be trusted. If they are wounded, they go into a coma and die, as this one did in my neighborhood.

In contrast, a church with open boundaries is all over the map. They act as though they suffer from Congregational Attention Deficit Disorder. One Sunday the preacher is proclaiming the missions call to foreign lands, and we all need to give sacrificially for this new vision. A month later that vision is forgotten and the preacher is off on a new crusade. It's not that they cannot get excited. They do that very well. They do not have appropriate boundaries. They haven't set their priorities and let them define where they are going.

Open-boundary churches lack ministerial boundaries. The Flirtatious Minister lacks boundaries around the messages he's sending. The Sexual Minister lacks boundaries around their sexual behavior. The Narcissistic Church uses members as a resource in a parasitic relationship. Some churches lack professional boundaries around confidentiality. Members would never seek help there because gossip is such a problem.

Consulting with an open-boundary church is challenging because they agree to a contract of work with the consultant and then are quickly distracted by other experts who have captured their attention. They agree to a healing process and then are constantly changing the rules. Open-boundary churches will fight any structure. They do not want to put up a back fence, which is exactly what they need.

Healthy boundaries are permeable boundaries. They allow the good to come into the system, while keeping the bad out. I tell my marriage and family therapy students to imagine they have just learned that an uncle has passed away and left them a beautiful resort in the Caribbean. "You fly down, anxious to see your new hotel on the beach. When you arrive, you're shocked to see guests at your resort running up from the beach bleeding and maimed. 'Sharks,' they cry as they rush past. Your beautiful beach harbor is infested with man-eating sharks.

"You have one of three options. Option one is that you go down to the print shop and have signs made that read 'No Sharks Here.' You then hammer those signs along your beachfront, get in your car, and return to the states, thinking the problem is solved.

"Option two is somewhat different. You go down to the harbor master and ask to rent a barge. You go out to the mouth of the harbor and pour a thick sea wall in the ocean and dam up waves as they are rolling in to shore. You then get in a row boat, take your shotgun, and go out and shoot all the sharks. Once again, you return to the states thinking your problem is solved.

"Neither solution is tenable. The first option represents churches with open boundaries. We're just going to act like there's nothing wrong here and maybe everything will be okay if we just leave it alone. They let the good in and the bad in without regard for the effects on the church. The second option represents churches with closed boundaries. We've gotten rid of our shark problem, but we've also eliminated the life-giving power of the sea coming into our harbor. The harbor will die because it is not being refreshed from the outside.

"Option three suggests that I install a shark net at the mouth of the harbor to prevent the sharks from entering my beach. The net keeps the bad out but lets the good in. The ocean is allowed to refresh the harbor. My guests are safe from shark attack. Healthy boundaries let the good in but keep the bad out."

SIGNS OF UNHEALTHY BOUNDARIES

- Trusting no one or trusting anyone.
- Telling everything, especially to people incapable of hearing the content.
- Not respecting the confidentiality of others.
- Walking out conflict on social media rather than interpersonally.
- Using anger and rage to intimidate others into compliance.
- Using guilt and shame to control others.
- Being offended when asked questions or challenged about a decision.

- Falling apart so someone will take care of you instead of owning personal responsibility.
- Letting other people direct your life and make your decisions for you.

Wounded churches include leaders, ministers, and members who have been subjected to boundary violations. This is one of the principal areas of healing that needs to occur and a key reason why the transition needs to give members time for restoration. In a later chapter I will discuss the important role that inductive preaching plays in the healing process. Boundaries are an important area to address and redefine in the consulting process.

TRIANGLES

If I stand a three legged stool up on two legs, you'll note that it sways from one side to the other and will eventually fall. If it is to maintain its balance, I'm going to have to stand there and constantly touch it to stabilize it. If I allow it to sit down on a third leg, it is balanced in a triangle.

Murray Bowen, one of the founders of Systems Theory, noted that a dyad (two people or two groups) is by definition unstable. When the relationship is going well, there is no tension (what Bowen called anxiety). However, when a problem arises, there is only one place for the anxiety to flow, and that's toward my partner. That means conflict, and we normally avoid that at all costs.

Bowen noted the tendency of partners in anxiety-producing dyads to reach out and draw in another person (or group) to hear their side of the story and thus restabilize the relationship. The new person hears their side of the argument and supports them, thus lowering the anxiety somewhat. This process is called triangulation. Bowen noted that this common process does not improve problem solving but complicates it.

If a couple is having an argument one morning and they leave for the day, they may both triangulate. He is upset and begins to share with his assistant at work what happened and why he is in a bad mood. She calls her mother and downloads her frustration to her sympathetic ear. By the time they get home, they both feel justified in their positions after talking with another person, and we now have four people involved in the drama, not two.

Jesus demonstrated an understanding of the power of triangles when he said, "If your brother or sister sins, go and point out their fault, just between the two of you. If they listen to you, you have won them over" (Matthew 18:15). The first step in resolving interpersonal conflict is between the offender and the offended. There are times when that is not possible, but the first step is still interpersonal.

People triangulate the church, and it wounds the congregation and keeps the conflict alive. A couple will not deal with their own issues or get counseling but will triangulate their individual prayer groups into asking for prayers for their spouse. A disgruntled church member will refuse to speak to the minister but carry out a campaign of slander against him behind his back. A church member will volunteer for every work assignment at church to avoid involvement at home, where they are unhappy. A staff minister will passive-aggressively refuse to do his ministry work and then complain to church members about how mistreated he is by the leadership.

A healing transition for a wounded church involves first education on triangles and how they occur in churches. The hard task of unplugging those dysfunctional triangles follows the educational process. The church will need communications and conflict resolution skills to help members deal "brother to brother."

Systems Theory offers a powerful and adaptable framework for understanding how congregations work. It focuses on process over content. The content of a discussion in a congregation will change over time. The process of how a church goes about communicating, resolving conflict, and negotiating roles will remain stable unless changes are made to the process. Systems Theory gives us the tools for changing process.

To complement Systems Theory, I draw upon six models that serve as a framework around key areas of congregational life. Those six areas are transition management, life cycle of the church, conflict resolution, church growth, trust building, and trauma. I will discuss each one briefly:

MODEL ONE: WM. BRIDGES MODEL OF TRANSITION MANAGEMENT

In 1994 William Bridges wrote the classic text on transitions titled *Managing Transitions: Making the Most of Change.* In it he proposed that change is an external process, while transition is an internal one.

It isn't the changes that do you in—it's the transitions. Change is not the same as transition. Change is situational: the new site, the new boss, the new team roles, and the new policy. Transition is the psychological process people go through to come to terms with the new situation. Change is external, while transition is internal (Bridges, 3).

Bridges makes the point that, if people fail to transition, the changes will not be successful. The internal process of transition is powerful and necessary to navigate change successfully. Though aiming his book at the business audience, Bridges makes frequent reference to the biblical text as a source for understanding endings, periods of wilderness wandering, and new beginnings. He proposes a three-stage model with endings, neutral zones, and new beginnings.

ENDINGS

"Transition starts with an ending. This is paradoxical but true. This first phase of transition occurs when people identify what they are losing and learn how to manage those losses. They determine what is over and being left behind and what they will keep."

NEUTRAL ZONES

"People go through an in-between time when the old is gone but the new isn't fully operational. This is a time between the old reality and sense of identity and the new one. People are creating new processes and learning what their new roles will be. They are in flux and may feel confusion and distress. The neutral zone is the seedbed for new beginnings."

NEW BEGINNINGS

"Beginnings involve new understandings, values and attitudes. Beginnings are marked by a release of energy in a new direction—they are an expression of fresh identity. Well managed transitions allow people to establish new roles with an understanding of their purpose, the part they play, and how to contribute and participate more effectively" (wmbridges.com).

We will discuss the application of the Bridges Model more extensively in chapter 14, "Healing through Death, Burial, and Resurrection."

MODEL TWO: MARTIN F. SAARINEN: THE LIFE CYCLE OF A CONGREGATION

Martin F. Saarinen proposed in *The Life Cycle of a Congregation* that churches go through two phases in the life cycle: growth and decline. There are eight stages in these two phases, and each stage is characterized by the use of certain energies in the church. Knowing where a church is in the life cycle is critical to healing a congregation.

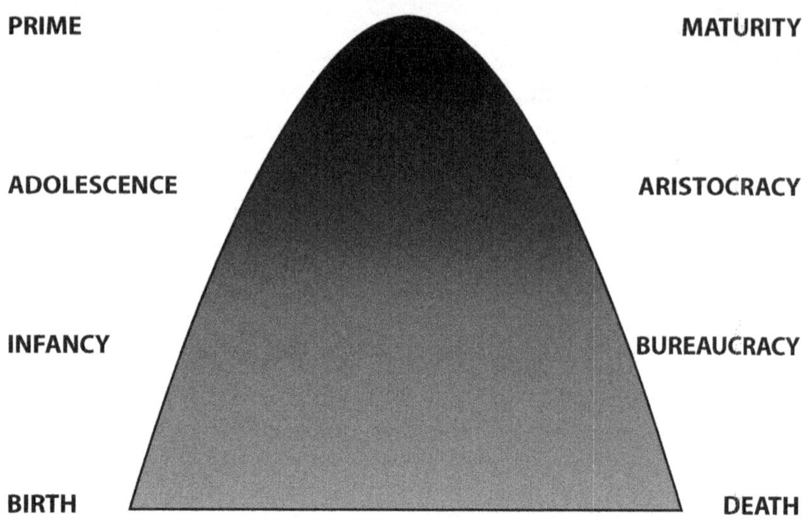

Birth

Every church begins with a gleam in the founder's eye. Someone has a vision for a new church. It is a culture integrated around the vision and charisma of the founder. There are high levels of enthusiasm but insufficient membership to support ministries. The church must expand and grow if it is to survive.

Infancy

The infant congregation has a strong need to survive. There is a great deal of enthusiasm and an attitude of "y'all come." The culture of the church is open and inclusive, and if you are a part of the congregation, you are expected to work. The church continues to be an extension of the "founding pastor or preacher."

Adolescence

Adolescence is a time when the church adds formal programs, ministries, and services. The focus of the church is on providing services to the families of members who have come to be a part of the church. It is a busy-bee culture that may result in program proliferation.

Prime

In its prime stage, the congregation is hitting on all eight cylinders. There is a balance between people and programs. There is positive energy directed toward the accomplishment of the vision. There is a strong sense of mission. These are the "glory days" that members reflect back on as the church begins to age.

Maturity

The congregation in maturity has settled into its life and routines. It has well-established structures and ways of doing things. It relies on the "tried and true." It begins to rely on momentum from the past to carry it into the future. Less attention is given to innovation, and the church relies on what it has always done. Members spend more time with one another than on the work of the church.

Aristocracy

It is a short step from Maturity to Aristocracy. The energy of Maturity now wanes as attendance and membership fall off. Power is vested in a few people. A "good ol' boy" club emerges that retains control of the church. The overall climate of the church has become stale. Members are nostalgic over "the good ol' days" when the church was busy and full of people.

Bureaucracy

The main concern in bureaucracy is maintaining one's turf and a general mistrust of others in various parts of the congregation. Boundaries are rigid, and a great deal of time is spent blaming others for the ills of the church. The strongest energy left in the congregation is administration—the rules, policies, and structures that provide the only memory of past vitality. These stubbornly refuse to change.

Death

The internal rules, policies, and administrative structures resist change for the longest time and continue until the death of the congregation. There is no memory of the original forces that breathed life into the founding of the church.

I have worked with congregations at all stages of the life cycle. The earlier they are in the life cycle generally, the more resources they have to devote to the healing transition process. The farther a congregation progresses into Aristocracy and Bureaucracy, the less congregational energy it possesses to address internal issues. The plane has been in a nosedive for too long. Congregations in decline also differ in their openness. Some congregational systems remain open, while others are closed to outside help.

MODEL THREE: LOREN MEAD: CHURCH GROWTH

Loren Mead, in his book *More Than Numbers: The Ways Churches Grow*, proposes four dimensions of healthy church growth. These dimensions are numerical, maturational, organic, and incarnational. Taken together, they form the basis of balanced church growth.

Numerical Growth

This is traditional church growth in terms of "nickels and noses." Growth numerically will include converts, transfers in, and births within the congregation. Decline numerically includes deaths, transfers out, and lack of conversions. Mead notes, "Any human institution that does not develop an effective method of recruiting new membership and leadership will die. There are no exceptions" (Mead, 16).

Maturational Growth

There are many churches that will never grow numerically due to location, change in neighborhood, or culture. This does not mean that they cannot grow in other ways. Maturational growth refers to growth spiritually in faith formation as the church deepens its walk with God. This may take the form of Bible study or following the spiritual disciplines.

Mead notes, "The case I am making is that dozens, hundreds, even thousands of congregations have not had that experience of explosive growth, and probably won't; they may, but it's not likely. Most pastors now working in congregations and most congregational leaders will live their lives without experiencing any dramatic change in church membership. With a few exceptions that has always been true of church growth. We celebrate the exceptions and we should work hard to be such an exception, but the chances are that we will have to work all our life without that experience. If our faith cannot handle that, we are in trouble" (Mead, 41).

Organic Growth

"Organic growth is about the task of building the community, fashioning the organizational structures, developing the practices and processes that result in a dependable, stable network of human relationships in which we can grow and from which we can make a difference" (Mead, 60). Churches that grow organically are focused on communications, conflict resolution, power, and decision-making processes and the roles of members and leaders. These processes are vital to the long-term health of the congregation.

Incarnational Growth

Incarnational growth refers to the ministry the church takes back into the world around it. How it plays out its role in the community may come in one of four ways. Civic congregations are those churches known throughout the community as being active and "good citizens." They hold the food drives and put on the Christmas activities for families. Activist churches seek to impact the social and political agendas of the day. They seek cultural change and see the church as a vehicle to enact that change in the culture. Sanctuary churches view the church as a body to move its members on to their final home in the next life. They are less concerned with the here and now and more concerned about "over there." Evangelistic churches view their role as being "to seek and save the lost." They are evangelistic battle stations for the conversion of the lost, so their focus is here and now. Any of the four will work, as long as there is agreement on the part of the church as to its mission. A church seeking to be evangelistic while at the same time activist will feel pulled in different directions.

Working with wounded congregations, I address all four of these dimensions. Decline in numerical growth is often the stimulus for congregational leaders to call for assistance. People are leaving out the back door, or the church has been in decline for many years. I have seen a healing transition restore the numerical growth of churches before the arrival of the next minister. People are attracted to congregational health and a renewal of spirit, not the announcement of a position filled.

A healing transition will focus a great deal of energy on organic growth. Areas such as communications processes, roles, and conflict resolution are often established and then never revisited to determine whether they are serving the congregation well. Systems Theory gives us the tools to look at those processes and make adjustments.

Maturational growth will occur though the preaching and teaching ministry of a transition. The church is fed a curriculum of text that examines relationships, change, and conflict resolution. Often members will say "This material not only applies to our church; it's exactly what's going on at my place of work." Incarnational growth is impacted as the congregation is allowed to talk about its vision for the future. "How do we see ourselves? What has been our role in the community in the past? How shall we incarnate the ministry of Christ in this place moving forward?" A healing transition allows the church to catch its breath and reflect on where it has been, where it is now, and where it is going.

MODEL FOUR: DR. JAMES CAIL AND DR. JANIS ABRAMS SPRING—TRUST AND FORGIVENESS

Congregations that are wounded are normally low in internal trust and high in doubt. They also possess a catalog of old wounds that have not been processed and are in need of forgiveness.

Dr. James Cail, in his *Lectures on the Family,* states, "Trust is the ashes from the logs of mutually shared experiences." In other words, trust is a by-product of a relationship. We do not automatically trust someone. Trust is built up over a period of time as people share experiences and, importantly, do what they say they will do. When I do what I say I will do, I put a stick on the fire of the relationship. When my partner or co-worker does what they say they will do, that adds a stick to the fire. Trust is the by-product of our consistently over a period of time doing what we say we will do. It is the ashes from the logs of those mutually shared experiences over an extended period of time.

When churches are wounded, often trust has been shattered. It is as though someone took a wet/dry vacuum to the fireplace and sucked all the ashes out. There is no trust left. A healing transition starts the process of people rebuilding trust with one another. But this process takes time. That is why, when church leaders ask me "How long will this take?" a part of my answer is "That depends upon how badly the trust has been damaged."

Arrogant church leaders will attempt to rush through the trust-building process. They want immediate trust restored because "We are the elders." I encounter this false rationalization in the case of extramarital affairs when the person guilty of having the affair demands that immediate trust be restored. They want to "put this all behind us and get on with our marriage." They refuse to do the hard work of burning some new sticks and reigniting the fire and instead stomp on the ashes and wonder why the flames don't return.

A healing transition will allow all parties involved to step back and grieve the loss of old relationships and consider how to ignite new ones. It gives the church time to heal and a process to say "This is how trust can be restored with me as your partner here in ministry." Impatient church leaders will rush through this step and later wonder why no one in the congregation trusts them. They have failed to do the hard work of trust rebuilding.

Dr. Janis Abrams Spring makes the case in her excellent book *How Can I Forgive You?* that forgiveness is an interactional process. Two people who are at odds with one another are bound together by the offense. The offender and the offended are bound together by a negative bond, which is the wound they have experienced. A church may be filled with members who are bound to one another in negative bonds from past wounds. The congregation may be bonded to its leadership through negative wounds.

Dr. Spring maintains that the path to healing these old wounds is for both the offender and the offended to "do the work of forgiveness." There is work to do on the side of the offender and on the side of the offended. Both must engage in the hard work of forgiveness to heal the wounds of the past.

The Gospel of Luke gives us several illustrations of the preaching of John the Baptist. Luke 3:8 quotes John as calling his audience to "produce fruit in keeping with repentance." In other words, don't show me—tell me. John understood that a relationship can be so damaged that people will not believe what the other person says. Actions are the only thing that will convince the other person that the offender has changed. And those actions must be consistent over time. There must be time to burn some more logs and let ashes of trust rebuild in the fireplace.

Dr. Spring's model of the offender and the offended bound together by a mutual wound would look like this:

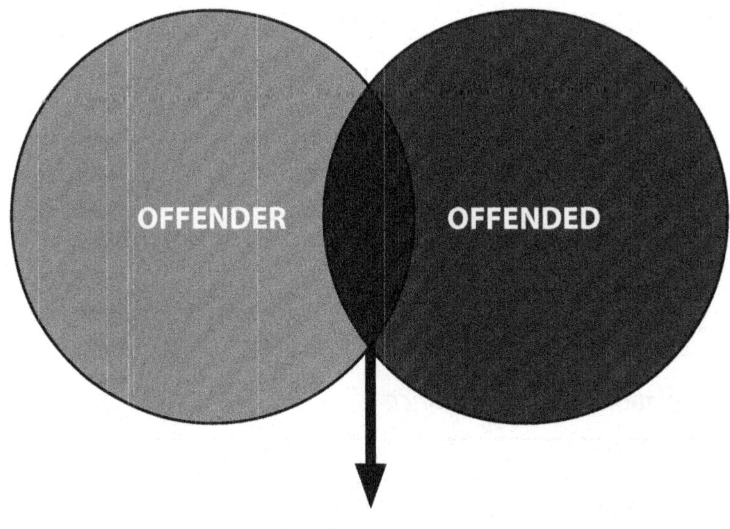

Binding Wound

A healing transition allows the church time to rebuild trust in its leadership and in itself as a congregation. Preaching and teaching on the process of forgiveness encourage members to learn the skills necessary to practice forgiveness on an interpersonal level. Process consultation allows leadership, staff, and ministries to examine ways in which groups or ministries have wounded one another in the past. The congregation forms a bond with the interim preacher/consultant and experiences trust in that relationship. That trust then forms the basis for a new relationship with the next minister. The deeper the trust wound has been, the longer it will take for the congregation to be restored from the pain. There are no magic wands to accelerate the hard work of forgiveness and rebuilding trust.

MODEL FIVE: CONFLICT RESOLUTION

In chapter 3, I shared the conflict resolution model proposed by Mouton and Blake. It defines conflict resolution along two dimensions: commitment to the relationship and commitment to personal gain. Combining the two elements, we get four conflict styles: Problem Solver, Tough Bargainer, Friendly Helper, Empty Tank.

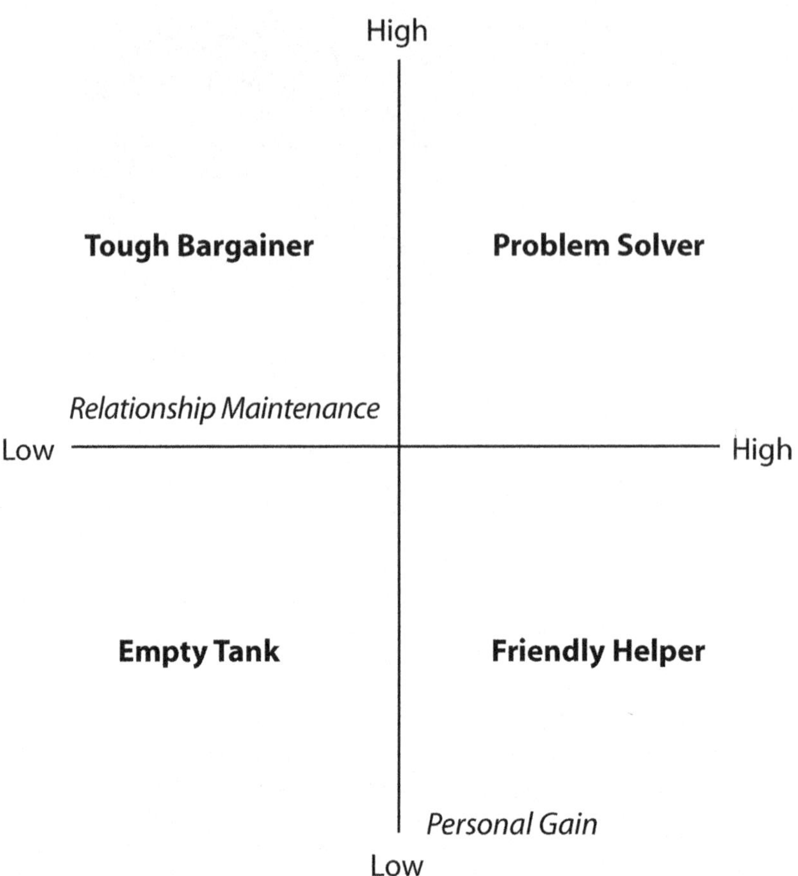

Problem Solver

This individual has a high commitment to the relationship and a high commitment to personal gain. They value their own viewpoints and value the relationship. They will speak in ways that are respectful, yet clear and direct. They are an asset to the healing process in a church.

Tough Bargainer

This individual has a high commitment to personal gain and a low commitment to the relationship. They value their opinions over relationships and are driven to get their way. A tough bargainer can do damage to a church if they are in a position of leadership. In a healing transition, they must be removed from leadership to allow restorative work to begin.

Friendly Helper

The friendly helper has a high commitment to relationships and a low commitment to personal gain. In church, as in other areas of their life, they will bend over backward to avoid conflict and keep the peace. In a healing transition, they will carry invisible scars from mistreatment they have received and put on a "happy face," acting as though nothing has happened.

Empty Tank

These are individuals in the church who are on their way out the back door or simply marking time until they resign from leadership. They are depressed and discouraged. They do not want to engage in the church system any longer and are waiting for the proper time to leave. A healing transition can give some Empty Tank people hope that things will change for the better. The departure of this group will be the final signal that a church needs outside assistance.

A healing transition will teach and model effective conflict-resolution skills. It will attempt to move leaders and members toward a Problem Solver stance. It will disempower Tough Bargainer as a conflict style and attempt to empower Friendly Helpers in the church. Finally, it will attempt to restore hope among those in the Empty Tank camp who are contemplating leaving the church.

MODEL SIX: TRAUMA

In my counseling, I often work with clients who have a quick trigger. Their emotional response to situations is accelerated. An event will occur in their lives in which the normal response, on a scale of one to ten, would be a one or a two. It is upsetting, but the event is not worth losing one's mind over. Instead, this individual goes from "zero to eighty" in three seconds. The event that should signal a response from the individual at a two is producing a ten. When I see that response, it is normally a telltale sign of trauma in the life of that client.

Pioneering researchers like Dr. Bessel Van Der Kolk, in his game-changing book *The Body Keeps the Score*, states that three new disciplines—neuroscience, the study of how the brain supports mental processes; developmental psychopathology, the study of the impact of adverse experiences on the brain; and interpersonal neurobiology, the study of how our behavior influences the emotions, biology, and mindsets of those around us—are changing our understanding of humans and trauma.

Van Der Kolk states, "These changes explain why traumatized individuals become hypervigilant to threat at the expense of spontaneously engaging in their day to day lives." Our churches are filled with individuals who have unprocessed trauma. That trauma does not simply go away. It remains in the brain and requires tremendous energy to keep tamped down. Like a software program I've opened and then minimized on my laptop, the trauma may not be on visible my screen, but it is open and running. At any moment, environmental stimuli can trigger it, and it pops up on my screen. The trauma gives me a fight-or-flight response, resulting in a reaction that is a ten to an incident that called for a one or a two. This is why severely wounded churches keep being retraumatized by members who lack emotional regulation. It is not a question of spiritual maturity. It is an issue of dysregulation of the brain. Church leaders can get stuck in processes of responding to dysregulated church members. In the process the "emotional tail starts wagging the dog."

Peter L. Steinke, in his book *Teaching Fish to Walk: Church Systems and Adaptive Challenge*, writes that churches will face issues. Those issues, which may involve church, family organization, or personal matters, are projected on the church. People may respond in a reflective manner, using higher-order thinking and a wise mind, or they may react out of fear and anxiety. Individuals who continually "go off the chart" and react chronically will become upset often and go from "zero to eighty in three seconds." This is a sign of trauma. These chronic reactors will also rope others into their drama and intensify the conflict.

Steinke notes that leaders who respond in a reflective way will pause, listen, gather options, and weigh a course of action. Leaders who fall victim to a reactive response to match the person's reactive challenge will make the situation worse.

A healing transition assists the church in unplugging the reactive-conflict cycles that have led to wounding. It educates the church on the need for reflecting problem solving and decision making that are based upon a wise mindset. Church members and leaders who have been traumatized in the past can be seen for what they are: hurting individuals in need of professional care. They should not be allowed to set the agenda for the church or dominate leaders' attention.

This chapter has presented the theoretical framework for healing a congregation. It has made the case that we need to understand why we are doing what we are doing in order to make long-term change in a church. Systems Theory provides the scaffolding for understanding how churches function. It is complemented by six other powerful models that address core issues of any church that has been wounded and is seeking a season of healing.

CHAPTER 10

HEALING AND THEOLOGY

"After the death of Moses the servant of the LORD, the LORD said to Joshua son of Nun, Moses' aide: 'Moses my servant is dead. Now then, you and all these people, get ready to cross the Jordan River into the land I am about to give to them—to the Israelites. I will give you every place where you set your foot, as I promised Moses. Your territory will extend from the desert to Lebanon, and from the great river, the Euphrates—all the Hittite country—to the Mediterranean Sea in the west. No one will be able to stand against you all the days of your life. As I was with Moses, so I will be with you; I will never leave you nor forsake you. Be strong and courageous, because you will lead these people to inherit the land I swore to their ancestors to give to them. Be strong and very courageous." (Joshua 1:1–7)

REMEMBERING AT THE RIVER

The campfires were burning, and the shadows of the evening were growing longer. Thousands of Israelites were gathering in their tents for the night, but their voices were low. The events of the past few weeks had changed everything. Tomorrow they would break camp and set out across the Jordan River headed for Jericho. But tonight, each man was taking a close personal inventory. It was gut-check time.

It had only been days since Moses had left the camp, never to return again. God had taken him up on Mt. Nebo and allowed him to look over into the promised land. Moses died, and God buried him in a place hidden from man's sight. Moses died at 120 years of age, still possessing strength and clarity. Joshua, Moses's trusted aide, took up the reins of leadership.

Israel had been in mourning in the plains of Moab for thirty days. They were mourning the passing of the leader who had taken them out of the grip of slavery in Egypt. They were mourning the forty years they had spent in the wilderness, wandering, after rebelling against God and refusing the conquer the promised land. They were, perhaps, mourning the ending of their own age of innocence. Ahead lay the land of the Philistines.

The Philistines had giants, walled cities, and more sophisticated armaments. They were trained in combat and had more experienced warriors. They occupied the land and had built fortified cities to defend against foreign invaders. A conquest against an adversary as formidable as this would not be simple.

But God was on a mission. His task was to change a group of former slaves from Egypt, who had spent the past forty years wandering in the wilderness as Bedouins, into a group of conquerors. This would not be an easy task.

It is important to note what God and Israel did not do at this critical moment in their history. Option one would have been to return to Egypt. They could have done this. Walk back across the Nile and give themselves up to their former masters. They had considered doing this when Moses first took over and led them into the desert. They rebelled and considered returning to the safety of their former lives.

People in transition often choose this option. When confronted with a challenge that may change their lives, some people run back to their self-destructive patterns. Like my client who proclaimed "I may live in a swamp, but it's my swamp, and at least I know where the alligators all live," Israel could have returned to the swamp of slavery.

The second option they could have chosen would have been to stay stuck in the desert. "Bedouin life wasn't so bad," they might have rationalized. "We've been doing this for forty years now; what's a few more?" Israel could have remained east of the Jordan and never risked the conquest of the land, regardless of God's promises.

People in transition may choose to keep doing the dysfunctional things they've always done because those things are familiar to them. They may believe that, if they do them just a little longer, a little harder, maybe this time they will work. There was security staying in one's tent that night and minding the sheep.

The third option they could have chosen that night would have been to organize a big pep rally, get all fired up about conquering the Philistines, and go storming across the Jordan in an emotional frenzy. "Let's go kill us some Canaanites!" And the walls of Jericho would have certainly fallen down on their heads.

People in transition get impatient. They want to see some change. They believe it would be better to do something—anything—rather than to sit here and do nothing at all. So, they take "decisive action." They make a big decision. They quickly hire a new preacher. They start a new program. And in the process, they miss out on the greatest opportunity for renewal, leaning, and rebirth the congregation has.

What did God do? He had them sit at the Jordan River for thirty days and transition. They were transitioning from being slaves and Bedouins to becoming conquerors. That change had to start internally, within each man's and woman's mind and soul.

God gathered his people and called on them to remember at the river. Behind them lay forty years of funerals. A whole generation of people who had refused to conquer the land had died and lay buried in the desert. They remembered the long years of waiting and looking west, wondering when the day would come that God would order them to march. They remembered Moses, the leader who had taken them through every trial and had now been replaced on the eve of the conquest.

God understood that, before his people could be conquerors, they needed to transition. There needed to be a deep-soul-level shift in their identity before they could take the land. So, he gave them a season of transition to remember at the river—who they were, where they had been, and where they were going. The seeds of success in the conquest were planted in those thirty days of transition at the river. God knew exactly what he was doing.

Israel needed time to grieve. They had lost their legendary leader, Moses. They had lost a generation of people: mothers, fathers, and grandparents had been laid to rest in the desert. They had lost forty years of time that could have been spent in the promised land. Now they were losing their self-identity. They knew how to be wanderers, but could they be warriors?

Israel needed time to open their eyes to new possibilities. What kind of leader would Joshua be? *What kind of warrior will I be? What will I do when I face combat for the first time? What will life be like living in my own town with a sense of permanence?* Israel needed to confront the reality of the soon-to-be-realized dream on a personal level.

In Joshua 1, God makes a speech to Joshua. He promises Joshua that he will faithfully subdue all of Israel's enemies. He will give Israel all the lands he had promised their forefathers. There was really one point to God's speech: his people needed to be strong and courageous. He repeated this three times in the chapter, and it was the last statement he made to Joshua. God was saying, "Have faith in me through this transition, and everything will be just fine."

As God's churches stand in difficult transitions, they need to hear the same message: be strong and courageous. There will be temptation to go back and do things the way you have always done them or make quick decisions because it somehow seems to relieve the anxiety we all have about the unknown. But the hard work is found in remembering at the river. The soul work for the church is done by sitting with the transition and allowing it to transform us from the slaves of our past into the conquerors of the future.

"Be strong and courageous," was God's message for his people in transition. He commanded his nation, Israel, to sit down and remember at the river—who they had been, where they were now, and what they might become with his divine help. The transitions our churches and our lives face provide us with the same opportunities.

THE WOUNDS OF MY PEOPLE

"From the least to the greatest,
all are greedy for gain;
prophets and priests alike,
all practice deceit.
They dress the wound of my people
as though it were not serious.
'Peace, peace,' they say,
when there is no peace.
Are they ashamed of their detestable conduct?
No, they have no shame at all;
they do not even know how to blush.
So they will fall among the fallen;
they will be brought down when I punish them,"
(Jeremiah 6:13–15)

The church's Associate Minister, Carl, asked me to visit a family in their home. The woman was in hospice care dying of cancer. Her second husband was caring for her at night after work, along with her two teenage boys. When I arrived, the nurse greeted me and showed me to the living room that had been converted into a hospital room for Mary.

Mary was in her mid-fifties and in the final stages of a long battle with cancer. She could no longer speak and used a letter board to spell out words. Her blue eyes still had some strength, and I immediately liked her. She had been the rock in this blended family, carrying the financial load for a husband who was chronically underemployed. The two boys had never accepted their "new dad," and Mary's illness just intensified the conflict.

Leaving the house, the nurse caught me in the foyer and in whispered tones said, "Someone's got to do something. We're finding her with bruises in the morning after her husband takes care of her. The boys come home from school and lock themselves in their rooms, and they have guns. There are fights, and this thing is spinning out of control. Her husband doesn't have the capacity to deal with this situation, and Mary is suffering because of it."

I talked with Carl, who knew Mary and her second husband well. We consulted on the best plan of action to recommend to the family. We spent hours talking with the boys, Mary's husband, doctors and nurses, and Mary's extended family. Our primary goals were the peaceful ending of Mary's life and the safety of everyone in the family.

The family agreed upon a plan whereby Mary would be moved into her sister's home. The boys would continue in their school and live with a favorite uncle, minus the firepower. Mary's husband would remain in the home, and everyone would be given access to visit with her. We enacted the plan, and the stress levels went down immediately.

Carl and I were thrilled, . . . until I received a call from the "chief elder of the church," commanding me to a lunch in the private dining room of his firm as quickly as possible. David was a successful Tough Bargainer who had purchased his position at the church and campaigned for the eldership before dominating everyone with his aggressive, dictatorial style.

"You are destroying families in this church," he blustered as the food was served. "I've heard you have recommended tearing up a Christian family and moving them into separate homes! What kind of example does that set for the rest of our church? What gives you the right to do this?" David was raging, dysregulated and making a scene in the dining room.

I tried to reason with David, explaining to him that if we did not step in and give this family some distance, we were going to be carrying people out of the house in body bags. Did he want that on his conscience? This was a "blended" family that had never actually blended, and the stepfather had no resources as a caregiver or as a father. He couldn't even hold down a job. David would hear none of it. I was to go back and reunite this family, or he would see to it that my work with the church ended. I informed him that I had taken the responsible steps to protect everyone in the family and would do nothing of the sort. He was welcome to do whatever he saw fit regarding my future role with the congregation.

Jeremiah speaks of prophets and priests who "dress the wound of my people as though it were not serious. 'Peace, peace,' they say, when there is no peace." The kingdom of God has always been haunted by so-called religious leaders who do not know how to treat the wounds of his people. They offer platitudes and sweet-sounding words but refuse to roll up their sleeves and get into the tough business of ministering to hurting people. Jeremiah's clear indictment could be offered today as churches are led by pastors and leaders who do not know how to pastor God's people.

There is nothing more devastating to a hurting person than for others to offer simplistic answers to complex problems. David was an expert in this. It was his default position. He wasn't willing to learn about the complexities of blended families. He wasn't willing to admit the potential for violence. He wasn't interested in the reality that this "Christian" family was being "led" by a man who couldn't hold down a job and that its foundation was now dying of cancer. He certainly didn't step up to the plate and offer to spend a few nights at her bedside to see what was happening. His pathetic prescription was "Everyone go home and be a Christian family." Was it any wonder that David's two grown children would have nothing to do with him?

There is nothing more reassuring to a wounded person or church than to say, "I hear you, and I take what you're saying very seriously. I'm not going anywhere, and we are going to figure out a way through this." I may have no idea what to do at that moment. I may say, "I don't know what to do, but I'm going to find someone who does." People will gladly accept that because I have taken their wounds seriously. The only way David might gain some insight would be to experience wounding in his own life. Even then, it is questionable whether he would understand.

Jeremiah is shocked as he points out, “Are they ashamed of their loathsome conduct? No, they are not ashamed at all. They do not even know how to blush.” This is a stinging indictment of the religious leaders of his time. The prophets and priests who were assigned to be the healers of Israel were completely devoid of empathy! You couldn’t trust the spiritual leaders of God’s community because they just didn’t care. They lacked the empathy chip and were not interested in acquiring it.

Simon Baron-Cohen, in his book *The Science of Evil—Empathy and the Origins of Cruelty*, studied individuals who lack “the empathy chip.” Dr. Cohen, a professor of developmental psychopathology, defines empathy as a two-step process. First, we must identify what someone else is thinking or feeling, and, second, we must respond in an appropriate manner. Empathy means that the person suspends their single-minded focus of attention and adopts a double-minded focus of attention.

Dr. Cohen developed an Empathy Scale that rates individuals on the extent to which empathy exists in their personality on a scale of 1–6.

Level Six

These are individuals with remarkable empathy. Their empathy radar is constantly turned on. They are aware of the intellectual and emotional needs of others around them and respond in highly appropriate ways. They are very comfortable with the feelings of others. We want our churches to be led by individuals who are on this level.

Level Five

These individuals are above average in their ability to empathize with others. While their radar is not on all the time like those at Level Six, they are able to turn on the empathy chip when someone begins sharing a situation that requires an empathetic response. Individuals at Level Five can also function well in church leadership if they continue to use their skills.

Level Four

People on the low-average end of empathy are more comfortable with relationships based upon activity rather than intimacy. They are more comfortable talking about things instead of talking about feelings. They will struggle to respond to someone who is wounded and want to care only for their external needs. Individuals in church leadership on Level Four will draw the group toward the instrumental aspects of leadership—the budget or building rather than expressive needs like empathy. The apostles in Acts 6:2 said, "It would not be right for us to neglect the ministry of the word of God in order to wait on tables." They were defining their work on Level Six and empowering deacons to work on Levels Four and Five.

Level Three

Level Three is composed of people who know they have difficulty with empathy, mask it, and pretend to be normal. They will avoid jobs that demand lots of interaction with people, preferring to work with things. They like to keep their heads down, avoid others, and get home to be alone. These individuals avoid church leadership and will avoid situations in which they will be called upon to exhibit empathy. They do not know how.

Level Two

Level Two is where I encounter severe problems with church leaders who lack "the empathy chip." At this level people lack both empathy and the recognition that the things they say and do are having a negative impact on the people around them. They blunder through life. They destroy relationships with their family, church members, and co-workers. Their spouse or friends try to offer them constructive feedback, but they do not listen. Spouses spend their lives cleaning up their messes. These are the Tough Bargainers described in chapter 2. The wiring is in the wall, and they do not, in my experience, change.

Dr. Cohen reserves Levels One and Zero for those individuals who commit heinous acts of violence against society. He notes that the verbal violence of Level Two can be as painful as the physical violence of Levels One and Zero.

Jeremiah's words are spoken, I believe, to a very targeted group of individuals. They are spiritual leaders who lack "the Emotional Chip." They function in Level Two of Dr. Cohen's model of empathy and do great damage to the body of Christ. They wound people with the things they say and stubbornly refuse to listen to any corrective feedback. So, Jeremiah's prophecy of their fate continues: "'They will fall among the fallen; they will be brought down when I punish them,' says the LORD."

JOSEPH: SITTING WITH THE AMBIGUITY

As a young man, Joseph's life seemed to have been mapped out nicely. He came from a wealthy, prominent family. He was his father's favorite son. He was surrounded by stepbrothers he looked up to and admired. He was destined to marry a nice Jewish girl and be a country gentleman farmer.

In one day, his life changed forever. The downward spiral began when he walked into his brothers' encampment and was beaten by them and sold into slavery. He tried to stabilize himself by performing his tasks in Potiphar's house to the best of his ability, but Potiphar's wife falsely accused him of rape. Now he was far from home, sitting in a jail cell, with no chance of parole.

Two fellow inmates enter the picture. Pharaoh had thrown his chief cup bearer and baker in prison. Joseph was charged with caring for their needs. One morning both men looked dejected. They had each had a dream, and there was no one to interpret them. Dream interpretation was a prized function in Egypt at that time.

It is at this point that we hear the confidence of Joseph: "Do not interpretations belong to God? Tell me your dreams" (Genesis 40:8). The baker and cup bearer share their dreams, and Joseph provides them with the interpretations. Later we hear the doubt in Joseph's voice: "But when all goes well with you, remember me and show me kindness; mention me to Pharaoh and get me out of this prison" (verse 14). In his pain and frustration, Joseph was begging for help. But the text reports that "the chief cup bearer, however, did not remember Joseph; he forgot him" (verse 23).

I work with clients who are facing difficult problems. When confronted with such challenges, an individual has three options. First, the person can attack the problem. They can marshal their resources and hit the problem head-on to effect change. Sometimes attacking the problem is not the best solution because the fallout from the attack would be a disaster. Second, the individual can choose to accept the situation and move on. They realize that the other person or situation will never change, so there is no point in "fighting city hall."

Joseph could not enact options one or two. He could not attack the problem because he was powerless in a prison cell. He could not accept the fact that God had created him to be an interpreter of dreams and that he would waste that skill in a jail in Egypt. He knew he was capable of more.

There is a third option. It is one I call "Sitting with the Ambiguity." Joseph found himself sitting for two years waiting for the cup bearer to remember him. He couldn't attack the problem. He couldn't accept the problem. He sat with the ambiguity of the situation. He was willing to live in a condition of being "in between," along with the pain that the condition produced inside him.

Churches that are wounded find themselves in an in-between moment in their history. There are problems that they cannot immediately solve to move beyond. There are problems that, if they just accept them, will come back to destroy them later on. Transitioning a church allows us to sit with the ambiguity and do core soul work. If used to its full advantage, it is the most opportune time for congregational transformation in the history of the church.

What can congregations learn as they "sit with the ambiguity" of the transition? Like Joseph in Genesis 40, they can discover five lessons:

I Am Not in Control

Joseph was forced to give up control of the direction of his life and all his dreams. It had seemed that he was destined to be a gentleman farmer, living on the ranch with all his brothers and their families. That dream was gone. Sitting with the ambiguity helps me realize that I am in control of myself and very little else. Coming to terms with that is a powerful lesson for church leaders who overextend their span of control and think they can dictate a church through a transition. I have learned to give up control and, as a leader, opt instead for influencing others.

I Can Endure Pain

The main reason churches abandon the transitional process is that they cannot or will not endure pain. They will not deal with the anxiety of sitting with the pain and learning from it. It is a core lesson that there will be a certain amount of pain and that no amount of money, prestige, or power will exempt us from that. Churches discover that they can walk through a healing process and endure the pain of not knowing exactly who their next minister will be. Or what the exact timetable will be for the healing to be finished. Christians who embrace the passion of Jesus often want to move from the Garden of Gethsemane to the empty tomb and skip the pain of Calvary.

My Plan Didn't Materialize, But That Doesn't Mean There Isn't a Plan

Joseph no doubt had a plan for his life. That plan was blown apart, but that did not mean God didn't have a plan for him. He laid his plans at God's feet and humbly accepted God's sovereignty. I am amazed how many churches will claim to pray for God's leading and then lose faith when their own plan falls through. They refuse to lift their eyes and see the possibility that God is about to do a great work among them, not recognizing that they first must crucify their own willful plans.

I Can Still Be Positive and Productive Sitting with the Ambiguity

Joseph was positive and produced results wherever he went. At home he was the responsible son his father trusted. In Potiphar's house he was entrusted with the oversight of all his household and business affairs. The jailor put him in charge of the other prisoners. After one interview, Pharaoh made him his second in command of the country's affairs. Joseph used his time in ambiguity in a powerful way. Churches in transition have important work to do before the next era of congregational history begins. The transitional time can be the most creative time of church renewal. Joseph did not miss his opportunity for growth by being lost in misery.

Living in the Ambiguity Gives Me Time to Do the Work I Need to Do

Joseph needed to do his own core work and give up control in order to rely upon God. God knew Joseph was about to be in charge of famine relief for the entire world. So, he placed him in a jail for white-collar criminals. Joseph heard the inside talk from Pharaoh's enemies in that jail. Joseph was given a graduate course in white-collar crime in Egypt that would be invaluable as he managed millions of dollars in famine-relief funds! This was not wasted time. It was preparing him for his next era.

There is important work for congregations to do in transition. There will be healing for relationships and resolving conflicts. There may be changes in leadership or staff. Informal rules that have been hurting the church will need to be addressed. The church may craft a new vision before it hires another minister. There is a rule of core work: life will keep bringing it around until it is done.

Dr. Maureen Lumley, a Jungian Analysist in Dallas, says, "If you sit with the ambiguity there will be the appearance of a third option. The third option will come. It will not be what we expected or anticipated."

In Joseph's case the cell door opens one day, and he is escorted into Pharaoh's court and presented with his dreams. When Joseph finishes divulging God's interpretation, he hears Pharaoh say these unbelievable words: "Since God has made all this known to you, there is no one so discerning and wise as you. You shall be in charge of my palace, and all my people are to submit to your orders. Only with respect to the throne will I be greater than you" (Genesis 41:39–40). Joseph's time "sitting with the ambiguity" had prepared him for his mission in life.

TELESCOPIC NATURE OF SCRIPTURE

The biblical story routinely passes over large segments of time with an economy of words. Many events that occurred within those years are summarized in a few short sentences. It is left to the reader to understand that the story moves on with the passage of these large blocks of time when many significant events occurred:

- ***Joseph is left to languish in prison (Genesis 41:1)***
  "When two full years had passed, Pharaoh had a dream."

- ***Joseph and his generation dies as a new pharaoh ascends to the throne (Exodus 1:6–8)***
  "Now Joseph and all his brothers and all that generation died, but the Israelites were exceedingly fruitful; they multiplied greatly, increased in numbers and became so numerous that the land was filled with them. Then a new king, to whom Joseph meant nothing, came to power in Egypt."

- ***Israel groans under Egyptian masters (Exodus 2:23–25)***
  "During that long period, the king of Egypt died. The Israelites groaned in their slavery and cried out, and their cry for help because of their slavery went up to God. God heard their groaning and he remembered his covenant with Abraham, with Isaac and with Jacob. So God looked on the Israelites and was concerned about them."

When we look at the sky through a telescope, it brings things into a close perspective. The telescope passes through millions of miles of space to achieve this view. We take for granted the journey that it takes to get to our destination.

The same holds true of churches in transition. The process of healing takes time. Often leaders want me to pull out my magic wand and transform the congregation overnight. They want the healing process to skip over the many miles it takes to get to our final destination. Patience with the process is not only practical—it is biblical.

PAUL AND A TROUBLED CHURCH

People sometimes ask, "Where is the biblical justification for healing troubled churches?" I refer to the ministry of Paul to the church in Corinth. Corinth was a deeply troubled church. Paul writes to them, addressing a catalog of concerns they have written him about. However, he begins his letter with an important statement: "For I resolved to know nothing while I was with you except Jesus Christ and him crucified" (1 Corinthians 2:2). Paul stated that the crucifixion was center stage in his theology.

However, from that point forward in his epistle, Paul confronts challenges in the life and ministry of this troubled church. A brief catalog of concerns include:

- Divisions in the church
- Sexual immorality
- Lawsuits among members of the church

- Marriage problems
- Food sacrificed to idols served at meals
- Problems in the worship assembly
- Problems during the Lord's Supper
- Correct use of spiritual gifts
- Resurrection of the dead
- The resurrection body

Just reading this list makes someone tired thinking about the difficult discussions that had to occur for this church to work through its problems. It would be no easy task to help heal this church and set it on track for healthy growth. But Paul walked into the challenge.

Paul writes in 2 Corinthians 11:28 concerning the pressure he felt ministering to the many needs of the early church, "Besides everything else, I face daily the pressure of my concern for all the churches." Paul was a model of ministry who placed the cross of Christ center-stage in his theology and ministered to the broken spirit within the early churches.

SIX CONCLUSIONS FROM THE BIBLICAL TEXT

This chapter has explored the biblical basis for a ministry of healing to congregations. Six major principles explain my approach to healing hurting churches. They are:

1. God transitioned his nation, Israel, at the Jordan River as they transformed from being slaves and Bedouins to becoming conquerors.
2. Authentic ministry demands that we take the wounds of God's people seriously.
3. Authentic ministry flows from deep empathy.
4. God's people are called to sit with the ambiguity during seasons of transition.
5. Time is required to heal.
6. Healing hurting congregations has historically been a part of ministry.

CHAPTER 11

HEALING THROUGH INDUCTIVE PREACHING

The voice on the other end of the phone said very simply, "We won't need you for the parenting seminar this weekend." I had been scheduled for several months to give a parenting seminar at a church in town, and my host was canceling just two days before the event. It was rather unusual. He was a very organized guy.

It had been a tumultuous week in the city. The summer heat was bearing down. Schools would be opening soon. Families were running out of town for their last trip to the beach. But the city was gripped with a story that had broken on Monday of the murder of a man at the hands of his daughter and her boyfriend.

The details of the murder were ghastly and unbelievable. These two teenagers had satanically tortured and murdered the girls' father in his home with a knife. He had suffered unbelievably before succumbing to his wounds. What made the murder more heinous was that he suffered from multiple sclerosis and was confined to a wheelchair. Two teenagers "in love" had carved up the girl's father, who was defenseless in a wheelchair. A normally tough city was brought to its knees by the thought of two teenagers committing such a brutal act.

"I guess you've heard about the murder?" my host inquired. "It's all anyone is talking about over here. We don't think it would be a good time to be having a seminar in light of what all has gone on.

We do have another request, though." He paused and took a deep breath. "The two teenagers who committed the crime are members of our church. The elders and the ministers would like you to come this Sunday and preach at our morning service. We'd like you to help us process everything that has gone on." I was quiet for a very long time.

"The two teenagers were in our youth group. We don't know what Sunday morning will be like. There may be news outlets here in the auditorium covering the worship service and doing stories on the church. Likely at least one of the families of these kids will be in attendance. Our minister is overcome with grief. He doesn't think he can handle this. Would you be willing to come over and speak to us?"

I agreed and hung up the phone, knowing I did not have a "satanic murder sermon" in my repertoire. Somehow, we hadn't covered that in Preaching Methods back in college. I felt the weight of the occasion pressing down on me. I knew I had very little time to prepare for perhaps the most challenging speaking engagement of my life.

What I did have was an approach to preparing for this message. The approach was based on starting where the audience was and establishing common ground with them. We were all in shock and grief. From there I could draw upon my experiences with clients who had been the victims of violent crimes. I had also worked with parents of young people who had been sent to prison for a variety of reasons. My brain began assembling stories, illustrations, and memories around these various themes. I thought about what it must feel like to be the widow in shock, the youth minister asking what he had missed, the minister preparing to conduct a funeral, or the parents who were in shock—especially the one woman who was burying her husband.

I was drawn to a reality in the text. From Genesis 4 forward the Bible is bathed in violence. Cain murders his brother Abel. Joseph's brothers seek revenge for their sister's rape by wiping out a village. The early church is persecuted, and Saul holds the coats of the men responsible. God's people had faced this many times. As David said, "Though I walk through the valley of the shadow of death, you are with me." We would be walking through the valley together that morning.

I have clear memories of preaching that morning. Standing in an old, wood- paneled auditorium behind a massive pulpit, I looked into the faces of members who were in shock. As I spoke, the tension began to ease, and people started to lean into the message. The church was motionless as I spoke. Tears flowed, and the long, difficult process of healing began. Thankfully, there was no media presence. It was like a close family conducting a private, difficult family meeting.

Afterward, the ministers and members thanked me for speaking from the heart and having the courage to address the situation with clarity and compassion. The week following, I received a letter from the mother of the teenage girl, thanking me for the words I'd shared and expressing how she would remember them as they moved forward in this horrible process. The church had already begun ministering to her family. God, in his providential wisdom, had filled that church with people who had already experienced profound grief. The message had connected with these veterans of loss and released them to begin healing the body.

I cannot take credit for what occurred that morning. It was a combination of three variables. First and foremost, God's Spirit was active and working on that occasion. Second, there was a profound readiness on the part of the congregation to hear a word from God. They were wounded and in need of healing to begin to move forward. Third, I had discovered a methodology for preaching and teaching that turned the traditional approach upside down. It is called Inductive Preaching, and it revolutionized my speaking to churches in transition.

INDUCTIVE PREACHING: THE LEWIS AND LEWIS MODEL

In 1983 Ralph Lewis and Greg Lewis published *Inductive Preaching: Helping People Listen*, one of the most important texts on preaching ever written. I had just completed my dissertation on the subject of public speaking to adult audiences, and I was reading everything in print on the subject. This book changed my approach to public speaking and gave me the tools I needed to address wounded churches in a biblical and practical manner.

Lewis and Lewis argue that the problem with most preaching is that it focuses on the situation four thousand years ago and then tries to bring people back to biblical times and apply the scenario to our contemporary scene. Inductive preaching begins with common ground, where people are living, and then walks them back to the text. This is a major shift in perspective and one not easily made by most ministers. I began my sermon that morning by acknowledging that we were all in shock and grief and then moved into the text. Starting with common ground helps people listen.

Traditional deductive preaching is jokingly built around an introduction, three main points from the text, with some cute illustrations thrown in, and a memorable conclusion to wrap it all up. The focus is on the main points. The stories are the cherry on top. An inductive approach turns this upside down. It begins where the audience is with common-ground experience and uses story, illustrations, analogy, and metaphor to deliver the listener to the text. It is, in Lewis's words, "helping people listen."

Inductive preaching is built upon several important principles:

Adults Learn Inductively, Not Deductively

Deductive learning moves from general to specific. It is the way we are taught in school. I learn about English writing in high school and then apply it to writing this paragraph later in life. There are rules of grammar, and I apply them later in specific situations.

In adulthood, we learn inductively. I move from specific problems to general principles. When an electrical socket goes out in my home, I don't take a course in electrical repair and then pay special attention to the "residential repair" chapter. I watch a YouTube video, go to Home Depot, and talk to a guy in an orange vest to learn how not to electrocute myself. I may call up a friend who does know electrical repair to quiz him. In the process I will learn some things about electricity, but my driving motivation is socket repair.

Wounded church members come to the preaching event carrying a lot of baggage. They have specific questions, concerns, and stories. They need to know that the preacher is "speaking right to them." Inductive preaching allows me to craft a sermon that speaks to their questions and addresses their concerns, while moving them into the biblical text for solutions to their problems.

Jesus Preached Inductively, Not Deductively

Jesus used inductive preaching as the main vehicle to preach to the masses in his ministry. Lewis and Lewis point out, "We might call Jesus the Master Storyteller. He wouldn't preach without a story, and most of those were parables. The New Testament records thirty-three to seventy-seven parables of Jesus, depending on your definition. He doesn't use them as merely teasers, light introductions to get his hearers listening for what he really wants to say. They are often the primary expression of his message" (Lewis and Lewis, 69).

Jesus used analogy in his speaking. He referred to light and darkness, salt, houses built on rocks and sand, and shepherds and sheep. "Jesus repeatedly returns his listeners to common experiences by his references: forty-nine times to sheep, twenty-seven times to sowing, twenty-two times to reaping and harvest and twenty times to water imagery. All are every day, crucial parts of the agrarian culture he lived in" (Lewis and Lewis, 69).

Jesus let his audience set the agenda for his speaking. The authors point out that, of the 125 incidents of Jesus communicating with others, 54 percent of those encounters were initiated by his hearers. "It is interesting that the Son of God, who came to earth to convey the most important message of all time, who had the clearest channel to God, and the deepest understanding of the message, let the audience determine his communication agenda more than half the time" (Lewis and Lewis, 72). Preaching in wounded churches requires that the message be co-crafted by audience involvement.

Simply hiring an interim minister to come in and preach his best candy-stick sermons misses the point entirely.

Stories, Metaphor, and Analogy Deliver the Freight in an Inductive Sermon

Rather than a story being a nice add-on to a point in the sermon to illustrate the text, stories become the vehicle to deliver the freight to the audience. This follows the model of Jesus's preaching and matches the adult audience's inductive way of learning.

Stories work because people match their own story with the story they hear. When I stand at the back of an auditorium greeting people as they leave, it is not uncommon to have a line of people waiting to tell me a story from their life that reinforces a story I shared in the sermon. People match their story to the ones they hear.

Stories work because they address difficult situations in a nonthreatening manner. This is especially important when treating a wounded congregation. They may have experienced toxic abuse, affairs, financial mismanagement, or lying from leaders. There is a minefield of difficult topics that need to be addressed. Stories allow us to do so in a non-defensive way.

Stories involve the audience in the sermon. Watch an audience when the speaker begins to tell a story. Everyone begins to lean in and listen a little more intently. I did a preaching internship during my undergraduate degree and experimented with the power of stories. I placed two cameras in the church auditorium. One filmed the preacher, and the other filmed the congregation's reaction to the sermon. Each time the preacher started telling a story, the nonverbal response in the audience was clear. People looked up, they straightened up in their seats and leaned forward slightly, and they nodded in agreement. The effects were clear. Stories engaged the audience in a way that no other part of the sermon could.

Stories go "under the wire" and connect with a hostile audience. Dr. Dan Mitchell was my clinical supervisor as a marriage and family therapist. Dan had spent years on the mission field and as a brilliant psychotherapist. He taught me that there are two doors that open the change process. The front door gives people an explanation of what we are doing. It is the deductive approach. The back door stimulates change through story and metaphor. People consider new options because a story is just a story. We are not asking them to change; we are just relating what happened to someone else.

Stories are a powerful tool in our toolkit when healing hurting churches. Congregations will match their story to the stories they hear from the pulpit. Stories address difficult situations in a nonthreatening way. Many congregations have members who aren't convinced they need a healing transition. Stories are a way to build a relationship with a hostile audience. Finally, stories go under the wire to stimulate change by going in the back door, not the front door.

Great Preachers Use Inductive Preaching Methods

Lewis and Lewis note that, historically, great preachers have always used inductive methods, whether they have called them that or not.

"D. L. Moody collected stories loosely around a theme as he aimed his simple, basic message at common people. He felt there was great need for a ministry to those who knew nothing of the Word of God and cared even less for it. So he gathered everyday experiences and stories in envelopes and shuffled these items into various orders as he preached from city to city in evangelistic campaigns" (Lewis and Lewis, 35).

As a young preaching student, I was given the assignment of preaching to the inmates in the Dallas County Jail one Sunday afternoon in the fall. The inmates were in a large fenced room with picnic tables and a TV. I was to stand in a small, three-foot by three-foot, fenced-in "pen" in the corner and attempt to preach. To make matters worse, the Cowboys' game was on! From a communications standpoint, I didn't have a prayer.

On the spur of the moment, I discarded my sermon and waited for a commercial. I then called out to the men and started telling them a story about the Cowboys: "Dallas Cowboys' defense backfield coach Gene Stallings was standing on the practice field one day looking from side to side. He then began walking across the field from sideline to sideline, stepping off paces. He stopped the practice and called a trainer to get him a tape measure. He laid out the tape and discovered to everyone's astonishment that the field was three feet too narrow. A professional football team had been practicing on a field that was the wrong size! The players were astonished that Coach Stallings, by just looking at the field, could see that it was too narrow. He'd played defense so long he could just feel it."

I finished my brief talk by asking them what field they were playing on. Was it the right size for their life? Maybe they needed to make some changes and stretch their field out before returning home. To my great surprise, every man in that holding room was quietly listening to me tell the story. In that moment we connected.

Inductive Preaching Takes a Therapeutic Approach

When I begin working with a client, I base my work on the relationship we develop in the counseling sessions. I want to be a compassionate co-struggler who accompanies them on their path of healing, discovery, and change. I must take these same attributes into the pulpit as I'm working with a wounded congregation.

Fred Craddock, in his book on inductive preaching, *As One Without Authority*, wrote: "The inductive preacher becomes the group leader of an exploration party. He doesn't profess either to know everything or to know nothing of the territory or tribal problems the listeners face in daily life. He only seeks to guide them from where they are to where they need to be without any great show of authority or coercion" (Craddock, 37).

Inductive preaching is highly respectful of the listening audience. It lays out evidence, examples, illustrations, and stories. It postpones the conclusions and declarations until the listeners have a chance to consider and weigh the evidence based on their own experience. It is truly a "Come, let's reason together" approach that respects those who agree and those who are not sure yet. Lewis and

Lewis state, "A preacher can't preach an inductive sermon without an attitude of tolerance, charity, respect, trust, cooperation and patience toward the hearers" (Lewis and Lewis, 44).

The attitude of the consultant/preacher working with a wounded church is vital in the healing process. Wounded churches have already been hurt or disappointed by leaders who have walked through situations wearing combat boots. They are in need of preaching that conveys an attitude of acceptance, compassion, and reasonable respect for their perspectives as church members.

Inductive preaching and consulting attitudes from the consultant include:

- Accepting
- Asking
- Compassionate
- Courageous
- Dialoguing
- Directing
- Encouraging
- Engaging
- Humble
- Inquiring
- Involving
- Respecting
- Resourcing

Inductive Preaching Review

- Begins with particulars—facts, examples, stories, illustrations, experience.
- Builds bridges to the listener's life rather than asking to join them in the past.
- Builds bridges with examples, illustrations, and questions.
- Inductive examples lead to assertions and conclusions.

"The deductive preacher begins with truths and sets out to prove them. The inductive preacher seeks to help listeners see the truth in such a way that they are ready to accept and respond to the truth at the end of the sermon" (Lewis and Lewis, 81).

Inductive Preaching Sermon Structure

This is not a textbook on preaching. However, it is worth noting that inductive preaching follows a creative structure that is not typical of the traditional deductive approach. The traditional deductive approach utilizes three main points, illustrated by a story, along with the bookends of an introduction and conclusion.

An inductive sermon flows in a spiral or circular manner, beginning with common ground and leading to a conclusion or assertion at the end. In the process, the listener is led through stories, illustrations, examples, analogies, and metaphors from life and the biblical text. Along the way, the preacher may offer tentative conclusions, but the audience is invited to join him in the journey and reach their own conclusions.

The process is powerful and shows tremendous respect for the listening congregation, who have often been "preached at" but have experienced very little "real communication." For some wounded churches, it is a breath of fresh air to receive authentic communication that is respectful and believable. This was the approach I took when addressing the congregation following the murder. I had to acknowledge the difficulty of saying anything helpful. My simply saying "Yes, this is awful, and I am without words to fully address this" was a comfort to them. Only a fool would pretend to know what to say on such an occasion.

An inductive sermon follows a spiral or flow process, as illustrated below:

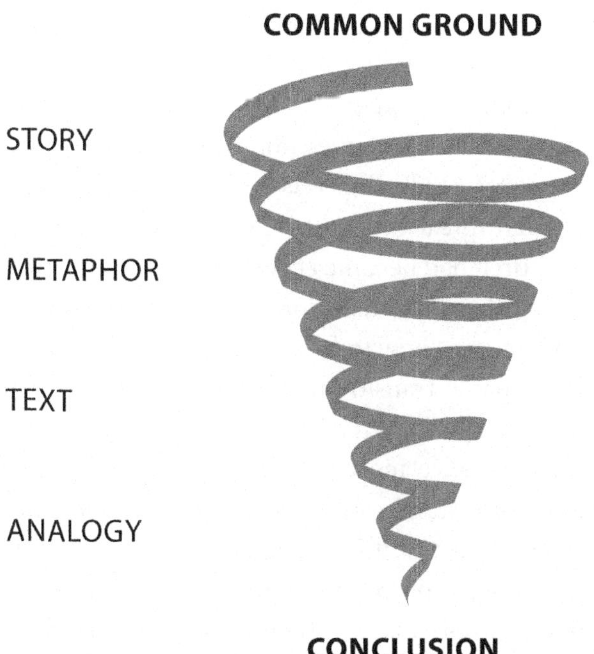

REPLACING A LEGEND IN THE PULPIT

The chairman of the elders stood with me behind the pulpit in front of the entire congregation. It was my final Sunday with the church, and he had just presented me with a Vietnam-era flak jacket and a combat helmet. "We wanted you to have these because you've taken our congregation through so much flack in the last year and seen us through this transition." We all laughed, and I treasure that gift. That church had not been too sure about my ability to see them through the transition. I was replacing a preaching legend.

Mark had been the only preacher the church had ever known. As a young man, he had been a rising star in the denomination's firmament. The church exploded as people flocked to hear his preaching. A talented staff was built around him, and for years the church grew. The core of the growth, clearly, was Mark's dynamic preaching. Then one day he was gone. Out of the blue, he announced that he had accepted a job as preacher in another town. The church was devastated. Their hero, their leader, was gone.

I received a call from their elders, asking if I would help them through this transition. The "big question" was: Can anybody follow Mark in the pulpit? Leadership was concerned that, after a few weeks of substandard preaching, people would be flowing out the back doors. The church had become accustomed to "home run" preaching. There were other tasks to accomplish in the transition, but the most pressing one was how to follow a legend in the pulpit. This was not my first at bat in transitioning a church that had been blessed with excellent preaching.

Inductive preaching gave me the tools I needed. My style was totally different from Mark's. Mark was a gifted expository preacher. He preached in a traditional, deductive way and was excellent at it. I just chose to approach the preaching event from a totally different vantage point. It's like pitching to all right handers, and suddenly you have a southpaw at the plate. The approach is totally different.

The second difference was the content of my sermons. People who hear my transitional preaching often say, "This applies to my whole life. You are talking about our church, but it sounds like things going on where I work and at home." Inductive preaching doesn't try to be relevant because relevance is built in to the entire sermon preparation process.

A third reason inductive preaching worked in replacing this legend was that the congregation had been blessed by a gifted inductive minister on their staff. One to the associate ministers traveled nationally, speaking, and was himself a gifted inductive speaker. His speaking had influenced me greatly, and the church delighted to hear his messages, which were a contrast to Mark's. When I began my interim preaching, the messages sounded "like home" to the congregation's ears. They gave me a rough time for a little while, and I eventually earned my flak jacket, but it turned out to be one of the finest transitions I was involved in.

In my experience preaching to wounded churches, there are five approaches I use that accelerate the healing process. They are passion and good information, listening before speaking, making them laugh, cry and think, wise men and women and the reality principle. I must come in and build a trust relationship with the church in a very short period of time and ask people to make major shifts in their congregational life. Approaching preaching in the following five ways has helped me connect with a church quickly and build a relationship from the pulpit that is positive, meaningful, and enjoyable for us both. Church members often tell me that they have enjoyed the transitional preaching so much that they are sorry to see it come to an end. Others will say, "I know you're talking about all of our church problems, but this stuff also relates to the rest of my life."

PASSION COMBINED WITH GOOD INFORMATION

I did my doctoral dissertation on public speaking to adult audiences. At that time very little research had been done on the effects of lecturing and public speaking when used with adults, as compared to with college students, who were easily available for university research. I secured a professional speaker, filmed them giving a speech, and then showed it to multiple adult audiences and asked for feedback on its effectiveness.

Two characteristics stood out in the feedback from adults who listened to the speaker. First, adults like speeches that give excellent information. If they are going to invest thirty minutes listening to a speech, they want to come away from that event with something that really causes them to think. "Give me some great information to take with me," they were saying. Second, adults like speakers who deliver their message with a great deal of passion. Adults want to catch the passion of the speaker and experience that with them. They want to be moved in the speaking event. So, speaking and preaching are about touching the mind and the heart.

I realized that preaching that addresses affairs, personality disorders, and conflicts among church members and leaders would have to come with excellent information delivered in an emotionally authentic manner. Because I am always a newcomer to the congregation, I would have to risk vulnerability with the church and leave it to them to accept or reject relationship with me in the preaching event.

LISTENING BEFORE SPEAKING

Dr. Paul Faulkner, my professor in marriage and family therapy, said, "Good preaching is good therapy." Dr. Faulkner understood the power of the pulpit to heal wounds, provide good information, and restore hope to people. He maintained that the preacher and therapist are doing the same work, just walking down opposite sides of the street. Both are attempting to stimulate positive change in the lives of people.

I studied to be a preacher before Dr. Faulkner invited me into the graduate program in Marriage and Family Therapy at Abilene Christian University. I was trained in my undergraduate and master's degree programs to be a preacher, prepare sermons, and minister to a congregation, using the tools of homiletics, hermeneutics, and pastoral care. There was not an emphasis on listening. The emphasis was on telling, speaking, sermon preparation, and "digging into the text." I was to have all the answers and proclaim them with clarity on Sunday mornings. Yes, there was a nod given to audience analysis, but the main thrust was speaking.

A dramatic shift occurred when I changed sides of the street and became a therapist. Now my job was not primarily speaking; it became listening. I quietly listened for thousands of hours as people poured out their hearts about broken marriages, broken lives, and broken dreams. I had a fifty-yard-line seat for forty years at every major life "train wreck" one can imagine. This has been a profound experience that has changed forever the way I approach preaching.

I discovered that I loved hearing the stories of people's lives. I love being a co-journeyer through their disappointments, surprises, pain, and successes. It is an honor to walk with people into the stories they have never shared with any other person. I didn't know it at the time, but those years of listening were transforming me as a preacher. By the time I began transitioning churches, I was no longer the same man. I had a different set of eyes and a different heart.

As a preacher/consultant, my greatest tool of healing is listening. My "client" is the church. It is sharing with me its collective story. Sometimes those stories are painful, sometimes they are endearing, and many times they have never been shared before. As I listen, the words resonate with the thousands of hours I've spent in therapy with clients experiencing guilt, grief, resentment, and anger. People are people, and those experiences don't magically change just because we walk into a church building.

My greatest asset in my ability to facilitate a healing process in a church is the ability to suspend judgment and listen to folks who are hurting. Too many leaders I work with are too concerned about what they have to say. That is why so few people are really called to minister to hurting churches. I am not saying that one has to be a licensed therapist to do this work. What I am saying is that those who have a calling to help wounded churches will have the gift of listening.

MAKE THEM LAUGH, CRY, AND THINK

Congregations love preaching that engages their hearts and their minds. I call this "make 'em laugh, make 'em cry, and make 'em think." It is my gold standard of excellence I have applied to my preaching throughout my career. From my perspective, my preaching has been effective if I have touched people's minds and caused them to think about something from a new vantage point.

In my counseling I use the Meyer's Briggs Type Indicator to help analyze people's personalities. Based on the work of Carl Jung, it defines the personality along a continuum of four scales. One scale is Thinking vs. Feeling. Thinkers make decisions based on facts, logic, data, and rational analysis. The problem is "out there," and they attack it with their minds. Feelers hold the problems close and address them from an internal set of values and beliefs. Feelers enjoy "warm and fuzzy," while Thinkers like "cool and detached."

A church auditorium is going to be filled with a combination of Thinkers and Feelers. To connect with all of them in a sermon, I'm going to have to appeal to both groups. Inductive preaching connects me with both. Its explanations, discussions, and exploration of the text appeal to the mind of the Thinker. The stories, illustrations, and metaphors of inductive preaching are right down a Feeler's alley. They connect immediately with humor and emotion in the message. Both Thinkers and Feelers are moved by passionate preaching. So, inductive preaching, with its circular flow, appeals to both types of personalities.

Inductive preaching allows me to "create moments" in the sermon. The combination of stories and text can produce powerful moments of connection between the minister and the congregation. I'm often surprised by the congregation's emotional reaction to a point I'm making. They may laugh, cry, or grow very still at moments I did not expect. Those responses may be clues to me as their consultant indicating places of corporate congregational pain that I need to address. Like a doctor gently pressing on a patient's tummy, asking "Does it hurt here?" the message becomes an exploration into the emotional condition of the church.

Inductive preaching has allowed me to involve the church in the delivery of the sermon. My kids used to tease me that I would preach for multiple services and the sermon was never the same from one service to the next. I told them that the reason for this was that the audience changes from eight o'clock to ten o'clock, and that changes the dynamics. The church will alter my lesson at the moment of delivery. The audience may look confused, and I have to add a story to clarify a point. Inductive preaching gives me a storehouse of illustrations I have at my fingertips and can drop into the sermon at the moment of delivery. The church gets to participate in the crafting of the message. For me, this is very exciting because there is an aspect of the preaching that is truly left up to God, the body of Christ assembled that morning, and the cues I pick up at the moment of delivery.

Transitional preaching can involve the church so naturally that people answer back to me from the pews. Inductive preaching involves the church through the use of questions. I ask a lot of rhetorical questions when I preach. Early in my preaching with a church, a shift may occur. I will be sharing a story or point in the sermon, and the congregation is very still. It's as though the church has been frozen. Speakers are familiar with this phenomenon because it indicates that an audience is tracking with the message. I'll often ask at the end of my point, "Does that make sense?" It is not uncommon for people to answer me out loud. The audience has joined in the message. From then on, we have an informal dialogue created within the preaching event. The church is no longer simply listening to a message; they are a part of crafting it.

WISE MEN AND WISE WOMEN

I have a secret weapon in my lesson preparation. I do not do it alone. I am blessed with a cadre of "wise men and women" on whom I call to consult on topics I know nothing about. Early in my career, I received a call from a well-known preacher. I was surprised at his call because we had never met, but I had great respect for him. He was preparing a series on the family and wanted to pick my brain for a few minutes to get a Christian counselor's perspective. I was flattered by his call and impressed with his humility. His ego wasn't so big that he couldn't ask for help.

That phone call made a huge impact on me as a young man. I thought, *If this guy who is nationally known needs help sometimes, what does that say about me?* I slowly began assembling a small but powerful group of wise men and wise women whom I give permission to speak into my messages. They have been an invaluable resource to me over my career in transitioning churches.

There is no way I can be an expert on all the issues that a church or leadership will present to me. I encounter problems with ethics, human resources, finances, leadership styles, and conflict resolution. The combination of these issues in some churches could drive Solomon to get frustrated and cut the baby in two, giving half to each mom and heading to lunch!

When I am stuck, I will run my messages and consulting by my small cadre of wise men and wise women to solicit their spiritual feedback. And I give them permission to speak to me so I can hear the things I need to hear. They hold me accountable and have told me on more than one occasion, "I think you're crazy for doing that." I have found the contrast between a woman's perspective and a man's to be so valuable. In the counseling profession, I am required by law to seek supervision when I encounter a client situation that I'm not sure how to address. The same should be required of the minister—when you don't know what you're talking about, it's a really good idea to get some wise counsel.

THE REALITY PRINCIPLE

Jesus's preaching dealt with real-life issues. Lewis and Lewis list the topics Jesus preaching on: adultery, anger, anxiety, death, debts, doubts, eternity, faith, giving, greed, honesty, hypocrisy, joy, kindness, legalism, life, lust, marriage, money, parenting, pretense, respect, responsibility, rulers, sex, slander, speech, taxes, trust, and wisdom.

They note, "Just reading this list of subjects from our pulpits would no doubt create a stir in our sanctuaries next Sunday" (Lewis and Lewis, 69).

Churches in transition are in need of preaching that deals with reality. The transition has laid the problems of the church front and center. They must be dealt with. They cannot be ignored any longer. The church can either return to a position of denial or confront the reality of the situation and move forward.

In my speaking, I have always found that people do better when I apply "the Reality Principle." Simply put, people do better when they know what they are dealing with and what's at stake. Several years ago, I was out running and thought I had blown out both my hamstrings at once. It was extraordinarily painful. I rested for a few weeks, went out to run, and found that it happened again. I stumbled into my doctor's office, who laughed and informed me that I hadn't blown out my hamstrings. I had injured my back. He referred me to Dr. Richard Naftalis, one of the best neurosurgeons in Dallas. Dr. Naftalis examined my back and told me, "Your spinal cord is pressing against your spine at lumbar three. I've got to repair it, or you'll eventually be unable to walk. And, by the way, you need to buy an elliptical bike and stop running on the streets." What! The Reality Principle hit home. I had a decision to make. Change my life or suffer the consequences? I now do my miles on an elliptical.

Churches often ignore "the Reality Principle." They believe that if we speak the truth about a situation, it will somehow make it worse. That talking about the reality of a situation will empower it. So, we ignore the decline in attendance. We sit silently by as leaders make poor decisions. Maybe it will all magically go away with prayer and few more potluck dinners.

My clients also suffer from the "You can't tell Grandma syndrome." We can't speak the truth to people about the reality of their situation because they are just too fragile to deal with it. I've found that people are many things, but fragile is not generally one of them. My clients do best when I respect them enough to tell them the truth. "If you keep letting your son talk to you in that disrespectful way, that's how he'll treat his wife."

Transitional preaching must courageously and compassionate present the reality of a situation to a church and give them the opportunity to decide how they will respond. This is the adult thing to do. It respects people's judgment and the choices they make. I had the difficult assignment of presenting the congregational assessment results to a church that was aging. There were very few members under the age of fifty. The truth was that in ten years half of the congregation would be gone. Their choice was to rebirth or choose to die gracefully. They needed to be respected enough to make that choice as a congregation. When they chose to grow younger, this was a decision made and owned by the church, not one small group.

The combination of passion, good information that touches the head and heart, input from wise counselors, and the power of reality provide the foundation for excellent preaching to a wounded church in transition. However, when I enter most churches to begin my work, I am fighting a host of barriers to effective transitional preaching.

BARRIERS TO TRANSITIONAL PREACHING

In a healthy church, the worship service "sets the table" for the sermon. Technology and media are checked ahead of time to ensure they are working. Worship leaders are instructed on the theme and how much time they will have to speak. The preacher is allowed to do his job and preach. Staff ministers are not vying for control of the pulpit, and the eldership is not dictating the content of the messages.

Wounded churches are often dysfunctional systems. I have spent a career overcoming an hour-long worship service that drains the church's attention. By the time I get up to speak, the congregation is lulled into a coma or ready to head out the door in frustration. Most churches I transition give more planning to the noon potluck than they do preparing for the Sunday morning worship service.

Preaching by Committee

Healing a wounded church is *not* the time to invite all our favorite guest speakers in to fill the sermon calendar and enjoy candy-stick sermons. The church may be entertained, but when they get to the end of the transition, the work has not been done by the church. It has been an exercise is self-delusion.

Healing a wounded church is both an art and a science. It is a delicate process that changes week-to-week. I've even changed sermons from service to service because the dynamics of the congregation have changed that fast. We are doing major surgery, and you don't want to change surgeons in the middle of the operation. When Dr. Naftalis visited with me in pre-op, he did not introduce me to six other surgeons who were going to be helping him out. I put my spinal cord in Richard's hands because I trusted him. The same trust must exist between the leadership team and me.

Over-functioning church leaders tend to think they know what's better for the church and will schedule a beauty pageant of guest speakers. Or the leaders will use the Sundays as an opportunity to roll in their favorite candidate to take the position. This politicizes the healing process and destroys any likelihood that we can make progress. The church must deal with its Tough Bargainer leader, or it will repeat the same pattern once again.

Leaders Dictating Sermon Content

There is a fascinating phenomenon in counseling. Often the sickest, most dysfunctional clients I work with are also "know it alls." You would think that someone who had been married four times and have had children from three different fathers would be asking, "What's wrong with my man picker." Instead, these self-assured marriage experts come in and proudly act as though they know everything about relationships and instruct me on how to conduct the session. We don't last long.

Churches are the same way. I have discovered that, the sicker the church, the more likely they are to try to control the consulting and dictate the sermon process. I've worked with church leaders who are shepherding congregations that are literally "bleeding out." Members are leaving, staff ministers have resigned, and the budget is in the toilet. But they are so convinced that they are the experts that they spend their time giving me instructions on how to conduct the consulting process and how I should be preaching my sermons. They have never transitioned a church and are now captains of a ship that is sinking on their watch, but they are going to manage the individual who is piloting the Coast Guard cutter coming to their rescue. The absurdity of the situation is a testimony to their lack of leadership ability.

Cleaning Up Others' Messes

As a transitional minister, I am constantly cleaning up other people's messes from the pulpit. Leaders send mixed messages publicly or informally, and those communications must be cleaned up in front of the entire congregation. One of the reasons the church is in the position it is in is that its leaders are doing a very poor job of communicating.

Another reason I insist on being the primary preacher working with a wounded church is that the transition leaves a gap in the pulpit that invites every "junior minister" to volunteer to step in. Staff ministers who secretly desire the job want to fill in for preaching assistance. Former ministers now dust off their favorite sermons. Elders now feel amazingly "called to the ministry of preaching." The Shadow Church runs its spokesperson into the pulpit to set the stage for the selection of their next minister. Members now claim to have been given a message from God to share with the church. The cages have sprung open, and the monkeys are running the zoo.

The confounding variable for me is this: everyone has their unique formula for what needs to be happening in the transition. They are going to use their five minutes of fame to set the agenda for the church. Or, dangerously, they are going to have their say and dump twenty years of frustration onto the church; now the congregation has been re-traumatized. Their formula is the exact opposite of the work I am trying to do in healing the entire church system.

It is tragic that wounded churches will re-traumatize themselves at the very moment they need care in the ER. They have been hit by a truck and will stagger back into traffic, dodging cars and getting hit again by some amateur speaker who is working their agenda on the church publicly. This practice is unethical and constitutes leadership malpractice, and I will not participate in it.

Technology That Gets in The Way

When a speaker begins a message, he or she has about one minute to connect with the audience and answer the questions "Will I listen to this lesson today?" and "What's in it for me?" I was taught a firm rule: when you start, . . . start! Those first few minutes between the preacher and the congregation are priceless.

I'm a great believer in technology because, when used correctly, it heightens the effectiveness of the message. But that's the key. When it's used effectively, technology is in the background to facilitate the message.

Today we have what I call "Technology Moments" distracting the audience from most presentations. Microphones do not work because the media ministry forgot to change the battery. PowerPoint slides are out of order, or the person running the slides simply cannot keep up with the speaker. The preacher cannot start the sermon because there is a "glitch" in the sound system that wasn't checked ahead of time. A new mixer board operator is being trained on Sunday morning, and the slides go down. The list of technology failures goes on and on, and we just smile and act as though this doesn't affect the preaching event. It does. And it is inexcusable in my opinion.

In the past twenty years, we have raised up a generation of speakers and listeners who have become accustomed to wasted time, technology miscues, and general sloppiness in public presentations. It is embarrassing to watch. As a speaker, I can say it is maddening to experience and inexcusable.

When I am transitioning a church, I have a very limited amount of time to talk with them. I have a long list of highly difficult and emotional topics I need to visit with the church about. I am trying to create a moment that is open, quiet, well planned, and uniquely crafted to walk into that conversation with up to several thousand people. To say that this is a difficult undertaking is an understatement. When I am fighting with the media, the sound, the new guy running the mixer board, and worship leaders who preach sermons before I ever stand up, I'm dead before I get started.

Do Not Take the Job

The first rule of transitional peaching is that the transitional preacher never takes the long-term job. Period. I've been offered many preaching jobs over the years. It's not because I would make a good long-term match for that congregation. I would not. I'm a therapist, a professor, and an interim minister. I tell the leadership and the congregation at the beginning that I would never myself take the job.

My external consulting position allows two things to happen. First, it explains transference when it occurs. When my clients come in and have never experienced a healthy relationship with someone who listens to them, they can often "fall in love" with the therapist because those unmet needs are suddenly being met. I must maintain my professional boundaries and be their therapist and not their new boyfriend.

Churches that have not experienced a healthy relationship with their minister or leaders may also transfer their unmet needs onto me as their interim minister. Retaining my boundaries as a helper from the outside allows me to assist the congregational system without getting pulled into it.

A second reason my independence from the system is important is that I will need to speak into the system in order to change it. Speaking as an outsider coming in with a fresh perspective can be powerful in the change process. "Since I've been here, these are some of the strengths of this church I've noticed, and here are a couple of work areas I see." In the sermons I give, I am going to initiate some powerful conversations with the entire church.

Crafting those from a neutral stance is vital so that I don't become triangulated with one group.

Dr. Faulkner was right: "Good preaching is good therapy." Inductive preaching gives us the tools we need to open the most difficult conversations with a church and walk into them. I don't remember the words I spoke to that congregation in shock over the murder that Sunday morning. Sadly, whatever notes I made have been lost in the intervening years. But their faces looking back at me are etched into my memory. We shared a moment of profound grief together. The message simply said, "Let's walk through this valley together." So, we did. And that was enough.

CHAPTER 12

HEALING THROUGH PROCESS CONSULTATION

It was the fifth standing ovation the congregation had given me during my final weekend with them. Twice the Saturday-night-service crowd had risen to its feet as I began to speak, and three times the Sunday-morning group had done the same thing. New Day Community Church was overcome with emotion. We had "walked through the valley of the shadow" together and come out on the other side stronger.

Eighteen months earlier, New Day Community had experienced a blowout going ninety miles an hour and flipped three times before crashing into a ditch. It was a wonder anyone had walked out alive. They had been "the hottest growing church in town." New members were streaming in every week. Worship services were being added on the weekend. New staff were hired to keep up with the growth. The three-man leadership team was expanded with new leaders. Everyone in town knew New Days' reputation.

Their explosion of growth centered on a dynamic minister who had moved to town a few years earlier and taken the reins of the church. His charismatic preaching, combined with a tireless drive, had brought new life to the congregation. Soon everyone was bringing friends to hear his messages. The church, though, had been built on sinking sand. He was a combination narcissistic-sexual addiction leader. It wasn't long before his affair with a woman in the church went public, followed by another and another. Camelot was over.

I received a call from a colleague close to the leadership. Could I come and help hold the ship together while the church rebuilt? I inherited a congregation gut-punched with grief. They had lost the leader they idolized and were looking for a sense of direction. Many members were previously unchurched people new to the congregation, and they were especially traumatized by the events. Leadership had a huge budget, a new building, and significant financial investments made around the preaching of their "golden boy." Now he was gone. Could we build a healthy spiritual identity for this church? It would mean recasting the identity of the church from a personality cult into a mature congregation of God's people.

The thunderous applause that weekend was not so much for me as it was for each other, realizing they had made it through the transition. New Day really had a new day. They had done the hard work of healing. They stood at the river as former slaves and were now ready to march into the land as conquerors. They had embraced a process of healing and transition that had prepared them for the next era of their history. They were ready to welcome their next minister. They had even endured two attempts by their former minister to return as he attempted to abort the therapeutic process. Typical of a narcissist, he believed that the church belonged to him and not to the Lord. The church did not return to Egypt with him.

I tell my clients and the churches I work with that I do not have a magic wand behind glass hanging in my office. I can't break the glass in an emergency and wave it over hurting people and magically make it all go away. What I can do is recommend a process. A process that is tailored to the specific wounds the congregation is experiencing. That process involves consultation on the key areas of church life to ensure that patterns that have hurt the church in the past do not continue into the future.

PROCESS CONSULTATION AND DR. THOMAS A. EAVES

In 1982 I entered the doctoral program in Adult and Continuing Education at Texas Woman's University under the leadership of Dr. Thomas A. Eaves. Tom was a brilliant academic who had started his career with a PhD in nuclear physics and worked on the first nuclear bomb projects before World War II. He decided to pursue a second doctorate in Adult Education, and TWU hired him to launch a new program. Students were streaming from Dallas and Ft. Worth to study with him, and I had the privilege of securing him as my major professor for my doctoral degree.

Dr. Eaves's specialization was process consultation. He introduced his classes to the pioneering work of Edgar H. Schein, who had written one of the first books on Process Consultation. Human Systems Theory was ramping up as a driving force in understanding organizational behavior, as it was in understanding family therapy. It proposed that humans interact with one another in repetitive loops or circular causality. These loops tend to repeat over time and are responsible for the communication, conflict resolution, and roles people take in their relationships at home and work. Process consultation gave me a framework to use when a congregation was going through significant change.

Process consultation allows us to explore the process of how things occur in a church. Often, we focus on the content of what is occurring in a congregation. Who will be the next minister? When will the transition be over? Who will be the next leaders of the church? Those are appropriate questions, but a transition allows us time to change the processes of a congregation. We look at how we go about the business of being a church and explore ways to improve.

INITIAL AGREEMENTS

Dr. Eaves described the initiation of a consulting relationship as based on three agreements between the church and the consultant. Whenever I have ignored his advice, the consultation has always gone off the rails. The three agreements I make before beginning a consultation are:

1. **Agreement on the part of *all* top leadership to commit to a healing transition.** Unless there is agreement on the part of all leaders to enter into a season of intentional transition, we are doomed to failure. When I have accepted work with leaderships that were not completely on board, those individuals who were dragging their heels have detonated the process. Having one person or a small group within the leadership campaign for the consultation, hoping that once it is begun it will persuade the others, is a fatal mistake. Top leadership, including staff, elders, deacons, and the leadership team, must all agree to participate cooperatively and fully in the process, or we do not have a basis to work from.

2. **Agreement on the part of the leadership to a consulting relationship that is exclusive and confidential**. I work with churches that treat their transitions like a visit to the Golden Corral. They want a buffet of consultants and preachers. That might be fine for a traditional interim, but a congregation that has been wounded is in need of critical care from a consultant/preacher who is delivering a process that is custom-designed for their unique needs. That is very difficult to do with a rotation of the leader's favorite preachers sharing the pulpit. The work I do is also confidential. For people to be willing to share their stories, they need to know that I will respect the confidential nature of those communications.

3. **Agreement on the part of leadership to a consulting process and projected timetable**. I will lay out an approach to dealing with the church situation that is reasonable and designed to move the church forward as quickly as possible. Healing takes some time, and each

congregation has its own recovery pattern. No two are the same. We will agree to a scope of work to address the issues that the church is facing and that will be uncovered as a part of the assessment process. I reserve the right to end my relationship with a church if the leadership promises agreement to a process of work and then backs out of that agreement.

CHARACTERISTICS OF THE PROCESS

As I open a conversation with a church about a healing transition, leaders will often ask "What will this be like for our church?" Most have never been through this type of experience and wonder what it will entail.

Some of the characteristics of the process include:

- **Transparency:** I will model transparency in my work with them and ask leadership to adopt that as a primary characteristic of their new leadership style.

- **Trust**: We will want to rebuild the trust between the leadership and the congregation. As we learned earlier, this is a combination of doing effective things over an extended period of time.

- **Good Information**: People do better when they are armed with some good information to help them make sense of the situation they are in. Preaching and teaching arm the congregation with tools to grow spiritually, emotionally, and relationally.

- **Controlled Communications**: This is not a time for open-mike live. The worship services and preaching ministry must be crafted to achieve the healing goals of the transition.

- **Eliminating Distractions**: This is not a time to launch a new program or campaign or major ministry initiative. The church is in a season of rebuilding itself so it can then go forth to carry out its commission.

- **Borrowed Confidence**: Dr. Paul Faulkner stated, "Good therapists allow the client to borrow his confidence that tomorrow will be better." Churches need to borrow my confidence that we will move through this time into a better place for the church.

LEADERSHIP FEARS

As I began visiting with the leaders at New Day Community, they voiced concerns about the transition process. The fears they expressed were typical of church leaders I've talked with as they consider whether to allow a healing transition to occur.

What if no one shows up Sunday?

This fear is not often articulated, but it is implied. What if news of this situation has caused our congregation to lose heart, and members are all going somewhere else? My experience has been that members are tied to a congregation for a variety of reasons and that the loss of a minister or some other significant event will not immediately cause them to leave. Most people are fair minded and will come back to see what the plan is to get through the transition.

Shouldn't we quickly start a search for a new minister or announce a solution?

That is exactly what should not be done. As I stated in chapter 1, it may be too early for the church to assimilate a new leader as it grieves the loss of the former one. Moving too quickly through the transition misses the opportunity to process important changes that the church needs to make.

This will take too long. Will people actually stay through a transition?

Yes. People do stay through a church transition. Some churches I've worked with have actually grown numerically during a transition, and former members have returned when they learned that the church was getting healthier. It is not uncommon for members to tell me at the end of a transition that they are sorry to see it end.

If we "air our dirty laundry" with the church about our problems, won't we look weak?

No, you will look strong. And you will look honest. Dealing openly and honestly with the past and the present challenges is responsible leadership. People know when they are being lied to, and church leaders are just as guilty of lying to their membership as politicians in Washington. People need to know the reality of what they are dealing with so they can make informed decisions and important contributions to turning the ship around.

Admitting we need a transition makes us look inadequate as leaders, doesn't it?

My experience is that implementing a transitional process actually builds the credibility of leadership. When I can speak about the leaderships' openness to assessment and desire to be transparent, this shifts the perception of the congregation from mistrust to trust. The transitional process can make bank deposits into the trust account of the leadership every week.

The leadership at New Day Community had agreed to participate fully in the transition process. We agreed upon a scope of work and a timetable. I knew this would not be a quick fix, as news kept surfacing of one affair after another involving the former pastor. The leadership stood strong and remained transparent, even as they delivered additional "bad news" to the church. I was able to begin the healing process from the pulpit immediately and to stop some of the bleeding. The chemistry with the congregation occurred quickly, and they were able to borrow some of my confidence that there was light at the end of the tunnel.

The process I followed at New Day and many other congregations progressed through six phases of work: Pre-Consulting, Early Healing, Middle Healing, Late Healing, Termination, and After Care. Each phase contains its own unique body of work and builds upon the results of the prior phases. They unite to form a movement from wounded body to whole once again.

SIX PHASES OF PROCESS CONSULTATION

Phase One: Pre-Consultation

Primary Question: What do we do now?
Primary Emotions: Shock, fear, confusion
Consultant Goal: Orient church leadership to healing transition process.

In the Pre-Consultation Phase I am orienting the church leadership to the consulting and preaching process that will be used in the healing transition. I will explain the six phases of the work and what is to be accomplished at each step in the process. I will discuss the three main agreements I must secure in order to begin the ministry with them. This is the time for questions, concerns, and objections to be raised by the leadership team of the church.

The Pre-Consultation Phase is the most important step of the six. It sets the framework for all the work that is to follow. If I do not have consensus, or sense that I do not have consensus on the part of the top leadership of the church, I will not move forward. The church is not ready, and they need to continue in the patterns they are currently operating in until those patterns fail them and they are ready for change to occur.

Tasks of the Pre-Consultation Phase

- Initial contact and inquiry on the part of the church with consultant for help.
- Initial interview with church leadership to "hear the story" and create timeline of events.
- Begin to assimilate a congregational history of events leading up to current crisis.
- Orient church leadership team to the scope of process consultation and how that might apply to the current situation.
- Description of the consultant/preacher's role in the process.
- Description of the role of preaching in the healing process.
- Discussion of a tentative timeframe that might be applicable to the recovery of the church.
- Financial commitment to the transitional process.
- Consultant support required from office staff, worship ministry, and leadership team.
- The nature of the consulting/preaching relationship, including level of performance, exclusivity, and confidentiality.
- Questions regarding the process.
- Decision to move forward, discuss further, or decline.

Phase Two: Early Healing

Primary Question: What do we do now?
Primary Emotions: Anxiety, fear, anger, doubt
Consultant Goals: Establish a working relationship with leadership and congregation as preacher and consultant, begin the process of stabilization, and start to assess the church family system.

In Early Healing Phase, I am meeting the church for the first time and establishing a working relationship with them. I do not have the luxury of a long honeymoon period, as the work requires managing a transition that is already in motion. The consultant/preacher role will have to be established quickly, as access from the pulpit is vital to forming that initial bond of confidence and trust.

The Early Healing Phase will see the implementation of process consultation. The heart of that process is assessment. I will be assessing the church family from a systems perspective, looking at roles, rules, communications, and conflict resolution. The assessment will be both formal and informal. I employ tools such as the Congregational Health Assessment, developed by the Siburt Institute at ACU, as well as interpersonal interview assessments conducted with ministers, elders, and leaders.

The Early Healing Phase will be a time when the church will lean into my confidence that there is a path forward out of the current crisis. As an outsider, my perspective should not be triangulated by the different voices I hear.

Tasks of Early Healing Phase

- Introduction to the church.
- Orientation to the process with the church.
- Stabilization of the pulpit and begin preaching on the transitional process.
- Formal Congregational Assessment begins.
- Moratorium on new projects, programs, and ministries to allow healing.
- Church stabilization starts slowly.
- Informal assessment of congregational roles, communication, key subsystems, and conflict resolution.
- Assessment of cumulative damage from congregation's history.
- Emergence of opponents to transitional process on staff or in congregation and response.

- Continued practice of transparency, increased communications, and trust building.

Phase Three: Middle Healing

Primary Question: Are we doing alright now?
Primary Emotion: Emergence of old, unresolved emotions, beginning of trust
Consultant Goals: Provide an accurate description of some of the congregational processes and a plan for addressing them. In-depth treatment of congregational issues in preaching and teaching work. Begin implementing action plan steps with leadership.

The Middle Phase of Healing is an important one because it is the point where I begin to share the results of the Congregational Assessment with the leadership and the church. At this time, the leadership will signal its openness to moving forward by owning the results of the assessment or dismissing the results as inaccurate or invalid. A dismissal of the results is a clear signal that the leadership is taking the congregation back into denial. Few changes will be enacted in the system. New Day Community looked at the results of their assessment and owned the key areas that needed improvement. They enacted a plan to address their issues.

By the Middle Phase of Healing, opponents to the process will have emerged and begin to be active. They may take an active oppositional stance in meetings, a passive-aggressive stance outside the time I am with them, or work entirely behind the scenes as a shadow church to undermine the entire process. Conflicting messages given to the church by leaders or backtracking on agreements are signs of serious opposition and should not be ignored. If agreement to the process of work is not assured, then contract should be ended by the consultant.

The chemistry between the preaching and teaching and the congregation will be producing a level of change in the church by this point. A preaching consultant must be able to establish a trust relationship from the pulpit quickly to stimulate change. I must be able to get off a plane and make friends with a thousand people quickly. At New Day, as with many other churches, we were able to get in a groove quickly and make significant changes in a short period of time. The Middle Phase of Healing will continue for several months.

Staggered Disclosure

In therapy, I will be working with a couple when there has been an extramarital affair or another major offense that has destroyed trust in the relationship. During the early phases of treatment, we build a narrative of the events that occurred during the affair, and the offended spouse is able to wrap their mind around a "new history" of those months of marriage during which the affair was occurring. This is a painful process. Often, the spouse who had the affair does not fully disclose all the events that occurred, or the fact that there were other affairs. As a result, new information appears later in the process that blows the therapy process off track. The work in counseling is back at square one. This phenomenon is known as "staggered disclosure."

New Day Community's healing process was lengthened by the former pastor's lying with regard to the extent of his extramarital affairs. He denied the first, and then others began to emerge. He continued in his denial. Every time evidence of another affair would appear, the congregation was set back to Phase One in the process. We continued in the shock-and-recovery phase for several months while he took his wife and the church on a roller coaster ride of lies and denial. When people ask me "How long will this take?" my response is always guarded because as a consultant I do not know what skeletons are in the closet that will emerge during the process.

Tasks of the Middle Healing Phase

- Communication of the results of the Congregational Assessment to the leadership.
- Communication of the results of the Congregational Assessment to the church.
- Development of a Plan of Action based on the assessment results.
- Implementation of the Plan of Action in key areas of church life.
- Begin enacting systemic changes in communications, roles, and conflict resolution.
- Begin deeper analysis of leadership subsystem of the church and of the adjustments needed.
- Preaching on key themes to support the assessment and targeted changes.
- Teaching on key areas of the transition if needed to support changes.
- Evaluation of staff as a part of the assessment process and involvement in transition.
- Identification of opponents to the transitional process and development of a response.
- Preparation for staggered disclosure and effects on the transitional process.
- Continued open communications and authenticity to rebuild trust.
- Identification of key leaders and members who are burned out and in need of rest.

Phase Four: Late Healing

Primary Question: Are we really doing this well during a transition?

Primary Emotion: Hope

Consultant Goals: The goal of this phase is the continued implementation of changes into the congregational system, based on the assessment and the stabilization of those changes. The preaching ministry will be addressing core issues of the church now that a trust relationship has been established. Major changes called for in the assessment will be implemented.

The Late Healing Phase is a time when the congregational climate has improved. Once the church climate was overcast or stormy, but now the outlook is partly cloudy, and the sun has shown through the clouds. Members' spirits begin to be restored. Hope emerges as the focus of the congregation is less on the past and more on the future. If the congregation were a patient in the hospital, he is now out of surgery and sitting up in bed taking food and talking. The congregation is beginning to get its "swagger" back. If a church's sense of humor begins to emerge, that is a positive sign of recovery.

Late Healing is a time to address the harder issues of leadership. Are there leaders who are ready to step down? Are there leaders who are so burned out from the recent events that they need a break? Are there ministers who need to be reassigned? Are there ministers who are nonfunctioning and need to have a job performance review? We will explore changes in leadership that occur during a transition in chapter 15. The rollout of the Early and Middle Phases of Healing often provides stabilization for leadership and allows them an opportunity to reflect on their own effectiveness. In many cases, the entire leadership subsystem of the church resigns, and a new leadership is formed to move the church into its next era of history. As with Moses's era ending at the river and Joshua taking up the mantle of leadership, the transition gives the church an opportunity to make major shifts in leadership.

The Late Healing Phase is the time we enact the ministerial search process. The search committee is formed, and they begin the process of looking for a new minister. The Late Healing Phase has relieved the church of focus on crisis management, and they can begin the conversation regarding what kind of church they want to be moving forward. In New Day Community's case, they wanted a preacher who was strong in the pulpit but one who could also empower the use of all the church's gifts. They were moving away from the personality church model to one that was more balanced. Those conversations could not occur in the early phases of the healing process when the congregation was in pain.

Tasks of the Late Healing Phase:

- Continued stabilization from preaching and discussion of vision and minister to fit church.
- Continued implementation of changes based on the congregational assessment.
- Continued communications and trust building on the part of leadership.
- Evaluation of the leadership subsystem and its role moving forward.
- Evaluation of the ministerial subsystem and its role moving forward.
- Formation of the ministerial search committee and the launch of its work.
- Congregational conversation regarding future vision for the church.

Phase Five: Termination

Primary Question: Does it have to end?
Primary Emotion: Confidence
Consultant Goals: Consolidation of the gains made during the healing transition. Blessing the new minister and leadership assuming responsibilities. Stepping away from the church with a "good goodbye."

The Termination Phase is the time we land the plane before it takes off again. The church has come through a massive transition. It has survived and even thrived in some new ways. It is now ready for a new beginning. For me as the consultant/preacher, there are several key areas I want to address as we conclude our work.

First, during the Termination Phase I want to review the work we have done together. God reviewed the history of his covenant promises with Joshua at the river. We want to look at what we have learned as God's people during this transition. That review is a guard against repeating previous patterns in the future.

Second, I want to discuss leadership and followership with the church. Often a new leadership is emerging, and it needs to function in ways that are new and untested. A new minister may be coming on board, and I want to discuss the stages of assimilation of that minister into the life of the church. The chemistry I have established with the congregation I want to bequeath to the next person in the pulpit. As John the Baptist said, "He must increase and I must decrease."

Third, I want to strengthen the spiritual and emotional bonds I have developed with the congregation. Many of these people have been hurt. Many of them were spiritually disenchanted. They agreed to trust me and go on a journey of healing and transformation and did not know where our final destination would be. That is an awesome risk to take with someone you've never met before! Yet they do it because they love the Lord, they love their church, and they hope things will be different.

The outpouring of love and emotion during my final weekend at New Day Community was the release of months of pent-up emotion. The congregation needed to celebrate. They needed to own that they had been "through the valley of the shadow" and come out alive. They needed to say thank you. They needed to say "We are God's people ready to move forward once again. We are not wounded; we have been healed by God's grace."

When I am finishing a transition with a congregation, it is not uncommon to hear the following statements from members:

"I can't believe I'm saying this, but I wish this transition time didn't have to end."

"The things you've been preaching on not only apply to our church but are things I'm dealing with in my own life."

"I was against doing this. I thought we just needed to go hire a preacher. But I was dead wrong. This is the best thing we could have done."

"Thanks for helping our church. We have been through so much as a congregation. We have needed this for years."

"I have grown so much during this transition, and our church has too. We have come so far in such a short period of time—it's really amazing."

Tasks of Termination:

- Review of work done over the course of the transition.
- Consolidation of changes made during the transition.
- Preparation for launch of new leadership.
- Preparation for onboarding of new minister or staff.
- Celebration of God's grace and faithfulness.

Phase Six: After Care

Some congregations request my continued involvement with them as they onboard a new minster and launch a new vision for the future. The work moves to that of a consulting role, as I assist the leadership in continuing to implement changes started during the transition. I can also assist the new minister in establishing a working relationship with leadership and the congregation behind the scenes in a coaching role.

The Congregational Assessment we developed can serve as a baseline for health. Churches I've worked with will re-administer the instrument later on down the road to see how the church's overall health has improved. It is not unusual for a total package of transition and change to walk out over a period of three to five years in a congregation.

ROLE OF THE CONSULTANT/PREACHER

To introduce graduate students to the field of counseling, I recommend that they read *Psychotherapy: A Practical Introduction* by Dr. Adam M. Brenner and Dr. Laura S. Howe-Martin. It is a "Counseling for Dummies" introduction for a beginning therapist. Brenner and Howe-Martin make the point that helping someone comes out of a relationship between the helper and the hurting person.

"There are several basic things that make our initial meeting with a patient therapeutic. You take them seriously and showed their concerns matter to you. . . . You did not recoil in shock when the patient talked about the material they found disturbing. . . . Your response made a profound impression. In fact you probably even asked them to tell you more about things that they found are most terrible and off putting. The last fundamental element is that you seemed to have some (even if vague) idea about how to be helpful and conveyed some confidence in the process."

Change, according the Brenner and Howe-Martin, is stimulated by four elements in the helping relationship. First, the client feels they are no longer alone in the situation. The two of you are together in this. Second, their experiences make sense to someone outside the situation. They are not going crazy, and the things they are experiencing are valid and normal. Third, they are accepted as they are. They are not looked down upon for the things they are feeling. Fourth, they no longer feel desperate and hopeless. There is a path forward that can lead them out of their current situation.

"These four effects—(1) Together (not alone); (2) Understood (not incomprehensible); (3) Accepted (not rejected); (4) Hopeful (not demoralized)—will be repeatedly reinforced throughout the entire process." These four effects form the basis for the helping and consulting relationship.

My role as consultant demands that I wear several hats, depending upon the needs of the church. I will be an educator, providing new information. I will be an encourager, promoting change. I will be a confessor to people in doubt and a mediator of conflict. There will be times when I encourage movement forward or warn that marching in place is exactly what the church needs to do to catch its breath. Above all, I am a passionate defender of the process of producing positive change in the health of the congregation.

KEY ROLES OF THE CONSULTANT/PREACHER

Consultant to entire transitional process: Able to oversee the scope of the transitional process and implement the steps based on the response of church and leadership.

Change management: Timing the implementation of key changes in the church.

Congregational assessment: Implementing a congregational assessment to evaluate health.

Leadership coaching: Assisting leadership in dealing with specific conditions in the church. Assisting leadership with their internal dynamics and relationship with the congregation.

Preaching: Addressing issues of healing, transition, and major change areas from a theological and practical standpoint. Building momentum heading into the next phase of history.

Communications: Facilitating the process by provi-ding clear communications to the congregation.

CHURCH HEALTH ASSESSMENT, SIBURT INSTITUTE FOR CHURCH MINISTRY, ABILENE CHRISTIAN UNIVERSITY

The Siburt Institute for Church Ministry, under the direction of Dr. Carson Reed, provides resources for congregations and their leaders. Dr. Carley Dodd and Dr. Suzie Macaluso developed the Church Health Assessment as a tool to help churches identify their strengths and challenges. The CHA identifies nine areas of church health and provides a breakdown of each one in a comprehensive assessment picture. Congregational demographics and the areas members like most and least are also identified. Recommendations and best practices are given to each congregation.

The nine areas assessed by the Church Health Assessment are:

1. Vision, Mission, and Goals
2. Ministries, Activities
3. Perception of Family Stages
4. Spiritual Formation, Discipleship
5. Worship
6. Congregational Culture, Values
7. Leadership
8. Church Relationships
9. Finance, Facilities

I have used the CHA with congregations and found it to be an outstanding tool in providing an accurate picture of church life. It sets out priorities for the leadership to address. It is valid and highly accurate in predicting the processes in the church. Congregations that have used the results as a guide to their strategic planning have discovered that targeting change in the key areas produces long-term results for the church. The CHA is easy to administer and is straightforward to communicate to a congregation. Even when the results of the CHA are not good, they are not discouraging. The CHA provides helpful information that stimulates positive change. It normally confirms what most members in the pew already believed to be true about their church.

CHARACTERISTICS OF CONGREGATIONAL HEALTH

Healthy churches, like healthy families, have certain characteristics that are present across different congregations. Healthy church family systems may be characterized by:

Healthy Church Systems	Unhealthy Church Systems
Honesty	Deceit, Lies, Omissions
Reciprocity in Relationships	One Person or Group Gets Their Way
Resources Are Shared Across Congregation	Resources Flow to One Person or Certain Groups
Everyone Makes Efforts to Change	I'm Fine. This Is All Someone Else's Problem.
Transparency, Openness	Staggered Disclosure, Church Family Secrets
Fair Deals and Fair Use of Power	Double Standards, Game Playing
Mutual Support	Blaming, One Person Painted Black
The Past Used for Learning Only, Moving Forward	Stuck in the Past, Repeating the Past
Stable Emotional Moods, Predictable	Roller Coaster of Emotions, Unpredictable
Authenticity—The Person You See Is Who They Are	Dr. Jeckyl and Mr. Hyde Personalities

Process consultation gives us the powerful tools we need to address the church family from a Systems Theory perspective. It looks at the dynamic circular relationships that keep things stuck in a church and prevent it from healing. It assumes that no one is "to blame" and that everyone is doing the best they can with the information they have. The consulting process is based on a trust relationship with the consultant in a multi-dimensional role with the church. The church is trusted with the power of God's Spirit to heal itself and move forward.

CHAPTER 13

HEALING CONGREGATIONAL EMOTIONS

DO YOU WANT TO SEE OUR OTHER CHILDREN?

From outward appearances, Christ Chapel should have been in a season of celebration. They had purchased thirty acres of prime real estate on the new interstate for the location of their new campus. Their building, which was crumbling down around them, had sold to a Mexican restaurant chain in only ten days. The old neighborhood that was filled with used car lots, pawn shops, and tattoo parlors, requiring security guards to be posted at every service, would now be a distant memory. The drafty old auditorium that was hot in the summer and cold in the winter would soon be replaced by a handsome new sanctuary with the latest media technology and sound system, as well as comfortable seating to replace the worn-out pews.

But all was not well at Christ Chapel. The congregation was on the verge of revolt. Members were angry about the relocation of the church. Longtime members were pulling their contributions and considering moving to a different church. The mood was tense, depressed, and sad, as members struggled to make sense of the changes that were occurring beyond their control.

Christ Chapel's leadership had been hijacked by a Tough Bargainer. His authoritarian leadership style had dominated the decision making over the past few years. His confrontational personality frequently left members damaged in his wake as he worked the crowd in the foyer. He couldn't say good morning without offending people. It was his conviction that Christ Chapel needed to move, and he was the driving force behind the acquisition of the new property and the sale of the old location. He had convinced the congregation to buy into his vision and was quickly implementing changes before members could catch their breath.

Christ Chapel had a long and storied history in its current location close to the downtown center of a major city. It had ministered to inner-city homeless, the university teaching hospital, and the faculty and students of the seminary close by. Its members were some of the best thinkers in business, medicine, theology, and politics the city had to offer. Yet somehow, they were watching events unfold at church over which they had little control.

The consequences were quick and harsh. The beloved minister who had served Christ Chapel retired after a strong thirty-year ministry. He had grown tired of picking up bodies in the foyer after the Tough Bargainer every Sunday. To add insult to injury, following a six-month retirement he'd taken another preaching job with a neighboring church. The staff was in shock and trying to hold the church together. The eldership was split over the move and trying to uphold the image of unity, but that image was disintegrating. One deacon stood up in Bible class and announced, "If we move from this location that has been our home for 75 years, . . . someone is going to have to carry me over there."

I arrived in the middle of this complex transition and began putting the pieces together. The mixed emotions of sadness, anger, and depression were palatable in the auditorium every Sunday morning. Why was there such a strong emotional reaction to this move? I knew the church was in the process of rejecting the current leadership and grieving the loss of their minister, but it felt as though there was more going on below the surface. These were gifted leaders in the community, and they'd dealt with authoritarian bullies before.

The pathos seemed to be embodied by a member named Sally. I called her "Mad Sally," though not to her face, because she was angry about everything. Sally was angry about the move. She was angry about the sale of the building. She has angry that the leaders were a bunch of wimps being pushed around by a bully, and she was especially angry that they'd brought in an outsider like me to work with them during this transition. Her sounding board had been the former minister, and he'd abandoned her—so she was angry at him, too. Her spiritual gift was being pissed off at the world, and she was using her gift well.

I was shocked when I received a phone call one morning from Sally, asking me whether I could meet her for lunch and then go with her to make a visit to the cemetery. She briefly explained that she had lost her daughter several years earlier in a car accident and that the anniversary of that date was approaching. She always took flowers, and in the past her beloved minister had accompanied her to the graveside. Her husband was still grief stricken and had not been back to the grave since the funeral. Would I be willing to stand in for them? I agreed immediately.

We met for lunch at a local restaurant, where she began sharing the story of her daughter's death. Meagan had been a freshman in high school and had stayed late one afternoon after school. She had picked her up, and they were on their way home, crossing an intersection, when the car was broadsided on the passenger side by a large truck. The impact sent the car rolling, and the passenger compartment had been crushed. Both were trapped inside, and the mother watched as her daughter died in front of her, helpless to do anything to save her life. A part of Sally died that day in the car.

Meagan was buried in a beautiful old southern cemetery on top of a hill under a large tree. We stood at her grave on a bright spring afternoon holding flowers and a balloon bouquet. "There's a part of me that wants to be down there with her. Like it's not right for me to be here. I'm not suicidal, but a part of me is gone, and I don't know what to do with that hole in my heart. Terry, our old preacher, performed

Meagan's funeral service. He'd come out here with me. He knew the right things to say. Sometimes we didn't say anything at all. I'm just so angry at myself for not going quicker through that intersection. If I had, she just might . . . ," and her voice trailed off.

Then Sally looked at me and asked me a question I'll never forget: "Would you like to see our other children?" I was momentarily confused. "I'm sorry, what did you say?" "The rest of our children here from Christ Chapel that are buried here. Would you like to visit their graves as well? They're all around here. I can show you."

I was stunned. "You mean there are other children who passed away at Christ Chapel and are buried here?" "Yes—has no one told you? Our church has lost so many babies, children, and teenagers in the past few years, and they are all buried here around Meagan. I'll tell you their stories."

So began one of the most surreal experiences of my life. Sally led me on a sad tour, introducing me to the graves of more children than my mind or emotions could comprehend. There were infants who had died at a young age, children that had died of childhood diseases, teenagers like Meagan who had died in car accidents, and children who had perished in airplane crashes and were now buried next to their parents. At each headstone there was a new name and a new, gut-wrenching story. There were so many I lost count.

When we returned, I reflected on everything I'd just heard and seen. I asked Sally a question: "Where were the funeral services for these children?" "They were at the old building," she responded, "the one they are selling." Then it was clear to me. This was not a church in revolt. This was not a church resisting a new vision. This was a church in grief.

The final place those parents, family members, and friends had said goodbye to the most precious persons in their lives—their children—was that aging old church. Those old wooden pews and that massive pulpit held the memories and the tears of hundreds of members of that church. That old building had put its arms around them at their most vulnerable moment and walked them "through the valley of the shadow of death." They were not leaving a church building; they were leaving a piece of their soul.

It took only a sixty-minute walking tour in a beautiful southern cemetery for me to change my strategy. I was treating a church in grief. This was a church that had experienced too many "goodbyes" stacked on top of one another. They needed to grieve the loss of their beloved minister. They needed to grieve the loss of a building that had comforted them when there were no words to comfort. They were grieving the loss of their historic sense of place in the community. The deacon was right: someone needed to carry them for a while. My new strategy was very simple: to create a safe space for this church to grieve so they could then move forward into a new era of ministry. If I failed to do so, they would be forever emotionally stuck in that old building, grieving those old wounds.

CHURCHES ARE SPIRITUAL-EMOTIONAL SYSTEMS

Churches are living spiritual and emotional systems. They celebrate, they reflect, they regret, they become angry, and they can grieve. Congregations are more than a set of beliefs and doctrines (thoughts) combined with actions and ministry (behavior). Congregations have affect or emotion, and it is that emotional climate we often experience but have a difficult time describing. Someone will say "That's just a cold church. I didn't feel welcome." They are describing both the spiritual and the emotional climate of a congregation that can be either healthy or wounded.

Paul's farewell to the Ephesian elders in Acts 20:36–38 describes a church as a spiritual-emotional system. "When Paul had finished speaking, he knelt down with all of them and prayed. They all wept as they embraced him and kissed him. *What grieved them most was his statement that they would never see his face again*" (emphasis added). There was a powerful spiritual and emotional bond that had been formed between these elders and their preacher, and his departure prompted a strong grief reaction from these early church leaders.

In John's Gospel, it was Christ's experience of grief that prompted a healing so powerful and public that the chief priests and Pharisees enacted a plan to take his life. Lazarus, the brother of Mary and Martha, died in Bethany in the shadow of Jerusalem. John 11:35–36 records, "Jesus wept. Then the Jews said, "See how he loved him!" A public miracle at this point in his ministry, this close to Jerusalem, would have been crossing a point of no return. There would have been no coming back from having raised Lazarus from the dead. Jesus, fueled by the emotional power of love and grief, called "Lazarus, come forth!" Jesus embraced grief and his passion with that pivotal decision.

When I process difficult emotions with clients, I ask, "Are you mad, sad, glad, or fearful?" There are a wide range of emotions, both negative and positive, and they can be experienced mildly or powerfully. Churches also experience powerful emotions. In the case of Christ Chapel, the congregation was experiencing layers of grief. They were grieving the loss of their building, which represented their sense of place in the community. They were grieving the loss of a long-term minister who had served them faithfully as a trusted friend. Their grief was compounded by the loss of so many children in a brief period of time. This layered grief left them exhausted and unable to deal with the abuse of power present in the leadership. When I joined them, they were spiritually and emotionally incapable of moving forward into the next era of their history.

Wounded churches in need of a process of healing are experiencing one or a combination of many emotions:

- **Shock**: Disbelief over an event or series of events, decisions, or actions in the life of the church.

- **Sadness:** A sense of despair or despondency over the past, present, or future of the church.

- **Grief**: Mourning a loss or set of losses that may include people, things, or sense of purpose.

- **Anger:** Frustration over the inability to achieve certain goals or outcomes.
- **Depression:** Unresolved emotions may lead to a downward spiral emotionally and spiritually.
- **Shame**: Regret and frustration over the past—things that were done or things left undone.

MYTHS OF CONGREGATIONAL EMOTIONS

Ignore It and It Will Go Away Myth

There is the unstated belief among many church leaders that, if the church is wounded, all we need to do is ignore the problem, and maybe it will all just go away. That is akin to running over a dog and leaving it maimed in the street, hoping that it will drag itself into the nearest vet clinic. Jeremiah was correct when he said, "They dress the wound of my people as though it were not serious. 'Peace, peace,' they say, when there is no peace."

Ministry is grief work. Those who engage in ministry will be walking with people through powerful emotions. That means that we must be comfortable with our own emotions. The church leaders I've worked with who have helped their churches heal are leaders who are comfortable dealing with anger, conflict, sadness, and grief. These are not pleasant emotions, but they walk into them with wisdom and compassion, helping their church process the events so they can move forward.

There is a saying among therapists, "Deal with your emotions, or your emotions will deal with you." We know that powerful negative emotions that go unprocessed do not just disappear. They don't just go away over time by our ignoring them. They lie buried inside us, waiting for the right moment to retrigger them, and we then get a powerful new experience of the old emotion.

Christ Chapel had been trying to ignore the congregational pain for a long time. When the building sold quickly, this was the final straw, and their defense mechanism of denial failed. Christ Chapel needed a season to grieve before she could move forward.

Hurry Up and Get Busy Myth

Churches that resist spiritual-emotional healing may opt for the "Let's all get busy and we will get over this" myth. A church leader declares, "We all need to just get busy doing the work of the Lord, and all these other distractions will take care of themselves." They trot out the Great Commission and beat everyone over the head with guilt for not getting busy with the work of the church.

Let me be clear. I believe in the Great Commission, in seeking and saving the lost. I also believe that it as paramount to act on one's set of beliefs. And I believe that Jesus prefaced the Great Commission with a season of restoration with his apostles following his resurrection, during which he tutored them and reassured them of his presence through the Holy Spirit. The apostles were in shock following his crucifixion, scattered to the four winds, and needed a season of restoration with the Master before they were prepared to "get busy."

I work with many church leaders who want to move from crucifixion to the

Great Commission and skip the season with the Master. My judgment is that we have too many spiritual leaders who are disconnected from their own emotional life, so they do not know how to lead others. A minister cannot lead where he has not been. If a leader is uncomfortable with sadness, depression, grief, or anger, then he will not know how to lead a congregation through a process of healing.

Quick Remarriage Myth

Christ Chapel could have fallen into the "Let's go hire a new preacher and get on with things" trap. Church leaders will avoid the hard work of getting into the emotional life of the congregation and working on key issues that have resulted from the loss of the last minister, choosing to initiate a ministerial search immediately. They rationalize that a new minister will come in, and his presence alone will bring a fresh start. They hope that the positive momentum of finding a "new guy" will override the current negative emotional climate. It is much easier to blame the last minister or leadership than to look systemically and examine congregational processes.

In the first chapter, I described the insanity of a hypothetical ride home with my mother following the funeral service of my father and her saying she had arranged a date that night with the funeral director she'd just met that day. A scenario like that is ridiculous to imagine. Yet churches regularly skip over the healing process following a major event like the departure of a minister and quickly move on to the search process. They do not process the old hurt, disappointment, or anger. The emotional baggage does not go away. It is visited on the next minister, who comes in unaware of the events that preceded him or the entrenched processes that could undermine his work. This is a recipe for disaster and the reason many churches experience a revolving door of ministers.

Get Angry Myth

I was called to a meeting with Christ Chapel's Tough Bargainer. He was clearly not happy. "I don't understand what you are doing in your sermons," he shouted. "You're obviously not on board with the direction of this church! You are putting the entire building program at risk!" He was yelling at me in the front seat of his car, and I was stuck there with him throwing a temper tantrum.

I calmly explained that the church was grieving—on multiple levels. This was not permanent, but it was serious, and the congregation needed some time to transition. There were things we could do to minister to this congregation to prepare it to move forward. He would hear none of it. He didn't buy the assessment, and he rejected my assistance. I was now just another problem to be solved on his way to saving the church from itself.

I find people who, when exposed to difficult emotions, get frustrated and angry. They don't know what to do with them in the church, because they don't know what to do with them in their own lives. They are people who are disconnected from their own emotional life, so they cannot be connected to others. In the chapter on Sexual Wounds, Karen described Carl as "lacking the emotional chip" and being unable to relate to other people's emotions. This is a sign of someone who is disconnected from their emotional life.

I believe emotional maturity or the emotional chip is a necessary ingredient for any leader. When it is absent in adulthood, I've rarely seen it develop to the point that someone can be an effective leader. The leader who opts for denial, getting busy, or becoming angry needs to be replaced in leadership. The longer they remain, the more damage they do to the church and the harder the transitional process will be.

SOURCES OF NEGATIVE CONGREGATIONAL EMOTIONS

There are many reasons a church may be stuck in unprocessed negative emotions. A consultant working with a congregation will hear the pain as they listen to stories members share about the history of the church. Buried in those stories are the core emotions that need to be processed on a congregational level. We know from research on trauma that unprocessed traumatic events do not go away. If left unprocessed, they require great energy to tamp down for an individual or a congregation. Some sources of negative congregational emotions include:

- Loss of a minister.
- Loss of key leaders or a difficult departure of key leaders.
- Painful public meetings or announcements.
- Misuse of social media by members or leaders.
- Abuse of power by an individual or a group.

- Secrets kept by leadership regarding the affairs of the church.
- Unresolved conflict, resulting in personal attacks or threats to leave the church.
- Moves or retirement on the part of a minister.
- Building programs and fund-raising programs.
- Lack of protection of members from toxic leaders and members—lack of systemic boundaries.
- Accidents, natural disasters.
- Crimes.
- Change in community demographics.

EFFECTS OF UNPROCESSED EMOTIONS

Danny was a leader to whom church members turned for a listening ear. He had a deep passion for worship. Over the past two years, he had fielded more than his share of complaints about the Touch Bargainer. He had listened patiently to members' complaints. He had urged restraint and patience on the part of members. He watched sadly as lifelong friends moved their membership to other congregations. Danny was trying to hold the ship together with compassion and kindness.

The bright spot in Danny's life was the plan for the new sanctuary. He dreamed of a place where praise music would be offered every Sunday and worshipers could offer up songs old and new. As a part of the planning process, a church town hall meeting was called to discuss the new worship ministry. He made preparations as his excitement built. He was anxious to share his dreams and hear the dreams of the church regarding worship.

What I witnessed that Sunday afternoon was the ambushing of a church leader and the outpouring of years of congregational frustration. The meeting opened with Danny presenting ideas for the new worship ministry, but during the question-and-answer period it quickly disintegrated into a forum for members to threaten, accuse, belittle, and shout. Years of pent-up frustration were released on this unsuspecting man, who'd had no idea he was about to be run over by a freight train. Members' frustrations over unresponsive leaders, the loss of the minister, and the expected move to another location poured out in buckets as Danny absorbed blow after blow.

The meeting ended, mercifully, with nothing accomplished and another layer of hurt emotions laid into the record book of the church. Two weeks later Danny resigned, and not long afterward he moved to another church. This was one those tragic losses of a capable leader.

Emotions do not just melt away. If they are not adequately processed, they remain buried in the unconscious, waiting on the right trigger to bring them up. At Christ Chapel, the members had denied anger and frustration for several years toward their Tough Bargainer leader. Members found it impossible to deal with him. Danny, however, was safe to talk with. When the church reached its "Popeye Moment" and said "I've had all I can stand," Danny was a safe leader to attack. He took the brunt of the anger really aimed at the Tough Bargainer, and the church inadvertently drove off a healthy leader and was left with a toxic one.

This illustrates another principle of Systems Theory. Systems that do not address dysfunctional patterns will begin to spiral downward. They will lose healthy members who become frustrated with the church's inability to address dysfunctional patterns. The entire church system will spiral downward as less functional individuals step into positions of leadership. They recraft the history of the church as being "everyone else's fault," and the systemic pain becomes institutionalized. There are churches that have spiraled down so far that change is almost impossible. Too much damage has been done.

Danny passed away at a relatively young age of a heart attack. I know from our conversations that he had never recovered from the pain of that Sunday afternoon at Christ Chapel. He carried a broken heart to his death over the things that had been said to him from a church with unprocessed emotions.

SIGNS OF UNPROCESSED CONGREGATIONAL EMOTIONS

Low Energy Level

It takes a great deal of psychic energy for a person or congregation to keep pain tamped down in the unconscious. The old memories are constantly running like a program that is opened but not visible on the desktop of a computer. It isn't on the screen but is using up an incredible amount of storage space in the mind. Churches with unprocessed emotional pain find themselves "just going through the motions" of church. Conversely, congregations that process their pain and move on find that they can engage in new mission and relationships with new ministers that are authentic and free from pain.

War Stories

Congregations with unprocessed emotional pain tell a lot of old war stories. Like a couple coming in for counseling after many years of marriage and spending the entire session blaming one another, some churches are stuck in the past. As I begin consulting with a church, if members are constantly relating their "greatest hits" of terrible things the church has done, it's a sign that this is a group with unprocessed congregational pain. They will not be capable of embracing a new minister until that old baggage has been laid to rest. One question I ask is, "What stories are we as a church telling ourselves about who we are and what we have done in the past?"

What's Wrong with Us?

Churches with unprocessed negative emotions may rapid-cycle. Rapid cycle is the process of avoiding the emotional pain, quickly hiring a new minister in the hope that he can move the church forward, and visiting all the old issues on the new minister. He is powerless to do anything about the situation. The rapid cycle can occur in one to three years, producing a revolving door in the ministerial staff.

Members listen to announcement after announcement of ministers leaving and leaders stepping down. They begin to ask, "What's wrong with us?" They know intuitively that something deeper is wrong and that it cannot always be the minister's fault. The church develops a corporate self-esteem problem. "We will never find a guy who stays with us." Healing will involve processing the old emotional pain. It will also involve rebuilding the self-esteem of the congregation to the point that they feel themselves to be worthy of a mature adult relationship with all their leaders.

Symptom Bearers

Congregations with unprocessed emotions have emotional "symptom bearers" who carry the emotion for the church. "Mad Sally" at Christ Chapel was one of the symptom bearers for the unresolved anger aimed at the Tough Bargainer. The church was unable to carry on a conversation with him, and they were unwilling to remove him from leadership. Sally was angry at the leadership, angry about the loss of her favorite minister, and frustrated over the move. This was compounded by her grief over the loss of her daughter. Systems will informally "appoint" certain individuals to "carry the pain" for the group. They will voice, in powerful but destructive ways, the anger, grief, or depression of the entire congregation to anyone who will listen.

If the symptom bearer leaves, the system will appoint someone else to take their place. If Sally were to leave, in a short time someone else would step into that informal role. As with infantry flag bearers in the Civil War, if the colors were to go down, someone else would step in, pick up the flag, and carry it forward. Churches discover that unprocessed emotions produce powerful informal spokespersons who articulate the negative emotions of the congregation. Their presence is both maddening and necessary to keep the unhealthy balance of denial in place. The only sure way to heal the church is to process the emotion.

Growing Alumni Base

Amberton University, where I teach, has a fifty-year base of alumni. I meet our graduates in the community, and they proudly tell me the degree they earned and the professors who taught them. Our alumni base tells us a lot about the health or dysfunction of the system.

Churches with unprocessed negative emotions spin out members to other churches in town. New people come into the church, experience the dysfunctional processes, and move on. They may not be able to describe all the patterns, but they experience enough to cause them to move to another church. One leader who served a church with severe unresolved issues told me, "We have had so many members transfer out of here that I think we've built two other congregations in town."

Churches unwilling to deal with their pain will also spin out an alumni base of former staff ministers. One Narcissistic Church built a history room to commemorate its past, complete with a large portrait of the "founding pastor." I was sitting in the history room interviewing leaders, and we began counting the number of staff ministers who had come and gone during the narcissistic preacher's tenure. We stopped at fifty. The sad commentary on his leadership was a large alumni base of former staff ministers who had left, hurt, discouraged, and angry at the treatment they'd received from that church. I recommended they hang fifty additional pictures of former staff ministers in the room and take the portrait down.

HELPING CHURCHES PROCESS PAINFUL EMOTIONS

When I work with clients experiencing painful emotions, there are tools we can draw upon to help a person process the pain. Sally needed a safe space to deal with grief. She needed a season of time to process those old emotions that kept her up at night. She needed some good information about the nature of grief, anger, and depression. And she needed a trusted relationship with a healing person who would walk beside her to be a sounding board.

There are many healing tools that can be applied to the local church to help it resolve unprocessed emotions and move to a place of emotional and spiritual health. Some of these processes include:

Embracing Emotional Pain as Valid Human Experience

Some churches "live in their head." They approach spirituality from a strictly rational standpoint but have difficulty dealing with human emotions. When someone loses a loved one, a "head person" may struggle to respond. They offer an empty "Well, she is in a better place with the Lord," along with a formal hug to the grieving spouse.

I believe in approaching spirituality from a rational standpoint. I use a historical-critical approach to Scripture. However, life is lived in the head and in the gut. We are rational and emotional beings, and space must be made for the power of our affect to shape our lives. Christ at Lazarus's tomb was living in both his head and his gut. He was grieving, and he chose rationally to do something about it—even if it set in motion the wheels that led to his crucifixion.

At Christ Chapel, when we acknowledged that the church had been through multiple crises in a short period of time, the congregation heaved a collective sigh of relief. Finally, someone could see how much pain the church was in.

The first Sunday I transition a hurting church, I spend time in the sermon simply acknowledging the reality of the past and the pain the congregation is experiencing. I call this flying "wing tip to wing tip" with a group of hurting people. Without exception, I'm met at the back door by long-term members, saying, "We have needed this badly for a very long time." The first step in healing is validating the pain and someone saying "I get it . . . yes, this has been very difficult, but it doesn't have to stay this way."

Create a Season of Healing

Christ Chapel needed to stop, catch its collective breath and experience a season of healing. They had lost their preacher; their location; their building; and, sadly, a group of young children.

They were stumbling into the future burdened by grief. When individuals lose loved ones, we understand that they need time and space to recover from that loss. Why would churches be any different?

In order to process congregational emotions, I need the leadership to agree that we need a season of healing. During that time, the focus of the church will be on binding up wounds of the past and dealing with the spiritual wounds of God's people. Nothing new needs to be initiated during that season of restoration. No building renovations, no new ministry launch, and no big missions programs—we need to "be still and know that I am God." Church leaders fight me on this, and that is a critical mistake.

Church leaders want to know how long healing with take. I ask, "How long did it take you to get to where you are today? Perhaps we need to devote some serious time to undoing the damage that the past has caused before you move on." Churches that create a season of healing are able to stop and do the work that they need to do in order to move forward. Churches that succumb to the myth of the telescopic nature of Scripture will want to do important work in a brief period of time. They are searching for the magic wand of healing, and it does not exist.

Preaching and Teaching to Process Emotional Pain

The preaching ministry of the church provides great opportunities for congregational healing. For too long, the pastoral care of the church through preaching has been ignored by ministers who are anxious to promote growth and evangelism. Preaching as pastoral care is given a backseat to the more "important" mission of the church. A part of this problem stems from the inability of preachers to address their own internal core wounds. Preachers who are disconnected from their own emotional experiences cannot lead where they have not been.

The text provides rich examples of biblical characters experiencing loss, discouragement, anger, and depression. Dr.

Walter Brueggemann in his *Commentary on Genesis* views the life of Joseph in rich emotional and spiritual detail. He notes the emotional roller coaster Joseph experienced after having been betrayed by his brothers, betrayed by Potiphar's wife, and left to languish alone in prison. When Joseph is called upon to interpret the dreams of Pharaoh's servants, the chief cupbearer and the chief baker, he confidently proclaims, "Do not interpretations belong to God? Tell me your dreams." He has confidence in God and his standing with God to provide the interpretation. However, just a few verses later he pleads in despair, "But when all goes well with you, remember me and show me kindness; mention me to Pharaoh and get me out of this prison."

Brueggemann notes, "We are shown the personal struggle of a man still in prison. For all his ability to amaze others, he himself is in great need." Joseph is on a roller coaster of emotion, bouncing between faith and doubt. It is in that canyon between the two realities that faith is lived out. Biblical preaching that draws solidly from the text and then applies it to the wounded spirit of God's people provides spiritual healing to restore the soul of the congregation.

EMOTIONAL INTENSITY AND EMOTIONAL SPEED

People in churches process emotions at different speeds. Some move through emotions very quickly, barely experiencing them. Others process slowly and immerse themselves in the emotional experience. At Christ Chapel, the Tough Bargainer leader was processing so fast that members couldn't keep up with him. Sally, on the other hand, processed her emotions very slowly. One way to conceptualize emotional healing is on a continuum of fast to slow, depending upon the individual and the situation they encounter.

People also experience emotions with different intensity. A crisis may occur and an individual may react with "soft" emotions, such as sadness, anxiety, depression, and withdrawal. They are experiencing negative emotions, but when we hear them express the emotions verbally, they come across in a softer manner. When a crisis occurs, people may also experience hard emotions like anger, frustration, rage, or criticism. These harder emotions tend to be verbalized more intensely and are difficult to listen to.

When we combine emotional intensity, soft or hard, with emotional speed, fast or slow, we get four styles of emotional processing in a church.

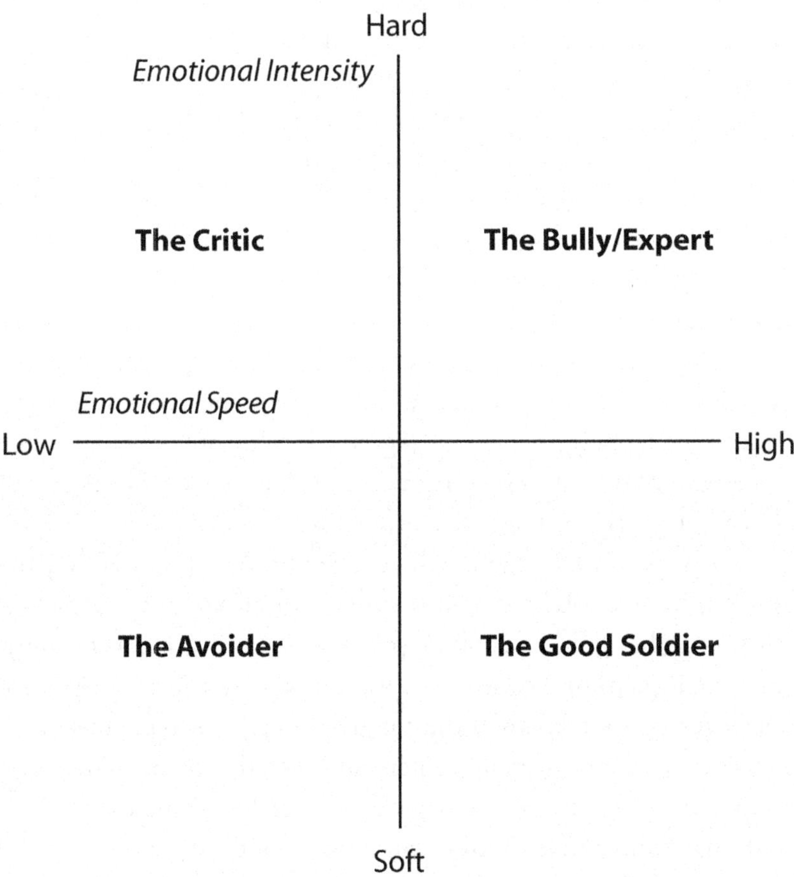

The Avoider

The avoider approaches congregational transitions with their default conflict-avoidant style. They take their emotions, especially the negative ones, and bury them deep inside. Asked if they are doing all right, they are specialists at saying, "You bet; everything is just fine." But inside, their lives are filled with a cauldron of unprocessed memories and emotions.

Churches are filled with Avoiders because we have developed the idea that conflict is inherently unspiritual. It is not. Conflict may be an opportunity for growth and change. It may provide the opportunity to stop old, dysfunctional patterns. But the Avoider wants nothing to do with conflict. Many members at Christ Chapel had slipped into the Avoidant role. Problems had built up, and they didn't have the will to engage in the conflict. The relationship between leadership and members grew progressively worse.

The Good Soldier

The Good Soldier can process emotions more quickly than the Avoider. They also experience difficult events by expressing more sadness, disappointment, and regret. Their default emotional life tends toward the softer spectrum of emotions like the Avoider's, but they tend to process them by getting busy.

In the midst of the death of their brother Lazarus, Martha was busy in the kitchen making dinner for all her guests. She was processing her grief by cooking pot roast! *Maybe if I just stay busy, this will all go away.* Danny was a good soldier at Christ Chapel. He was listening to the pain of the congregation and staying busy with his plans for a new worship center. However, the town hall meeting caught him by surprise as a group of hard-emotional members ambushed him and left him a walking-wounded leader.

The Critic

Critics tend to process emotions more slowly. They hang onto negative emotions and cook them in their Crock-Pot for hours before serving them up to guests as anger, frustration, and criticism. The critic will grab anyone who will listen and give them an earful of their latest complaints against the leadership. They may go on social media and carry out a campaign of social slander. They are some of the hardest people to deal with during a congregational healing process.

Sally was a congregational Critic at Christ Chapel. She had a long list of grievances to air. She was disappointed about the move to a new location, the departure of her beloved minister, and the inability of leadership to deal with a bully. Deep down, it was the soft emotions of grief over the death of her daughter and guilt over her inability to save her that drove her anger. Sally, the Critic, was in pain.

The Bully/Expert

People in transition may process hard emotions and do so very quickly. They experience crises or change and react with anger, resentment, frustration, and being overly controlling. They don't know what to do, so they hurry up and do *something*. They push everyone around them to follow their lead and accept their solutions. They come across as a Bully, and people describe themm as "a bull in a china closet." They also come across as a self-proclaimed "Expert." These are people who gain a reputation as someone "you can't tell anything because they know it all."

The Tough Bargainer at Christ Chapel was both a Bully and an Expert. He processed his emotions quickly, and they came out as verbally hard and aggressive. He knew more than anyone else. It is the aggressiveness of the Tough Bargainer style, combined with the more passive Avoider style, that drives members out the back door during congregational transitions.

CREATING CONVERSATIONS AND RITUALS TO REMEMBER

Following my tour of the cemetery with Sally, I returned to Christ Chapel and began designing a series of experiences that would help the congregation process their pain. We erected a series of blank murals on the walls outside the auditorium. One was prepared for each decade of the congregation's history. Then we invited members to bring pictures and place them on the murals. Sally took the lead in preparing a special commemorative mural for the children lost over the decades of the life of the church.

We invited key members from each of the decades to share stories about the history of the church during a special testimonial time each Sunday morning. The stories flowed as members laughed, cried, and remembered their shared history together. Leaders began to pause and stop pushing and started listening to their flock. The church began processing the pent-up emotion, and each week the atmosphere of the church lightened. People who just weeks earlier had been demonstrating in the streets were now smiling, laughing, and embracing the pain and promise of their collective past.

BUILDING A ROOM FOR THE MEMORIES

When I was in graduate school at Abilene Christian University, living on "the hill," my rental house burned to the ground. I came home to firemen with large shovels shoveling the ashes of my belongings out the window. Five years of undergraduate and graduate-level books and notes had gone up in smoke. A mentor had given me a beautifully-engraved set of the volumes of the William Barkley *Daily Devotional Commentary* that had survived the fire but were badly smoke damaged. The restoration company cleaned them, but I could hold the pages close and smell the fire in those pages and remember that day.

When my clients are processing painful emotions, I tell them that their life is like a beautiful Victorian home with three stories. Someone has just thrown a smoke bomb into your house, and it has damaged everything inside. You have to send the drapes to be cleaned, replace some carpet, and repaint the walls. Eventually, the house will look like new again. However, there will be some articles, like my commentaries, that will always smell like that day.

You decide to build a room up on the third floor. You are going to carefully place all those memories from that day in that room. You're free to visit that room any time you want to because it is your special place of grief. But the rest of your house will be restored, and it will be stronger and more beautiful than it was before.

Christ Chapel crossed their river. To their credit, we didn't lose a family during the transition after the healing process had begun. At the groundbreaking ceremony for the new sanctuary, we invited any member to come forward and turn a shovel of dirt. Most members attending stepped forward and took their turn. We provided small commemorative shovels, one for each of the children lost, and invited Christ Chapel's kids to break ground on a memorial playground to forever remember the children in that beautiful old southern cemetery. The congregation caught its collective breath, and in a short time a new generation of leaders stepped forward and the authoritarian Tough Bargainer resigned.

On the afternoon before the dedication of the new worship center, the dream Danny had been speaking of at that terrible town hall meeting, I walked into the auditorium. There before me in that empty sanctuary were a dozen white-robed nuns spread out among the pews standing perfectly still with their heads bowed in prayer. I was stunned and watched in silence, until one nun who seemed to be in charge spotted me, smiled, and came over. "We are from the Korean church. My sisters don't speak English well. We have been praying for this church. Our neighborhood is very poor. People are in great pain here. We need a church that can minister to people in pain." Perhaps Christ Chapel had its new mission because they were a church that had lived through pain and come to a place of healing.

CHAPTER 14

DEATH, BURIAL, AND RESURRECTION

FROZEN COMMUNION

It was 7:55 a.m., the service was scheduled to start in five minutes, and the deacon in charge of worship looked as though he were having a panic attack. The Gateway Church was in the middle of a significant transition. They were moving into a new facility, but the auditorium was not completed. The large Sunday morning crowd that enjoyed coming together in one service would be separated into three morning services in a modest fellowship hall while the auditorium was completed. This morning was the maiden voyage of the triplet-service schedule. The change to multiple services had everyone stressed out.

Gateway was a "go with the flow" kind of church. Regardless of its size, it still retained the relaxed atmosphere of a country church. The informal culture was being "stressed" by the demands of three back-to-back services that required a new degree of efficiency. Gateway was not happy!

The deacon in charge of worship asked me whether I'd looked at the communion trays that morning. "No—I typically don't inspect communion trays, announcement sheets, bathrooms. . . . I leave that to others," I joked. "Well, go take a look at them." It was now 7:57.

The stacks of silver-plated communion trays rested at the front, close to the pulpit. I looked at them and immediately noticed a layer of thin ice running up the sides of the trays. "Try to separate them," he instructed. The trays for the fruit of the vine were frozen tightly together, like a frosty mug of A&W root beer. "Go get a screwdriver," I urged him, but it was too late—7:59, The worship leader started leading the music, and our first worship service in Gateway's new location was off. Frosty mugs of fruit of the vine and all, just waiting to be served.

I sat on stage, my mind racing, wondering how we had managed to get ourselves into this predicament. It dawned on me: the moving crew had brought over the old coolers from the original building and installed them in the communion preparation room. The temperature dials must have been moved in transit. After the team prepared the communion trays on Saturday and put them in the coolers, they must have frozen overnight. Causation no longer mattered. I had to execute the service. Luckily for me, the Lord's Supper was after the sermon. I had some time to figure out my options.

I occurred to me that very few ministers in church history had encountered this problem. I could be breaking new ecclesiastical ground! I could have the deacons pass the communion trays and ask the congregation to hold the cups in their hands and defrost them. Wouldn't this be a form of a fellowship meal? We could pass out the little cups and ask people to partake of the fruit of the vine like mini-ice cubes. Would it be unscriptural to crunch the fruit of the vine? If I'd known earlier, I could have had toothpicks dropped into each little cup, and we could have had Gateway frozen popsicles on our first Sunday. Perhaps I could start a theological debate on frozen communion, write a book, and tour the country debating more conservative brethren who would oppose frozen communion. This could be big! The worship deacon appeared in the back waving a Phillips-head screwdriver, but I waved him off. No sense in traumatizing the church with excavation work on communion trays during the singing of "Blessed Assurance."

It occurred to me that the only two people in the house that knew we were in a pre-emptive emergency were the screwdriver deacon and me. Perhaps I could limit the damage. Luckily, I noticed little droplets of water running down the sides of the trays. Could it be the trays were defrosting? I waited until the opening prayer, and, while the congregations' heads were bowed, I snuck down to do a quick inspection. The trays were beginning to thaw! All I needed was time.

I returned to the podium with a plan. I was due up momentarily to preach. I quickly reworked my outline. It would have been poetic to report that I was preaching on Jesus turning the water to wine that day. Instead, I installed a series of prayers into my lesson. Prayers to lengthen the sermon, prayers for rapid thawing, and prayers to give me time to check the trays.

I would preach for a while and then ask the congregation to bow its collective head. I would lead the church in prayer and sneak go down to the communion trays and check on the thawing process. They were still too frozen to serve. Preach some more; then pray some more. They were thawing, but I was going to need to keep preaching. I should have prepared more material.

I ran out of sermon points, and prayers, about the time the lids came off the trays, revealing eighty little purple liquid cups smiling back at me. I ended the sermon, and the congregation was served communion with no one any the wiser.

After services, the deacon hugged me and ran off with his screwdriver to check the trays before the 9:30 service started. One elderly member remarked, "Dr. Don, that was the prayenest sermon I've ever heard!" And Gateway moved seamlessly into three morning services while it completed its auditorium. I missed my opportunity to introduce frozen communion into the annals of church history. Gateway was going through a major transition, and some things were just going to be messy for a while.

BIBLICAL MODELS OF TRANSITION

The Bible presents many examples of people going through an ending, a period of wilderness wandering, and a new beginning. Paul in Galatians 2:20 says, "I have been crucified with Christ and I no longer live, but Christ lives in me."

The passion of Jesus is understood in three separate but interconnected phases. There is his death on the cross, three days in the tomb, and his resurrection. There is an ending, a time in between, and a new beginning.

The nation of Israel encamped at the Jordan River in Joshua 1 was a nation of former slaves who had just spent forty years as bedouins before moving forward as conquerors. There was a former life, a time in the wilderness, and a new beginning.

After Jesus's baptism, Matthew records that he was led by the Spirit into the wilderness. "Then Jesus was led by the Spirit into the desert to be tempted by the devil" (Matthew 4:1). There was an ending to his private life, a period in the wilderness where he was tempted, and the commencement of his public ministry.

Jesus's apostles experienced an ending, a time of transition, and a new beginning. The crucifixion of the Master was an ending unlike any other the apostles had experienced. They were scattered, confused, and grieving. We normally turn to Acts 2 and hear them boldly proclaiming the gospel on the Day of Pentecost. We miss the time in the wilderness. Acts 1:3 records, "After his suffering, he showed himself to them and gave many convincing proofs that he was alive. He appeared to them over a period of forty days and spoke about the kingdom of God." Jesus's apostles needed a period of transition during which Jesus did remedial education with them. He had to explain again the things he'd taught them.

If Jesus, his apostles, and the nation of Israel all needed a time of transition, what about us? If God saw fit to provide a transitional period for his Son when he started his earthly ministry, for the nation of Israel when they were going to conquer the promised land,

and for the apostles when they were going to start the church—why would we doubt our need to transition today?

Working with churches, I find that some church people want to move from the ending directly to the new beginning. They want to skip the wilderness period. They want to move directly from the Last Supper and Gethsemane to the resurrection, while skipping the crucifixion. They want to move from baptism to public ministry and skip the wilderness of temptation. They want to move from rebellion coming out of Egypt as slaves directly into conquest, skipping the wilderness wanderings. I contend that each phase—ending, wilderness, and new beginning, contains important work for the church to do. To omit one phase is to have an incomplete transition.

MYTHS OF TRANSITIONS

Why do church leaders avoid going through an ending, wilderness, and new beginning? I find that they believe one of three myths surrounding the transitional process.

1. ***We are so unique the rules of transitions do not apply to us.***
   Churches are susceptible to the myth that they are so special the normal rules of human relationships do not apply to them. Their church will not go through grief because they are such a unique group of people. Narcissistic churches and Borderline churches are especially prone to this mythology because they excuse themselves from rules in general.

2. ***We are so spiritual we will not be affected by the transition.***
   Some churches fall victim to this myth because they see themselves "living on a higher spiritual plane" than other people. To admit that they suffer

from the same human struggles as everyone else would be to admit weakness. Forget that Jesus, the apostles, and the Israelites all needed some time to adjust to change. They have it all under control. Tough Bargainer churches will rely on their own power to get through the tough times and call it spiritual maturity.

3. ***I am such a great leader we can ignore all this talk of transition.***
   Narcissistic, Addiction, and Tough Bargainer churches are led by individuals who believe they possess all wisdom and knowledge. They can lead the church through any transition because they are such gifted leaders. This myth allows the leader to believe they could perform major surgery on themselves.

CHANGE VS. TRANSITION

William Bridges, in *Managing Transitions: Making the Most of Change*, writes: "It isn't the changes that do you in, it's the transitions. Change is not the same as transition. Change is situational: the new site, the new boss, the new team roles, and the new policy. Transition is the psychological process people go through to come to terms with the new situation. Change is external, transition is internal."

The rule of thumb "change is external, transition is internal" is critical for a congregation. Churches change preachers, change worship services, and change leadership. The internal processes of transition can take a long time. If the transition is not made internally, the change will fail.

The Bridges model of transition proposes that transitions go through three phases; endings, the neutral zone, and new beginnings. These phases overlap and are illustrated in chapter 9.

There are aspects of the neutral zone in the new beginning. There are characteristics of the ending in a new beginning. Each phase contains important work to be done. The Bridges model corresponds to the biblical model of death, burial, and resurrection, or of old life, wilderness, and new life. We will explore each phase separately.

The Ending Phase

"And Moses the servant of the Lord died there in Moab, as the Lord had said. He buried him in Moab, in the valley opposite Beth Peor, but to this day no one knows where his grave is. Moses was a hundred and twenty years old when he died, yet his eyes were not weak nor his strength gone. The Israelites grieved for Moses in the plains of Moab thirty days, until the time of weeping and mourning was over" (Deuteronomy 34:5–,8).

Israel was in the midst of a massive transition. They were shifting from former slaves and bedouins to being warriors. Moses was gone, and Joshua was taking command of the conquest. The first step in Israel's transition was to grieve the ending of Moses's life—"until the time of weeping and mourning was over." Wise church leaders allow time for the church to end eras of congregational history well.

I was in graduate school to become a marriage and family therapist with another student, Katy, who was already a gifted counselor. We were doing our practicums together at a clinic when I saw her leave with a client. They carried a shovel and a shoe box across the parking lot out into an open field. Sometime later, Katy returned with her client, and they hugged at the door. The client, a middle-aged woman, wiped tears from her eyes and turned to walk away. The shoe box was gone.

I couldn't wait for supervision that week to find out what had happened with Katy, her client, and the strange shoe box. What was in there? We had to dig for dirt in therapy, but usually not in an empty lot!

In supervision, Katy shared that her client had been through a painful divorce. She was holding her family together, working a new job, and caring for a dying mom. During the day she would keep it together. At night, after the kids were tucked it, she had a spot on her porch where she would sit and cry. She let all those emotions out and had a big garbage bag of used Kleenex tissues sitting next to her chair.

Katy stumbled onto an idea to help her client deal with the ending. She had her client take all those used Kleenex and put them into the sink and add water. It made a paste. She then spread it on cookie sheets and baked them in the oven. They made a crude papyrus surface. She then had her write all of her emotions on the papyrus, which had once held her tears. She wrote about her anger, her sadness, and her feelings of being overwhelmed.

Katy asked her client to bring the "pages of her tears" into a session and read them to her. They placed the pages in an old shoe box and walked out into an open field. Together, Katy and her client buried the shoe box and, in the process, ended the old life that had been weighing her down.

Katy had found a way to help her client learn from the past and move on. She marked the ending of the old marriage in a powerful way that was respectful of her pain and empowering to her potential to move forward. This was a wise and compassionate treatment of a woman's wound.

The first step in moving forward in a transition is ending well. I teach churches that we want to land the plane before we take off again. Some key steps in ending well include;

We mark the endings in important ways.

Katy marked the ending for her client with a shoe box funeral. When Israel crossed the Jordan River, headed to attack Jericho, the Lord commanded that a memorial of stones beset to commemorate the ending. "In the future, when your children ask you, 'What do these stones mean?' tell them that the flow of the Jordan was cut off before the ark of the covenant of the LORD" (Joshua 4:6–7). Churches would do well to consider important ways to mark the endings they experience to help members move forward.

Treat the past with respect.

Bridges encourages leaders to treat the past with respect. He stresses that leaders who connect the current changes with the history of the organization will win more hearts and minds. I worked with a church that was transitioning to a new location. It had a long history in the city as one of the pioneering congregations. The wise leaders constructed a history room in the new building that celebrated the faith history of the church over its life. New leaders will go to two extremes: they will try to ignore the fact that the past ever existed or stay stuck in the past. Both approaches generally fail.

Realize that people go a little crazy during endings.

Because transitions are emotional, people can go a little crazy when they are going through endings. When we apply that rule to an entire congregation, the potential for reactions that are all over the map is very high.

Endings are a time of grieving.

My father died of cancer. It was a long, painful death, and I had flown back to Dallas many times to help care for him. Exhaustion and emotions were high when he passed. He asked me to perform his funeral, and I, of course, agreed to do so. I was so emotionally spent, however, that I have no memory of that day. I cannot remember the service, the graveside service, or the family meal afterwards. Two weeks following, I was to speak on a panel at a university in Tennessee. It had been on the books for months. I showed up completely unprepared. I had not studied ahead of time and had nothing to offer. Graciously, my fellow presenters covered for me. My father had died and grief had temporarily depleted my coping skills.

Grief reactions in a church may take the following forms:

Anger: Rage, grumbling, sitting on resentments, sabotage, passive-aggressive acts.

Sadness: May range from sadness to tears. Preaching during transitions will often touch this sadness and allow it to find expression.

Bargaining: Unrealistic attempts to end the transition early. Making big promises that cannot be kept.

Anxiety: Anxiety may be silent or expressed.

Disorientation: Confusion, forgetfulness, feeling lost or insecure. Churches in transition need to communicate over and over because they lose focus easily.

Depression: The church may be situationally depressed because it views the past, present, and future negatively.

OBJECTIVE VS. SUBJECTIVE LOSS

Christ Chapel in chapter 13 was moving to a new building and selling its historic facility. That was an objective loss because it was tangible. The emotions tied to that building over the deaths of so many children resulted in a subjective loss. The subjective loss was more powerful than the objective loss.

Unresolved Issues Emerge

Endings are a time in churches when old, unresolved issues may emerge. Endings that have not been processed in the past will be tied to the current ending. People may tell stories of other ministers who have left. Members may complain about leaders in the past who have hurt them. When I hear congregations telling stories that are five and ten years old during an ending, I know there is unresolved anger and grief.

Monkeys Running the Zoo

Endings are a time when we want secure leadership to stabilize the church. People need something to hang on to during times of change. Often, the ending provides a gap that is filled by the very people who have no business running the show. Pseudo-leaders emerge with their own formulae for how to manage the transition, even though they've never done so before. Members volunteer to be guest preachers and deliver sermons that heighten the anxiety of the church. Splinter groups push their agendas on the church. Like Israel at Mt. Sinai, Moses is bringing the Ten Commandments down while the people are out building a golden calf.

Cutting the Alligator Tail

Leadership Magazine published an article suggesting that churches are notorious for the proliferation of programs that are never reviewed or ended. Churches grow a long tail like an aging alligator whose tail gets longer each passing year. Endings provide a time to "cut the alligator tail" and end some programs and ministries that have outlived their usefulness.

Helping Churches during the Ending Phase

In 1956, Buddy Parker was the head coach of the Detroit Lions. He noticed that at the end of the first and second halves of the football game, his offense could do certain things they couldn't do at any other time in the game. Buddy Parker invented the "two-minute drill," which is now a standard part of the game. Parker recognized that endings provide us with unique opportunities.

The healthier the church, the deeper the emotional pain they may experience during an ending. The church may have enjoyed a long, successful ministry with a preacher. When he retires, their feelings of loss are profound because they hold many positive memories associated with their time together. The signs of grieving may signal that the relationship that is ending was important, as in the case of Israel mourning the passing of Moses at the Jordan River.

How can we help churches process endings?

- Give people time and space to heal.
- Don't expect them to respond as you do.

- Allow people time to tell their story, and for some to tell it over again.
- Limit the number of major or minor changes during an ending. They have a cumulative, stress-inducing effect.
- Show how the past is tied to the present. The ending is a continuation of who we are.
- Get first-line leaders with high Emotional Intelligence and pastoral skills to speak.
- Normalize the transition.
- Give people lots of information, and do so repeatedly.
- Lower expectation levels for everyone.
- Assess presence of "skeletons in the closet" that may emerge morally, ethically, or financially.
- Rely on authenticity, tact, and timing to move people through the ending.

The Wilderness Phase

The children of Israel had to pass through a wilderness period before they could go into the promised land. Jesus went into the wilderness before the commencement of his public ministry. Moses was called by God from the burning bush in the wilderness to return to Egypt and lead his people out of slavery. The biblical narrative is filled with examples of an in-between time when the past was over and the new age had not yet begun.

In football, there is a time before the start of each play when the offense and the defense line up along the neutral zone. The old play is over. The new play has not yet begun. During those moments before the ball is snapped, both sides can make all kinds of adjustments. A man can be sent in motion, the back sprints out to the left, or a linebacker moves up to rush the passer. Once the play begins, everything is set, and it is impossible to change.

William Bridges writes about wilderness times and calls them "the neutral zone."

"Just when you've decided that the hardest part of managing transitions is getting people to let go of the old ways, you enter a state of affairs in which neither the old ways nor the new ways work satisfactorily. People are caught between the demands of conflicting systems and end up like immobilized Hamlets trying to decide whether "to be or not to be." If this phase lasted only a short time, you could just wait for it to pass. But when change is deep and far-reaching, this time between the old identify and the new can stretch for months or even years" (Bridges, 34).

Bridges recommends steps leaders can take to help followers navigate the neutral zone:

Recognize this is a difficult time.

During the wilderness phase, anxiety goes up. Leaders get impatient. People think about leaving. Motivation starts to fall off. Followers are polarized, as some want to rush forward and others want to return to old ways of doing things. This is a time to "sit with the ambiguity" and learn what the wilderness is trying to teach.

Recognize this is a creative time.

The wilderness or neutral zone has the potential to be the most creative time in the life of a church. The normal defenses preventing change are down. The congregation is now more open to new ideas than at any other moment in its history. The new play has not yet started, and we can make shifts and adjustments before the new quarterback comes in to call the play. If you have driven a car with a stick shift, the neutral zone is the clutch. We engage the clutch to select the next gear. We can choose our next forward gear before reengaging the gears. Too many leaders want to change gears in their church without engaging the clutch.

Give people support and encouragement.

Churches going through a healing transition need a lot of encouragement and support from their leadership. God reminds

Joshua repeatedly in Joshua 1 to "be strong and courageous." He promises Joshua and the nation of Israel that he will be faithful to the covenant he has made with them.

I have found that churches in transition will respond to the positive, reassuring messages they receive from their leadership. If they hear that everything will be all right, they will likely believe it. If they hear messages of doubt and concern, they will begin to believe that also. I often tell churches I transition that my role is to stand in the middle of the river and help people make the crossing from one side to the other. As the father of the boy possessed by an impure spirit in Mark's Gospel proclaimed, "I do believe; help me overcome my unbelief!" (Mark 9:24).

Recognize that this is a time when people engage and disengage.

I was working a transition that was extremely complex and busy. We were all spinning plates in the air. One Monday morning my assistant came into the office, saying that there was a member of the congregation there to meet with me. Johnny was retired from running a very successful home-building business. He was outgoing, friendly, and knew everyone in the church well. "You've got too much to do," he told me. Then he asked for a list of the members in the hospital. "I'm going to be visiting our folks in the hospital every week until this transition is over. It's the least I can do to help out." Johnny became one of our most powerful allies in the transition because he engaged in the process.

The wilderness is a time when members and leaders may move to the sidelines. People are tired. Leaders who have been holding things together have run out of gas. We will explore the effects of transitions on leaders in the next chapter. It is very common for the neutral zone to be a time when some people step up and others step back. This process is not a commentary on the transition itself. It is a natural part of the realignment and leads to positive change.

Questions to Ask in the Wilderness Phase

- Is there a policy or procedure that needs to be updated or eliminated?
- Is there someone on staff who needs to be evaluated or confronted so an issue is not passed on to the next person?
- Are we dealing with any ethical violators and violations that need to be addressed?
- Are there upgrades in the facility, technology, or media that need to be made?
- Is conflict now resurfacing among groups in the church that would threaten a new beginning?
- Is there polarization in the leadership that needs to be addressed?
- Are their Tough Bargainers who are disrupting the normal governance of the congregation?
- Is there disagreement regarding the overall direction of the church?
- Has this transition brought to the surface issues over events from the past that need to be processed before we can move forward?
- Is there a shadow church undermining the transitional process and seeking to control the decision-making process?
- Is the leadership willing and able to address the hard work of the neutral zone to transform the church's processes?

A Warning about the Wilderness

The wilderness is the place where the hard work of transition must be done. Churches will either do their work or run from their issues. If they chose to ignore the issues, they will roll them forward into the next phase of new beginning. They do not magically go away. They lie there like a landmine waiting to explode in the future. "Deal with your stuff, or your stuff will deal with you." Many church leaders hamstring their new beginning because they have not done the work of the wilderness. New ministers and leadership teams are left to clean up the mess from the past. They cannot launch a new era because they are weighed down by problems that should have been corrected in the wilderness. This is one of the main reasons transitions fail.

New Beginning Phase

A new beginning in a church may involve the onboarding of a new minister, selection of new leadership, or the launch of a new vision for the congregation. A new beginning for a wounded church will still involve those things, but they will have to be accomplished in a different context. The context may include rebuilding trust with the leadership; building faith in a relationship with a minister; and the practice of new processes in communications, conflict resolution, and decision making. The members will likely be recovering their sense of self-worth. After years of drama, they may believe, "No one would want to come here and work with us." The new beginning will be slower and more tentative in a wounded church.

The new beginning will include different goals, depending upon the wounding the church has endured. Some of the goals for each wound include:

Tough Bargainer Beginning

- Heal from verbal and power abuse from leadership.
- Identify new leaders willing to step in who are Problem Solvers, not Tough Bargainers.
- Install participatory leadership practices.
- Repair damage to Friendly Helpers.
- Give congregation time to build trust with new leadership.
- Encourage participation in the decision-making process.
- Discourage ruminating on past failures and "war stories."
- Get out of conflict-habituation mode.

- Remove Tough Bargainer from all leadership roles in phase two of transition.

Narcissistic Church Beginning

- Transition from a personality-driven church to a fully functioning church body.
- Remove old power structures from leadership.
- Deal with staggered disclosure as new information surfaces regarding church operations.
- Heal people hurt by power abuse.
- Remove ministerial family and friends from positions of leadership.
- Review finances and do a financial audit.
- Provide healing and restitution to members and ministers who have left the church under less than ideal circumstances.
- Repair the community image.
- Conduct a search for a veteran minister capable of handling complex dynamics.
- Give the church a long time to heal.

Sexuality Church Beginning

- Remove sexual offenders from leadership in phase one and assist them in finding healing.
- Prevent offending leaders from entering the church system again, following a "quick recovery."
- Establish new congregational boundaries regarding ethical practice of ministry, and review all programs for adherence to new rules and local laws.
- Be prepared for staggered disclosure that may compromise the new beginning.
- Rebuild trust in leadership and ministry so the next individuals stepping in do not inherit congregational doubt.

- Find ways to offer help and restitution to those hurt by the sexual misconduct.
- Set aside a long season of healing, and allow the congregation to recover its sense of equilibrium.
- Repair the public image of the church.
- Search for a veteran minister to assume leadership of the church following a sexual wounding.

Borderline Church Beginning

- Slowly open the church family system to outside help and information.
- Combat the "We have all the answers" mentality of leadership.
- Identify healthy leaders willing to step into leadership and replace the leadership core team.
- The shadow church must be removed from all influence on the leadership and church. This will be a slow, painful process, as they do not go away easily.
- Implement the transitional process before the resources of the congregation—time, money, and people—are used up.
- Confront issues of rage and passive-aggressive behavior on the part of staff and leaders.
- Urge the church to take ownership of their part in the narrative of their own failures and stop blaming everyone else for the events of the past.
- Find ways to make restitution to members, staff, and leaders who left after having been wounded by the former leadership.
- Confront pride and ego on the part of long-term members.
- The leadership must own a long-term rebuilding process led by someone outside—which is a difficult step to take.

Incompetence Church Beginning

- Build new internal structures for vision, work, and personnel, and to combat ethical and financial incompetence.
- Help the church take responsibility for itself.
- Build a congregational work ethic.
- Empower individuals in the congregation to own and execute important ministries.
- Point out incompetence when it occurs, and help address new ways of raising performance.
- Replace informal rules with formal performance standards and best practices.
- Do not allow over-functioning individuals to do all the work.
- Create an owned vision of the future to replace "just keeping house."
- Create accountability systems with real consequences to hold people accountable.

Exhaustion New Beginning

- Give the congregation time to process and heal from past events and the emotions associated with those events.
- Give people permission to process their emotions and an opportunity to share their story.
- Create a season of peace in the church, with no conflict and no major events.
- Have discussions of where to go from here as the church builds a new vision.
- Permit leaders who are tired to step down with dignity and appreciation.
- Deal with the effects of transitional density in the church.

I THOUGHT THIS WAS A CRAZY IDEA

I was finishing a transition when an older member of the congregation approached me in the foyer after services. She had been a member of the church many years and had sat patiently through the last years' process. "I thought this was a crazy idea when our leaders announced you were coming. I thought we just needed to go hire a new guy and get on down the road. But you know what? I was wrong! This has been great, and this old lady learned a few things." I often hear comments like that. Healing transitions make believers out of the most ardent opponents. Churches that start in a place of confusion end with a newfound sense of confidence.

CHAPTER 15

HEALING AND LEADERSHIP

The elders at First Colony Church were tired. When I met with them on a Monday evening, they looked like a group of defeated men. I admired them for the things they had survived over the past decade. They had held the ship together when it had taken repeated broadside hits. To their credit, the ship was still afloat.

When most of these men became elders, the church was at its prime. They had an experienced, energetic preacher who led the congregation well with his dynamic preaching and boundless energy. First Colony had a stellar reputation in the community as "the place to go because they help folks." The youth and children's ministry attracted young families, and the future looked bright.

Then a decade of change began. Their dynamic preacher retired unexpectedly and moved away, leaving a huge gap in the leadership of the church. Elders and staff who had relied on his energy and vision now found themselves at a loss to know what to do. They tried hiring a replacement for him. Four pulpit ministers later, they were between ministers and still looking for their "next messiah." The prospects for number five did not look promising.

The years had been tough on the church. There had been many false starts. There were a new preacher and a new vision every two years, and First Colony had grown weary of saying hello and goodbye to a stream of former ministers. The congregation grew impatient with the leadership they had once embraced during the glory years. Bonfires of controversy periodically signaled the growing tension between leaders and followers.

Internally, the eldership was split. There was disagreement on the kind of minister the church needed to hire. There was disagreement about the vision they needed to pursue. Some elders had become more controlling and fought for power as events spiraled out of control. Others seemed to recede into the wallpaper, trying to hide out and weather the storm. Men who had once enjoyed working together now dreaded meetings and the potential for more conflict. They feared making the wrong decision, so they made no decisions.

The transition had been healing for the elders. They had been in need of pastoral care more than any other group in the church. They had lain their bodies down on the tracks and been run over many times. They needed time to heal. After we had begun the transition with First Colony, the elders called me in and asked me to extend my time with them. They didn't want to move forward. "We just need some time to rest. Can we just take this slowly and catch our breath?" It was a wise request.

The chairman of the elders, a gifted leader and retired school administrator, asked me to join them for their meeting. He wanted to discuss where the leadership was in the transition. He put the question to the group. Each elder commented on where they were personally and how they thought the group was functioning. The group was out of gas. They owned their fatigue and discouragement. They also owned the low leadership reviews they'd received on the congregational assessment. They might be leaders without followers, one man commented.

After we'd gone around the table, he looked at me and said, "Don, you've been with us now long enough to know us. What do you think we ought to do?" The room grew very quiet. My reply: "I think you all have shouldered a lot of change in the last ten years. I think you are all very tired, and the church is saying a part of this transition is a shift to a new leadership."

The chairman smiled and immediately said, "I think you're exactly right. I think it's time we all stepped aside. The church needs to select a new leadership, and we need to step down." Within ten minutes the entire group had offered their resignations. The relief in the room was palpable.

First Colony went on to select a new set of elders. A talented group stepped up, and we began the transition of leadership. The church, to its credit, took time to affirm the former leadership for their years of service. The congregation could move forward into a conversation about its future and a minister search with the leadership that would be responsible for the new era.

In counseling, my clients often know exactly what they need to do. The answers are inside them. They just need to come out. My role is to give them permission to do what they know they need to do. I need to let it be okay in their hearts. At First Colony, a wise chairman knew his group was ready to make a change. They just needed permission to let go and trust that God would provide for the future of the church.

LEADERS' QUESTIONS

I have a great deal of compassion for church leaders. My father was an elder for 25 years for a church in Dallas, and we discussed "church politics" around the dinner table. Most elders and deacons come to the task of church leadership with very little training. They are thrown into the deep end and expected to sink or swim. Their backgrounds in business, military, law, or medicine do not translate to the unique world of church work.

Church leaders bring a set of questions to the transition process. Some can be addressed on the front end, and others must be experienced to be answered.

- What is a healing transition?
- How long will it take us to get through this?

- What happens in the various stages of healing?
- Who will do the preaching, and what will they preach on?
- Will we lose members and contributions during the transition?
- What about the rest of our staff?
- Has this worked in other places?
- What about members who are campaigning to bring in their favorite candidates?
- What is involved in the assessment process?
- How do we communicate this to the church?

These questions form the basis for and understanding of the transitional process. There must be agreement on the part of all the leadership in the church to enter a period of healing in order for the process to work.

REST, RETIRE, OR RECONFIGURE?

A transition is a pivotal time in the evolution of the leadership of the church. It will go through changes during this time because the entire system is changing. Those changes may be embraced by the leadership, if they are reflective, or forced on them by the church system if they are reactive.

As I work with church leaders during transitions, we move toward one of three goals individually and as a group:

Rest

A healing transition gives a leader or leadership time to rest. First Colony's eldership requested time to rest. They had been through a decade of dramatic change and needed some time to catch their breath. This was completely appropriate because it gave them space to reflect on where they were, both individually and collectively as a group.

We normally think of healing transitions as something for the congregation. However, they are a necessary step for leadership. Most congregations I work with are led by individuals who are in need of some care but don't know how to ask for it. If they can be provided with time and space to heal, they will likely make better decisions.

After a period of rest, some leaders choose to engage in leadership once again. Others may opt to move to the sidelines and assume a different role. Still others may be a part of a newly formed leadership team. Rest gives each person time to reflect on God's calling for their life.

Retire

A transition gives the leaders an opportunity to step away from leading in a way that his honorable and graceful. It is a perfect time for leaders to retire and be thanked for their years of service.

I encourage staff, elders, and deacons who are considering stepping out of leadership to do so during the ending and wilderness phases of the transition. The church is in a period of change, and they will normally accommodate the news quite well. Waiting until a new beginning is not preferred because it mixes news of an ending with a beginning. If we are going to cut the alligator's tail, it's better to do so in one operation, not ten.

First Colony was being led by an eldership that was ready to retire. They were worn out. No one was willing to be the first to talk about the elephant in the room. When the idea of retirement hit the table, it took ten minutes for the group to own their condition and make the decision. It was the best thing for the leadership and the church.

Reconfigure

Seventy-five percent of the churches I transition reconfigure their leadership and ministerial staff during a transition. This is very common because the leadership subsystem is the heart of the communications, decision-making, and conflict-resolution processes of the church. Those processes are being reconfigured; therefore, the makeup of the leadership will be impacted.

Transitions are times when people come and go. This is especially true of leaders. Some are tired and are ready to hand the mantle off to someone else. Others are on the sidelines and are eager to step up and take their turn leading the church.

Transitions are times when we need to honestly evaluate the ministerial staff. Are they the people we need to move us forward? Are they cooperating with the transitional process? Are they using the transition as an opportunity to further their own personal agendas? Are they using ministry as an easy place to "hide out from life?" My experience is that staff ministers polarize during a transition. They either support the transition and contribute to it, or they attempt to undermine it in passive-aggressive ways. I have also learned that, the less capable the staff minister, the more likely they are to use the transition to gain a higher prestige position for themselves.

LEADER CARE

I'm often asked by leadership teams to talk with them about how to survive and thrive in church leadership. I find that church leaders who are doing well are practicing five key habits: wear a small S on your chest, monitor your gauges, recognize personal pain, allow faith to evolve and pause decision making

Wear a Small S on Your Chest

Dr. Charles Siburt was a friend and mentor for many years. When I was working with a church and things became confusing, I would call Charlie and run the situation by him. He was a gifted church consultant.

One day, after I had explained the church's problems, he began laughing. "Don, the problem is you're trying to wear a big *S* on your chest. You're trying to be Superman, and no one can pull that off. It's okay to wear a small *s* on your chest, but you need to take off the big one."

Charlie was right. I had fallen into the trap of over-functioning. I thought I could solve all the church's problems and right all the wrongs. I was trying to leap tall buildings in a single bound, . . . and falling flat. I needed to pull down my expectation levels and let the church take responsibility for the work it needed to do.

Dr. Dan Mitchell, a former missionary turned therapist, was my clinical supervisor. Dan's favorite saying was "Sometimes folks are better at being sick than we are at getting them well." Church leaders who set reasonable expectations for themselves will survive leadership longer.

Monitor Your Four Gauges

My old 1965 Mustang had a series of gauges on the dash that showed me speed, temperature, tachometer, and voltage. That was before the creation of heads-up displays. I could glance at the gauges and know how the engine was running.

People have four gauges that tell how their "engine" is running. Those gauges are physical condition, emotional response, spiritual condition, and intellectual processing. When a person is healthy and well-functioning, these gauges are in the healthy range. Luke 2:52 says, "And Jesus grew in wisdom and stature, and in favor with God and man." His four gauges were operating very well.

When we are stressed, one or more of our gauges will register that. People cannot sleep, so the physical gauge goes down. People are stressed and get depressed, so the emotional gauge goes down. Problems cause us to ruminate, and the intellectual gauge drops. Relationships at church are strained, and the spiritual gauge is affected.

Church leaders are often so focused on meeting other people's needs that they neglect to attend to their own needs. Their gauges go down, and they are not aware of it. Friends and family point out that they are not doing well, and they minimize it.

First Colony had an eldership that was running on fumes. All four gauges were down, and the entire leadership needed relief. Each person needed time to recharge their battery. Church leaders who survive attend to their four gauges and know how to recharge their engines.

Recognize Personal Pain

When I was six years old, I had two very different accidents that left two very different scars. I was riding my bike on the gravel roads in my neighborhood in West Hartford, coming down a hill too fast. I came off the front of my bike and landed on my knees, grinding a sharp piece of gravel into one knee. It's there to this day.

Several months later, I was crossing the street in Torrington, Connecticut, with my parents after church services. It was a cold night, and the streets were icy. As I crossed the street, a young girl driving down it lost control of her car and ran me over. I woke up under the headlight of her front bumper. I was miraculously unhurt, but when I step off a curb to cross a street, I often remember that night.

Those two experiences left very different memories and very different scars. One was to my knee. The other is buried in my memory. Church leaders take hits that leave scars. Sometimes those scars are minor, like the gravel in my knee. However, the hits that leaders take are often significant and leave deep wounds in their psyches. The church leader didn't fall off a bike; they were hit by a bus.

Some of the most important transitional work I've done is giving church leaders a space to process the pain they've experienced in ministry. Many have no one to talk to, and they carry the pain and disappointment internally until it drives them to leave leadership entirely. I encourage leadership teams to care for one another while they are busy caring for the church.

Allow Faith to Evolve

I was visiting with Dr. Marshall Duke, a psychotherapist and professor at Emory University in Atlanta, about the impact of leadership on faith. I had been counseling for many years and was also involved in ministry. Those experiences had changed my own faith and Dr. Duke framed that as a positive thing. He explained that theology must inform our ministry, but our ministry must also shape our theology.

Jesus brought the Pharisees to a crisis of faith when his disciples picked heads of grain on the Sabbath. He told them in Matthew 12:6–8, "I tell you that something greater than the temple is here. If you had known what these words mean, 'I desire mercy, not sacrifice,' you would not have condemned the innocent. For the Son of Man is Lord of the Sabbath." Jesus was allowing his practice of ministry to define his theology.

Church leaders, if they are open to growth, will discover that their practice of ministry informs their theology. They will work with hurting people, and it will change how they read the text. They will engage in problem solving, and it will shape their theology. This is not a process to be afraid of. It is a process to be embraced as positive spiritual growth. Leaders who possess their "little box of truth" do not survive long in the complex world of local church work.

Pause Decision Making

Skipper Shipp was a public-school administrator and elder who hired me for my first ministry job. At 25, fresh out of graduate school, I became the family-life minister for a church of 1400 and joined a leadership team of 13 elders and 6 staff. Our leadership meetings were held after church services on Wednesday evenings, and the long-winded discussions often ran late into the night.

Skipper was an extrovert's extrovert and had a great sense of humor. As the discussion would drone on, he'd put his arms on his knees and lean forward as though carrying the weight of the conversation on his shoulders. He was bald, and the angrier he became the redder the top of his head would get. He was an emotional barometer for the entire group.

Finally, in frustration, Skipper would break into the conversation and say, "Gentlemen, we are not going to get this resolved tonight. I think it's time to head to the house." The tension was relieved, and we dismissed for the night. Normally, the next time we met the discussion would move ahead as though the logjam had never occurred. Skipper had an innate understanding of timing.

Wise leaders know that there are times we need to pack it in and call it a day. The problem is not going to be resolved that evening. The discussion is going to deteriorate. They answers are not going to come. It is better to step back and give people time to reflect with their wise minds than to react and say things they may regret later. I have seen this occur. The discussion that was causing so much difficulty last week now transpires smoothly, as though nothing had ever happened. Sometimes leaders need to follow Skipper's advice and "head to the house."

A LESSON FROM REINFORCEMENT THEORY

We all prefer praise over criticism. Most people seek roles and activities in which they maximize their positive reinforcement and minimize negative reinforcement. Church leaders are public figures who by definition will receive more punishment than rewards. To put this another way, in leadership you eat more veggies and less dessert.

There are two techniques for dealing with the high level of negative reinforcement that comes with being a leader. The first is to become a self-reinforcing individual. Leaders who survive are able to look at the job they are doing and say, "Yes, I did the best I could in that situation." The second is for the group to be able to reinforce one another. They provide each other with some positive regard that is missing from within the larger church.

The question is often asked, "How do I deal with unjust criticism?" Here are some useful tips for handling criticism, complaints, and personal attacks:

- Have a plan ahead of time on what you will do when this happens.
- Do not trust your spontaneous response.

- Step back or cool off before responding.
- Have an advisor to confer with who is outside the system.
- Determine whether this is a pattern for the person complaining. Certain personality disorders have a need to create crises.
- If possible, script your comments ahead of time.
- Consider all your delivery options, including face-to-face, group, alone, or with written responses.
- Avoid social media fights.

One of the most difficult positions to be in is that of the spouse of a church leader who is under attack. The feelings of defensiveness, powerlessness, and anger can be overwhelming. Here are some suggestions for spouses who are watching their partner being attacked in church work:

- Be aware of the tendency to lash out at the attacker, to stuff the negative feedback internally and become depressed, to disengage and avoid church entirely, or to take out your frustrations on your spouse.
- Take an adult stance. Be professional in your approach.
- Ask to be a part of the planned response to the situation.
- Define your role as the spouse of a church leader.
- Don't ruminate on the conflict. Don't let this thing eat you up.
- Value your identity. Keep being who you are.
- Make wise decisions. Which battles are worth fighting, and which ones do I walk away from?
- Relationship-mentor with someone who has been down the road in this role and can advise you.
- Forgiveness means sometimes letting some dumb stuff go.

ASSESSING LEADERSHIP

The healing transition is a time for leaders to assess themselves in their role and for the congregation to assess the leadership as a whole. This is where the formal assessment process provides value to the church.

The Church Health Assessment from the Siburt Institute for Church Ministry identifies leadership as one of the nine key factors in measuring congregational health. The areas of leadership functioning include:

- Church members respect leader authority.
- Leaders support teamwork.
- Leaders and members are on the same page.
- Leaders adapt to needs.
- Leaders use others' giftedness.
- Leaders take time to know the members.
- Leaders are approachable.
- Leaders communicate well.
- Leaders are not over-controlling.
- Ministers show mutual support.
- Ministers are supportive of elders.
- Elders are supportive of ministers.
- Leaders do well with processing different views.
- Leaders listen and respond appropriately to critics.
- Leaders implement vision well.
- Decisions are timely.
- Organizational structure is effective.
- Leaders understand the congregation's needs.
- Leaders are friendly.

Taken together, the scores of these subscales provide a useful picture of the health of the leadership subsystem. They also offer specific areas in need of improvement, such as communications or vision. The church and existing leaders can use this information to make informed decisions. The leadership at First Colony had scores on the leadership scale that were very low. When given an opportunity to retire from serving, they stepped aside as a group. That decision was highly influenced by the results of the Congregational Health Assessment.

SCAFFOLDING TO REBUILD LEADERSHIP

There are times when a church is so wounded that the leadership is not capable of seeing them through the transition, and a temporary "scaffolding leadership" needs to be commissioned. This leadership team will assist the church in the healing transition and give the congregation time to identify new leaders.

Congregations that are Narcissistic will benefit from a scaffold leadership because large portions of the existing leadership team need to be replaced. Congregations that have a Shadow Leadership will likely need a scaffold team to assist them in breaking the patterns of these unhealthy alliances.

The Scaffold Leadership may be composed of a combination of leaders from within the ranks of the church, along with members selected from outside the congregation. Those outside representatives can be vital in helping the congregation disengage from people and processes that have held them hostage and contributed to the wounding of the church.

Three years following that Monday night meeting at First Colony, I sat in the auditorium on a Sunday morning. I thought I was visiting a new church. The worship service was vibrant. New members filled the pews. Former leaders who had resigned from leadership that night shook my hand and related how they'd rested and found new ways to minister in the church they loved so much. The voices of new leaders were heard that morning giving hope to the church. That delicate balance of congregational climate had tipped the scales in a positive direction. This came because one leader had been bold enough to say, "I think it's time to step aside."

CONCLUDING THOUGHTS

I stand in a river and help people cross over. That is the role of a transitional minister. Some will run across the river; some will walk across very carefully; and others will wait on the bank, assessing the situation before stepping out. We all have our transitional style. My job is to help people get from one bank to the other, and then I am out of a job. Like a therapist with a client, my goal is for my client to be self-reliant and no longer in need of my care.

One of the great lessons I've learned, and there have been many, is that we are all transitional. Every minister, church leader, and congregation is a temporary holder of their position. I believe that God's sovereignty brings people together at the right moment in time to do important work in his overall plan. I also believe that those times pass and that we enter a transitional period, waiting on God to move in his mysterious way. We do all we can do and then wait upon the Lord.

Ultimately, each church and I will move in opposite directions. They will move into the promised land of a new beginning to accomplish the purposes God has in store for them. I will step out of the river onto the opposite bank. There is always a church coming out of the wilderness needing some time to remember at the river.

REFERENCES

Bridges, William. *Transitions: Making Sense of Life's Changes*. 2nd edition. DeCapo Press. 2004.

Bridges, William. *Managing Transitions: Making the Most of Change*. Addison-Wesley Publishing Company. 1991.

Brueggemann, Walter. *Genesis: Interpreter's Bible Commentary*. John Knox Press. 1982.

Craddock, Fred B. *Luke: Interpreter's Bible Commentary*. John Knox Press. 1990.

Clements, R. E. *Jeremiah: Interpreter's Bible Commentary*. John Knox Press. 1988.

Kruger, Roger. *The Proper Care of Snakes: Managing Personality Disorders in Congregational Settings*. Grace Point Resources. 2015.

Lewis, Ralph, and Gregg Lewis. *Inductive Preaching: Helping People Listen*. Crossway Books. 1983.

Mead, Loren B. *More Than Numbers: The Ways Churches Grow*. The Alban Institute. 1993.

Osburn, Carroll. *Lectures on Titus*. Digital.commons.acu.edu. 1997.

Saarinen, Martin. *Life Cycle of a Congregation*. The Alban Institute. 1998.

Spring, Janis Abrams. *How Can I Forgive You?* HarperCollins. 2004.

Steinke, Peter. *Teaching Fish to Walk: Church Systems and Adaptive Challenge*. New Vision Press. 2016.

Van Der Kolk, Bessel. *The Body Keeps the Score*. Viking Press. 2014.

ABOUT THE AUTHOR

Dr. Don Hebbard is a speaker, professor, and marriage and family therapist. He is Professor of Counseling, Human Behavior and Development at Amberton University in Dallas, Texas. He teaches Marriage and Family Therapy, Couples Therapy, Conflict Resolution and Leadership. He is the Director of Amberton's "My Learning Style" Quality Enhancement Plan and was formerly Academic Vice President. He has served on the faculty of Oklahoma Christian University, Abilene Christian University, and Harding Graduate School of Theology.

Don has served as a transitional minister for congregations nationally since 1988. He is a consultant with the Siburt Institute for Church Growth at Abilene Christian University. Don spent twenty years in local church work.

Dr. Don is a Licensed Marriage and Family Therapist and Supervisor and a Clinical Fellow with the American Association for Marriage and Family Therapy. He works with Restoration Counseling in Ft. Worth, where he leads Restoration Academy, a post-graduate institute for therapists. He founded the Family Center of the Metroplex in Dallas and the first Christian counseling center in Atlanta, The Genesis Center for Christian Counseling.

Don holds a doctorate in Adult Education with a specialization in Organizational Development from Texas Woman's University. His master's degrees are in Marriage and Family Therapy and Communications from Abilene Christian University.

He is a frequent speaker for colleges, businesses, and churches, and is known for his stories and passionate delivery. He is the author of *The Complete Handbook for Family Life Ministry in the Church*. His writings and research have appeared in *Ladies Home Journal* and *The London Sunday Times* and on PBS.

Don is a Cop Dad. His son Jared serves as an officer in the Ft. Worth Police Department. His daughter Hailey serves in the Guthrie, Oklahoma, Police Department. He considers being a Cop Dad his most important calling.

His professional website is donhebbard.com.

Made in the USA
Coppell, TX
01 July 2022